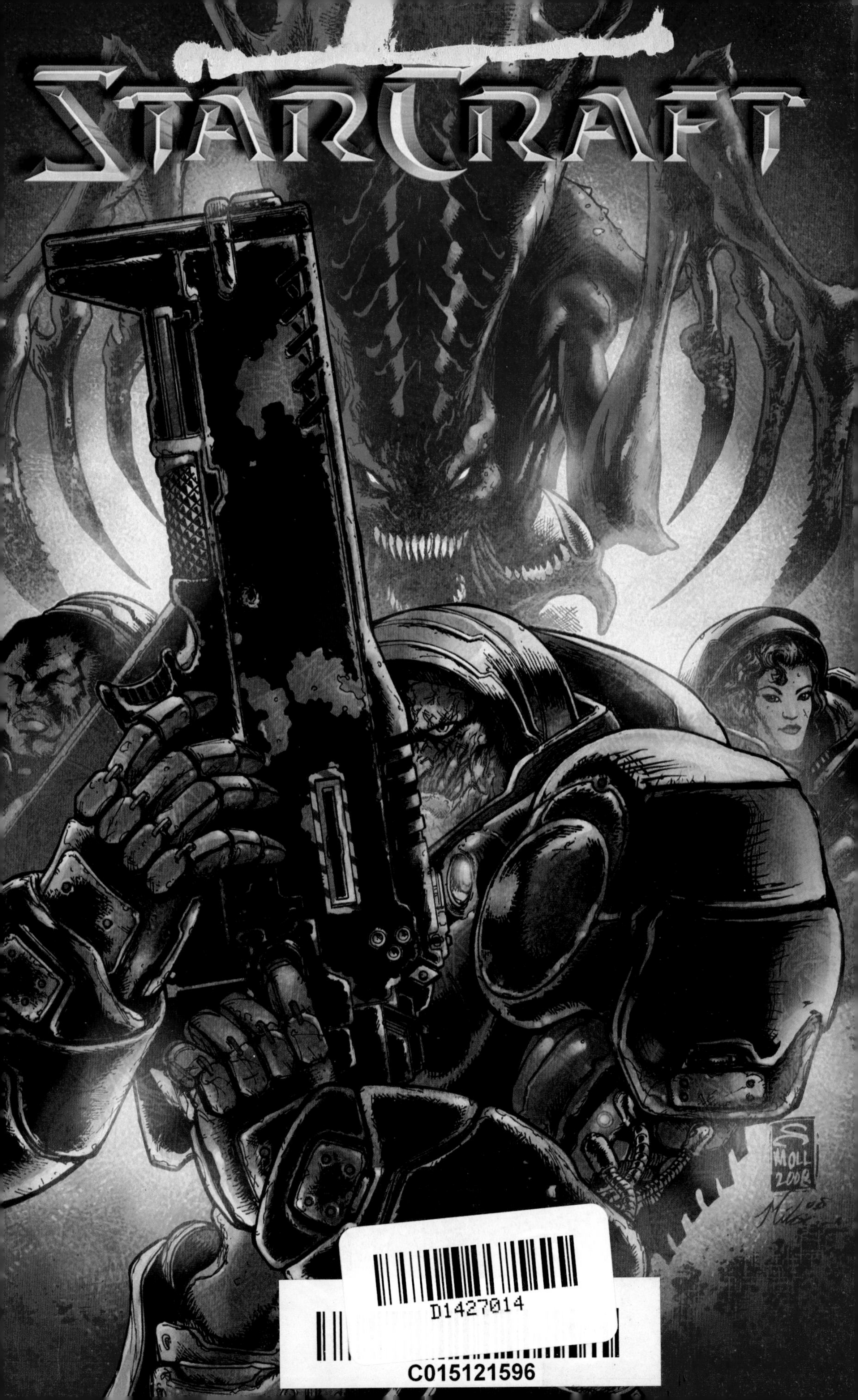
STARCRAFT

Story by
SIMON FURMAN

Art by
**FEDERICO DALLOCCHIO
BRIAN DENHAM
CARLOS D'ANDA
and MIKE S. MILLER**

Colors by
**MILEN PARVANOV, CARRIE STRACHAN
and WILDSTORM FX**

Letters by
SAIDA TEMOFONTE

Cover and original series covers by
**FEDERICO DALLOCCHIO
with MILEN PARVANOV and JONNY RENCH**

Variant covers and pinups by
**SHAWN MOLL, SHAWN MOLL & DOUG MAHNKE
SHAWN MOLL & SANDRA HOPE, CARLOS D'ANDA
FEDERICO DALLOCCHIO**

Story consultants:
**CHRIS METZEN, MICKY NEILSON,
ANDY CHAMBERS & JAMES WAUGH**

War Pigs concept by **JASON BISCHOFF**

Special thanks to **KEITH GIFFEN**

For Blizzard Entertainment:

Chris Metzen — Senior VP – Creative Development
Jeff Donais — Director – Creative Development
Micky Neilson — Story Consultant and Development
Glenn Rane — Art Director
Cory Jones — Director – Global Business Development and Licensing
Jason Bischoff — Associate Licensing Manager
Tommy Newcomer — Additional Development
Cameron Dayton — Additional Development

For DC Comics:

Ben Abernathy — Editor – Original Series
Ian Sattler — Director, Editorial – Archival Editions
Kristy Quinn — Editor
Robbin Brosterman — Design Director – Books

Eddie Berganza — Executive Editor
Bob Harras — VP – Editor in Chief

Diane Nelson — President
Dan DiDio and Jim Lee — Co-Publishers
Geoff Johns — Chief Creative Officer
John Rood — Executive VP – Sales, Marketing and Business Development
Amy Genkins — Senior VP – Business and Legal Affairs
Nairi Gardiner — Senior VP – Finance
Jeff Boison — VP – Publishing Operations
Mark Chiarello — VP – Art Direction and Design
John Cunningham — VP – Marketing
Terri Cunningham — VP – Talent Relations and Services
Alison Gill — Senior VP – Manufacturing and Operations
David Hyde — VP – Publicity
Hank Kanalz — Senior VP – Digital
Jay Kogan — VP – Business and Legal Affairs, Publishing
Jack Mahan — VP – Business Affairs, Talent
Nick Napolitano — VP – Manufacturing Administration
Ron Perazza — VP – Online
Sue Pohja — VP – Book Sales
Courtney Simmons — Senior VP – Publicity
Bob Wayne — Senior VP – Sales

STARCRAFT

INTRODUCTION

StarCraft.

It is a strange little universe.

Since the original game's launch back in 1998, we've been actively finding ways to continue the stories of the protoss, zerg and terrans—each locked in their seemingly endless war for dominance. Being a huge fan of comics myself, I always figured we'd get around to doing a comic—so long as we found the right creative partners. It took awhile (y'know—ten years or so), but the exceptional team at WildStorm proved to be the perfect match for what we had envisioned.

The book you hold in your hands started taking shape about two years ago. At that point, we were knee-deep in the development of *Starcraft 2: Wings of Liberty*—and still defining the characters and story elements that would form the narrative of that long-awaited sequel. Since there were still some lingering questions as to the fate of our major franchise characters (ie: Jim Raynor, Kerrigan, Zeratul, etc.), we decided to take a different track with the comic series and focus on characters and areas of the universe that would be fun to explore and be a bit less complicated to wrangle (*given the myriad plot complexities on the game-side*).

We realized very quickly that this choice provided us a great opportunity to show our fans the broader scope of the IP, giving them a glimpse at the political machinations at play inside the Dominion, letting them feel the plight of the rugged fringe world colonist, and all around really showcase what life in the Koprulu Sector is like when you're not harvesting crystals or trying to get your firebats to counter a massive zerg rush.

It was Blizzard's own Jason Bischoff wh[o] stepped up to the plate and pitched the idea o[f] a group of grim and gritty mercenaries makin[g] their way through terran space—one ste[p] ahead of the law (*personally, I think Jaso[n] watched a little too much* A-Team *as a kid— but then again…is there such a thing as to[o] much* A-Team?). Jason and the concep[t] team immediately jumped on this idea an[d] helped to flesh out the broad strokes of th[e] story—and define the various personalitie[s] (and fatal hang-ups) of the War Pigs.

Based on the brilliant scripts from Simon Furma[n] (Mister *Transformers* himself) and the gritty, heav[y] artwork from Federico Dallocchio—the STARCRAF[T] comic proved to be a fast-paced, hyper-kinetic rom[p] through the seedy, morally-compromised underbell[y] of the *Starcraft* universe.

Mission accomplished, indeed.

Chris Metzen
SVP, Creative Development
Blizzard Entertainment

INTRODUCTION

"They let you in the door?" (The honest-to-goodness first words spoken to me when I came to interview at Blizzard.)

Tell someone you work in video games and you're the "bee's knees." Follow with the fact that you're the licensing guy, and suddenly you're just another "business jerk."

Don't get me wrong, this strange industry I run around in is full of the above-mentioned stereotype. They can be the worm to the creative apple and sadly, at surface glance, you'd think me one of them. It's typecasting, I assure you, but an easy mistake.

My name's not in the title, nor found on the cover. On occasion (if I'm lucky), heck inside, near the legal. I hide there beside: "Associate Licensing Manager." It's a veil, a ruse to lead you off my path. I'm just a business jerk after all, like Bruce Wayne perhaps? Second glances won't be necessary. But don't believe it, don't buy into it for one second. Deep inside this façade lies a furnace burning for the chance to really creatively flex. You, friend, have just thrown a log onto that hungry fire.

Why? Skim the credits again: "War Pigs Concept by." I'm shaking as I type this. I feel the floodgates of chemical emotion swim in my face as I am thankful and unworthy, anxious and shell-shocked. *World of Warcraft*®, *Diablo*® and *StarCraft*® have always been titans of lore to me. How could I have expected to traverse even one of these worlds safely, nonetheless shaped them in some way? How could an "Associate Licensing Manager" have managed court-time with a cabal like Simon Furman, Chris Metzen and *New York Times* Best Selling Graphic Novel author Micky Neilson? (Sorry, Mick, I had to.)

Many years ago, in the primordial days of the mid 2000s, I silently contributed content to some of the biggest brands in pop culture. I cast off those gloves to do what I do now, never thinking that my writing ambitions would be encouraged once again in my new role. Little did I know it would be like being adopted by the family that had wanted me all along. Their patience was saintly. Their welcome astounding. Their opportunity generous. Cheers, guys. Thanks for letting me play.

The broken mess of Terran waste you are about to meet, the WarPigs, were born in seat 31 J (a sixteen-hour prison of my choosing as I flew to Hong Kong in the Spring of '08 for, you guessed it, business). You'll never find the original document that I entitled "Penance Detail" (what was I thinking?), but I can assure you that much of the setup and its stars survived the translation into the ride you're about to take. They were perfected in the weeks to come in Metzen's "Lab." Micky renamed Cole and made Turfa glow (literally). Chris christened the 'Pigs with a name (based off an early SC1 cinematic) and set them off into the fringe worlds on their own ship, the *General Lee*, and Simon—dear "Nemesis Part 2" Simon Furman—made them flipping fantastic.

For the seven issues that comprise this collection (of which I am extremely proud), I've been given a rare taste at what it is that a Senior Vice President of Creative Development does across the hundred-odd feet between our offices. I've got to say it, Mr. Metzen, I'm hooked. Wanna trade for a day…or a lifetime?

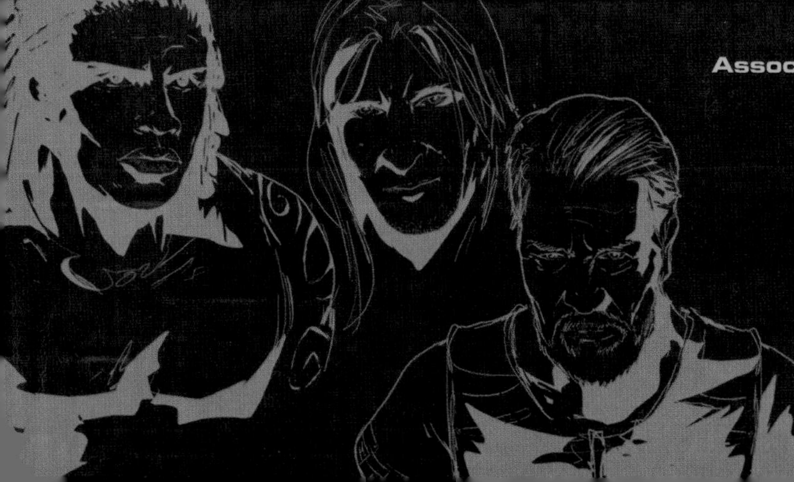

Jason Bischoff
Associate Licensing Manager
Blizzard Entertainment

Special thanks to Cory, Hank and James for your enduring wisdom and encouragement!

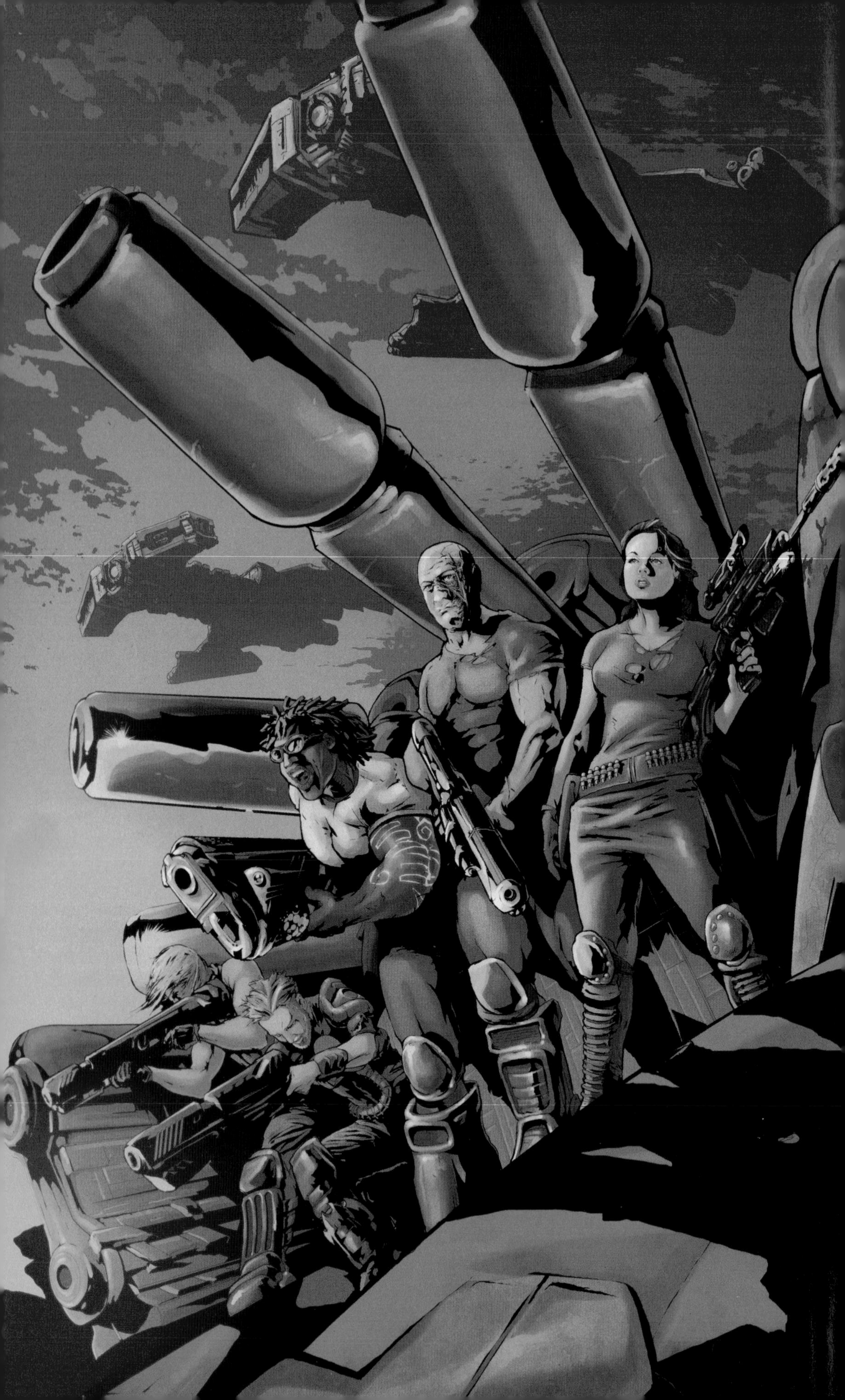

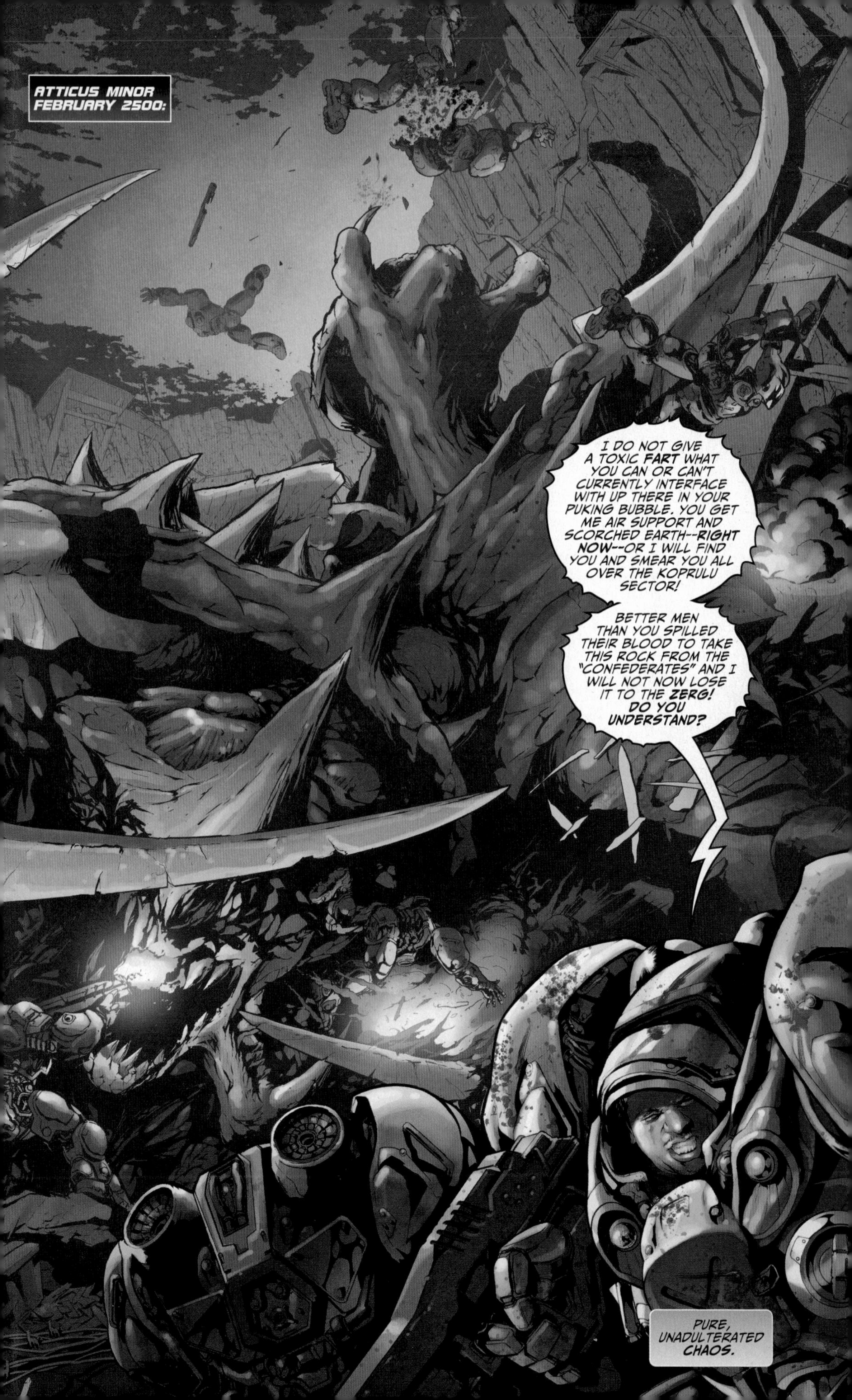
ATTICUS MINOR
FEBRUARY 2500:
I DO NOT GIVE A TOXIC FART WHAT YOU CAN OR CAN'T CURRENTLY INTERFACE WITH UP THERE IN YOUR PUKING BUBBLE. YOU GET ME AIR SUPPORT AND SCORCHED EARTH--RIGHT NOW--OR I WILL FIND YOU AND SMEAR YOU ALL OVER THE KOPRULU SECTOR!
BETTER MEN THAN YOU SPILLED THEIR BLOOD TO TAKE THIS ROCK FROM THE "CONFEDERATES" AND I WILL NOT NOW LOSE IT TO THE ZERG! DO YOU UNDERSTAND?
PURE, UNADULTERATED CHAOS.

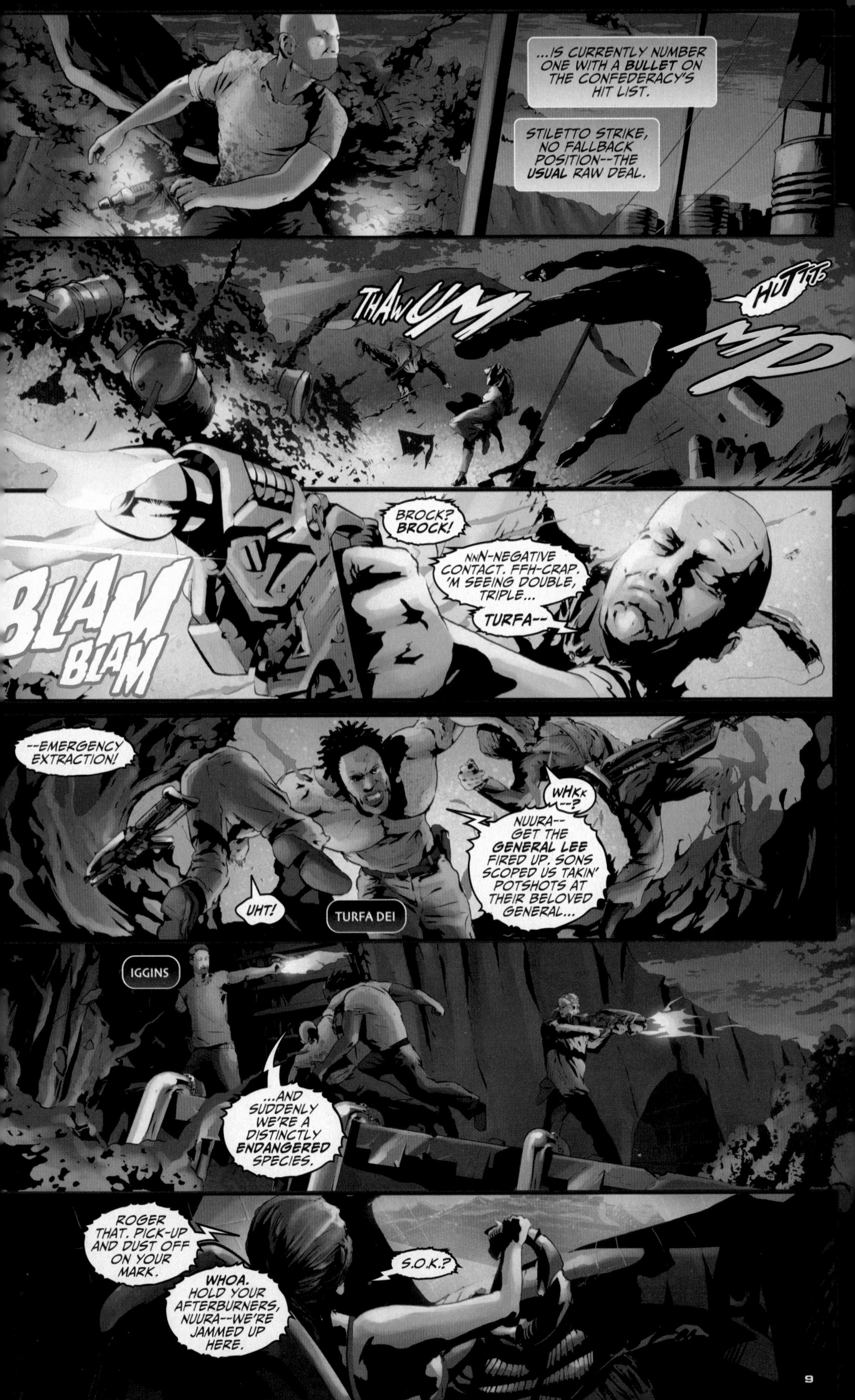

...IS CURRENTLY NUMBER ONE WITH A BULLET ON THE CONFEDERACY'S HIT LIST.
STILETTO STRIKE, NO FALLBACK POSITION--THE USUAL RAW DEAL.
THAWUMMP
HUTTT.
BLAM BLAM
BROCK? BROCK!
NNN-NEGATIVE CONTACT. FFH-CRAP. 'M SEEING DOUBLE, TRIPLE...
TURFA--
--EMERGENCY EXTRACTION!
WHKK--?
NUURA-- GET THE GENERAL LEE FIRED UP. SONS SCOPED US TAKIN' POTSHOTS AT THEIR BELOVED GENERAL...
UHT!
TURFA DEI
IGGINS
...AND SUDDENLY WE'RE A DISTINCTLY ENDANGERED SPECIES.
ROGER THAT. PICK-UP AND DUST OFF ON YOUR MARK.
S.O.K.?
WHOA. HOLD YOUR AFTERBURNERS, NUURA--WE'RE JAMMED UP HERE.

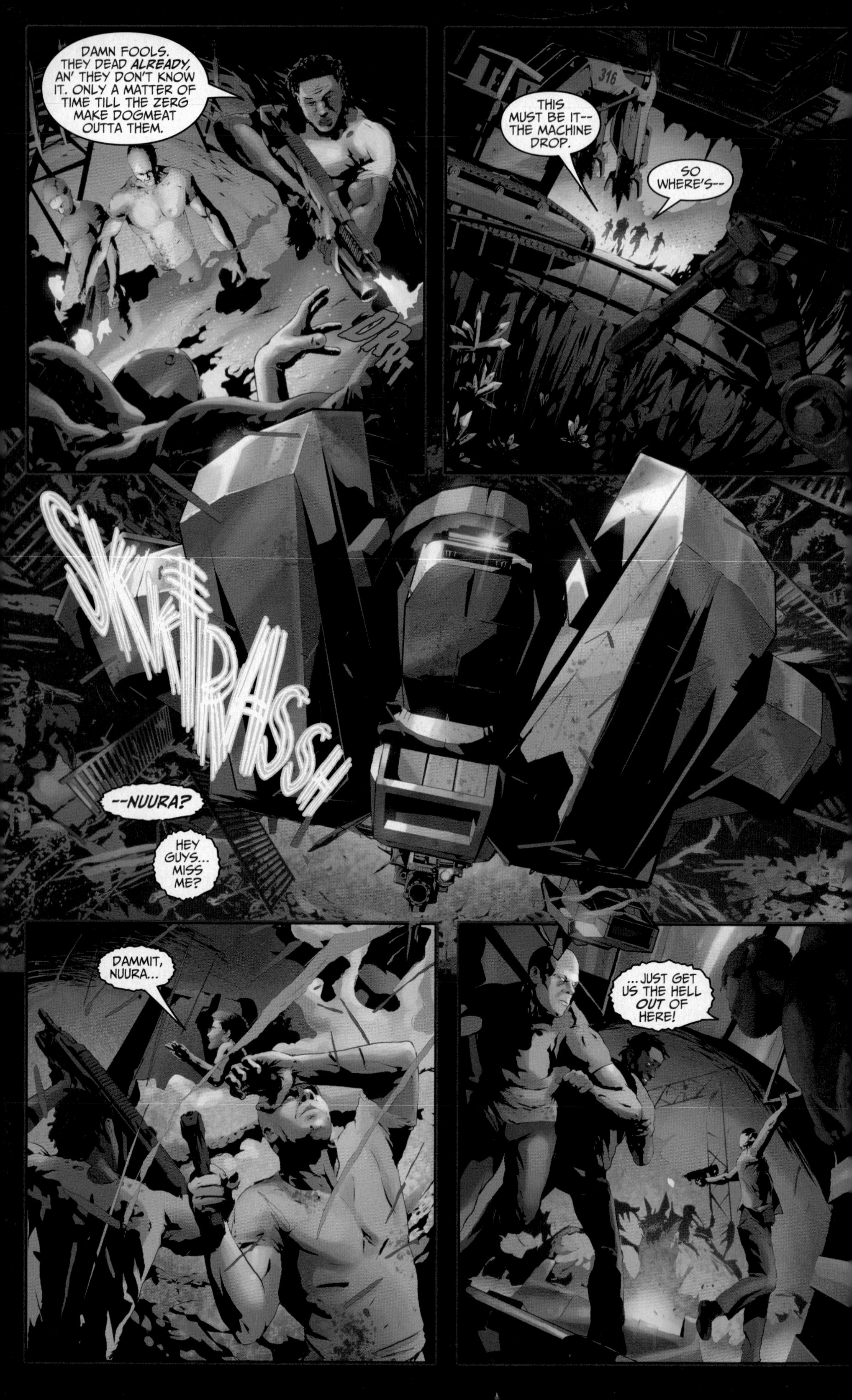
DAMN FOOLS. THEY DEAD ALREADY, AN' THEY DON'T KNOW IT. ONLY A MATTER OF TIME TILL THE ZERG MAKE DOGMEAT OUTTA THEM.
DRRT
THIS MUST BE IT-- THE MACHINE DROP.
SO WHERE'S--
SKTRASSH
--NUURA?
HEY GUYS... MISS ME?
DAMMIT, NUURA...
...JUST GET US THE HELL OUT OF HERE!

13

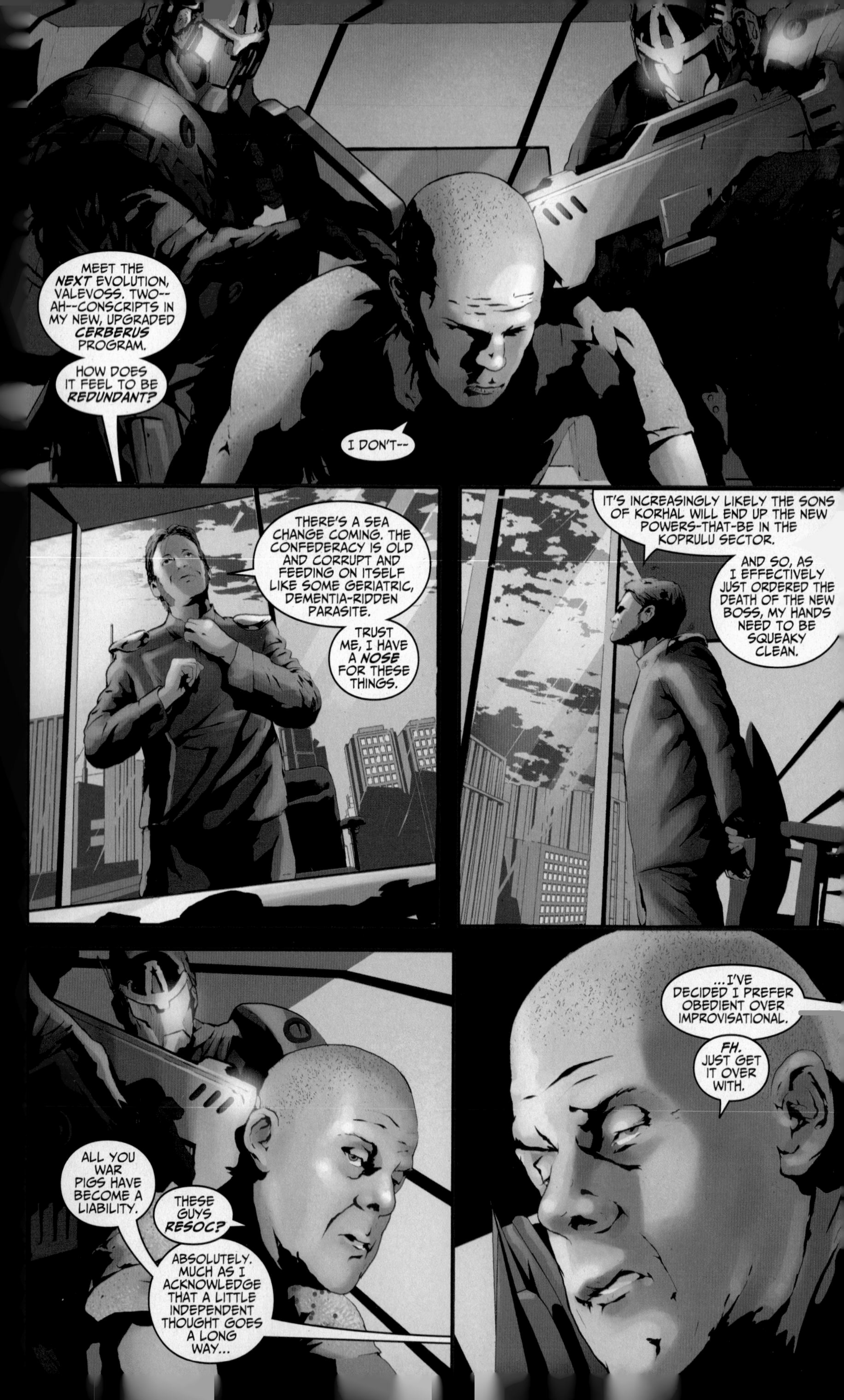
MEET THE NEXT EVOLUTION, VALEVOSS. TWO--AH--CONSCRIPTS IN MY NEW, UPGRADED CERBERUS PROGRAM.
HOW DOES IT FEEL TO BE REDUNDANT?
I DON'T--
THERE'S A SEA CHANGE COMING. THE CONFEDERACY IS OLD AND CORRUPT AND FEEDING ON ITSELF LIKE SOME GERIATRIC, DEMENTIA-RIDDEN PARASITE.
TRUST ME, I HAVE A NOSE FOR THESE THINGS.
IT'S INCREASINGLY LIKELY THE SONS OF KORHAL WILL END UP THE NEW POWERS-THAT-BE IN THE KOPRULU SECTOR.
AND SO, AS I EFFECTIVELY JUST ORDERED THE DEATH OF THE NEW BOSS, MY HANDS NEED TO BE SQUEAKY CLEAN.
ALL YOU WAR PIGS HAVE BECOME A LIABILITY.
THESE GUYS RESOC?
ABSOLUTELY. MUCH AS I ACKNOWLEDGE THAT A LITTLE INDEPENDENT THOUGHT GOES A LONG WAY...
...I'VE DECIDED I PREFER OBEDIENT OVER IMPROVISATIONAL.
FH. JUST GET IT OVER WITH.

I'VE BEEN LIVING ON BORROWED TIME LONG ENOUGH TO GET USED TO THE IDEA.

NO, NO. IF I'D WANTED YOU DEAD, YOU'D BE IN A CASKET BY NOW.

I'M OFFERING YOU A *DEAL,* VALEVOSS.

A DEAL.

YES-- A FULL PARDON, ANY REMAINING SENTENCE COMMUTED, THE SLATE WIPED CLEAN. *IF...*

...YOU GIVE ME THE *OTHERS.*

THE FRINGE WORLDS:

DAMMIT. YOU SHOULD *NEVER* HAVE LET VALEVOSS GO IN ALONE. CAULEY'S A SNAKE.

LIKE WE HAD A SAY IN IT, MAN. YOU KNOW BROCK, LAST OF THE LONE WOLVES.

YEAH, COLE, EXACTLY HOW MANY TIMES YOU GET IN HIS FACE WHEN HE'S IN THAT "ME, MYSELF AND I" *ZONE?*

I KNOW, I KNOW. BUT *THIS...*

IF TAMSEN CAULEY'S CLEANING HOUSE, THEN BROCK'S AS GOOD AS DEAD. PEOPLE TEND TO *DISAPPEAR* AROUND THAT MAN.

NOT BROCK. HE'LL *FIND* A WAY.

IF ANYONE CAN, HE CAN. BUT--

WHAT? YOU *SURE?*

WHAT IS IT? TURFA?

COLE HICKSON

17

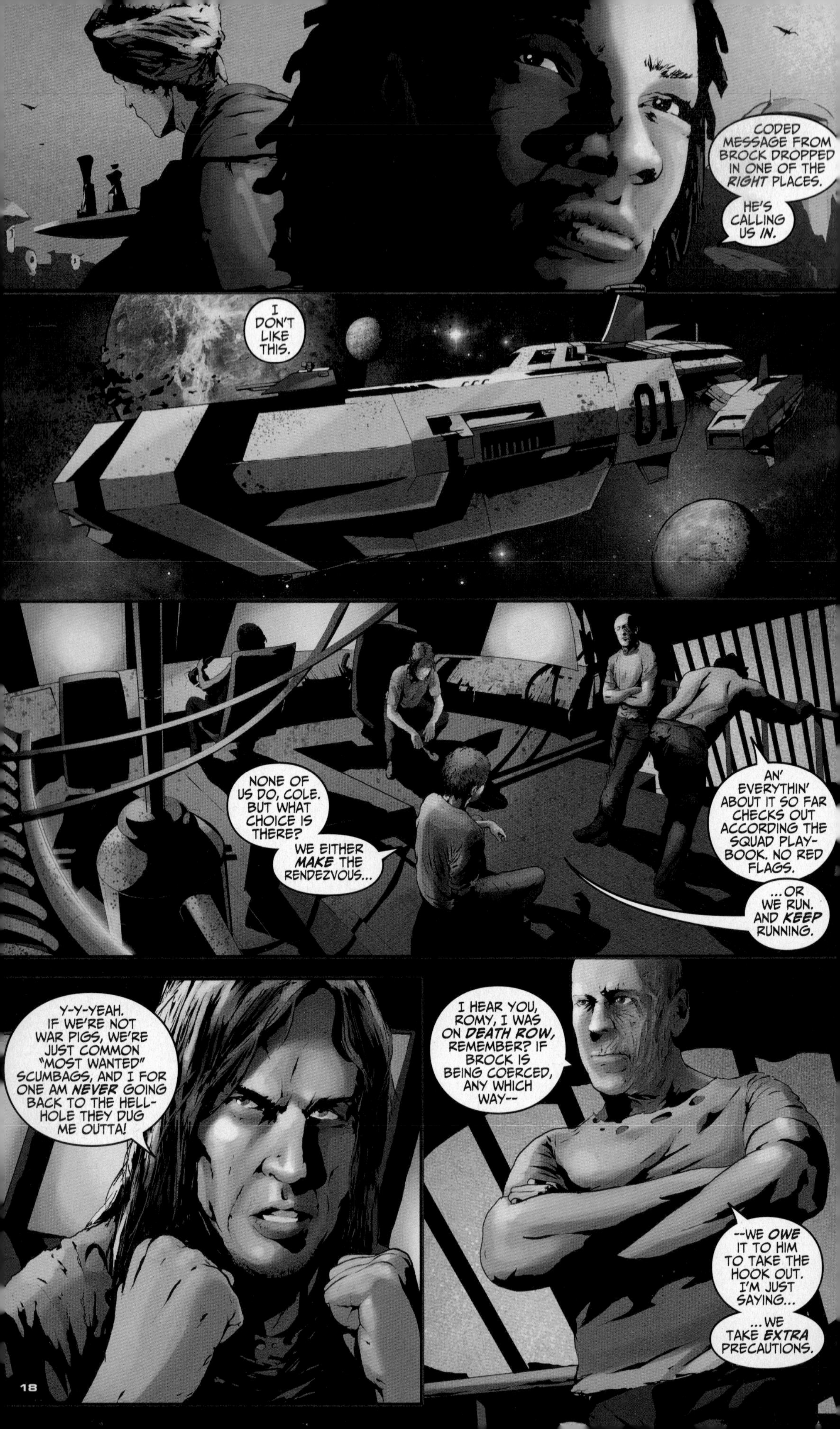
CODED MESSAGE FROM BROCK DROPPED IN ONE OF THE RIGHT PLACES.
HE'S CALLING US IN.
I DON'T LIKE THIS.
NONE OF US DO, COLE. BUT WHAT CHOICE IS THERE?
WE EITHER MAKE THE RENDEZVOUS...
AN' EVERYTHIN' ABOUT IT SO FAR CHECKS OUT ACCORDING THE SQUAD PLAY-BOOK. NO RED FLAGS.
...OR WE RUN. AND KEEP RUNNING.
Y-Y-YEAH. IF WE'RE NOT WAR PIGS, WE'RE JUST COMMON "MOST WANTED" SCUMBAGS, AND I FOR ONE AM NEVER GOING BACK TO THE HELL-HOLE THEY DUG ME OUTTA!
I HEAR YOU, ROMY, I WAS ON DEATH ROW, REMEMBER? IF BROCK IS BEING COERCED, ANY WHICH WAY--
--WE OWE IT TO HIM TO TAKE THE HOOK OUT. I'M JUST SAYING...
...WE TAKE EXTRA PRECAUTIONS.

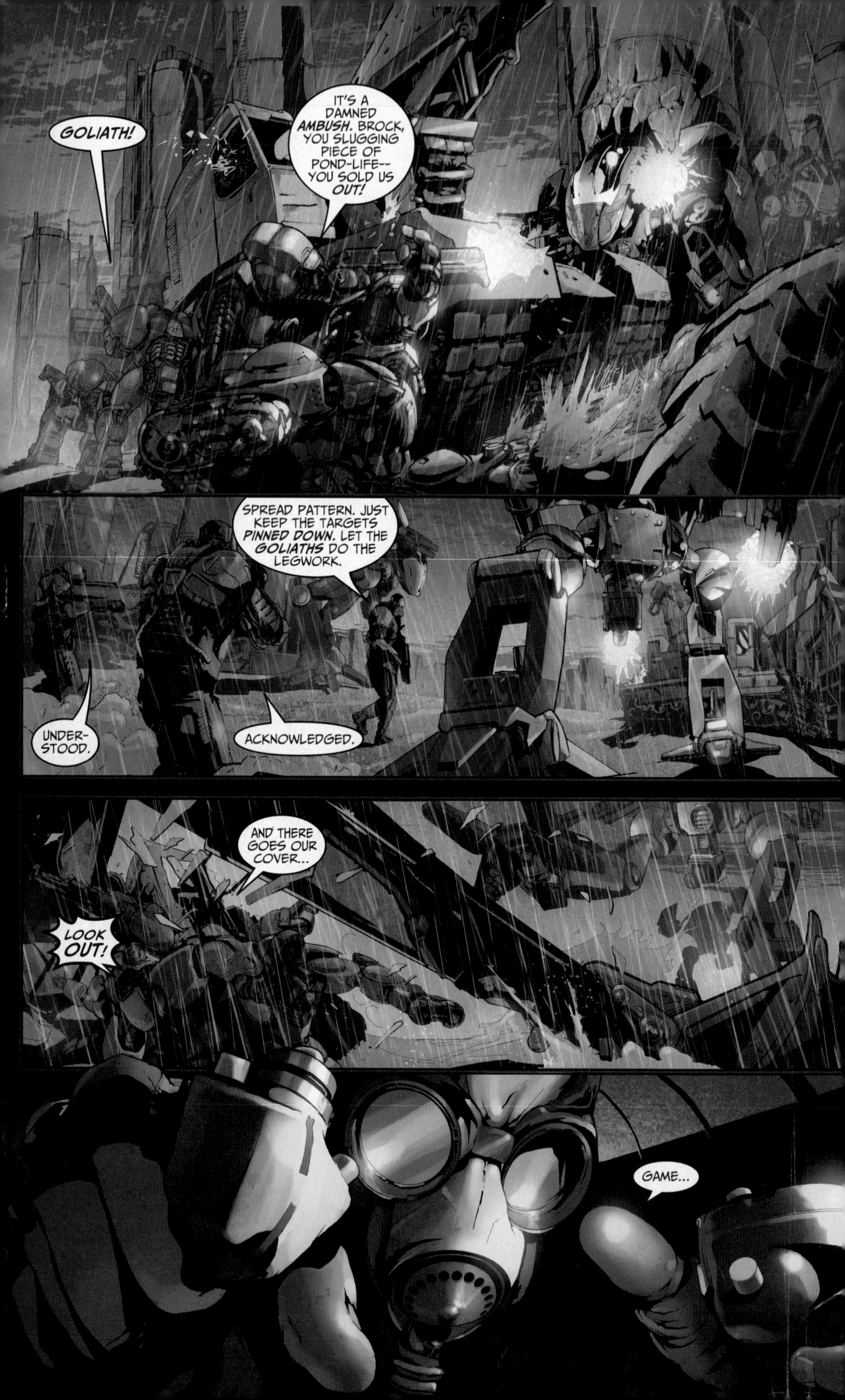
GOLIATH!
IT'S A DAMNED AMBUSH. BROCK, YOU SLUGGING PIECE OF POND-LIFE-- YOU SOLD US OUT!
SPREAD PATTERN. JUST KEEP THE TARGETS PINNED DOWN. LET THE GOLIATHS DO THE LEGWORK.
UNDER-STOOD.
ACKNOWLEDGED.
AND THERE GOES OUR COVER...
LOOK OUT!
GAME...

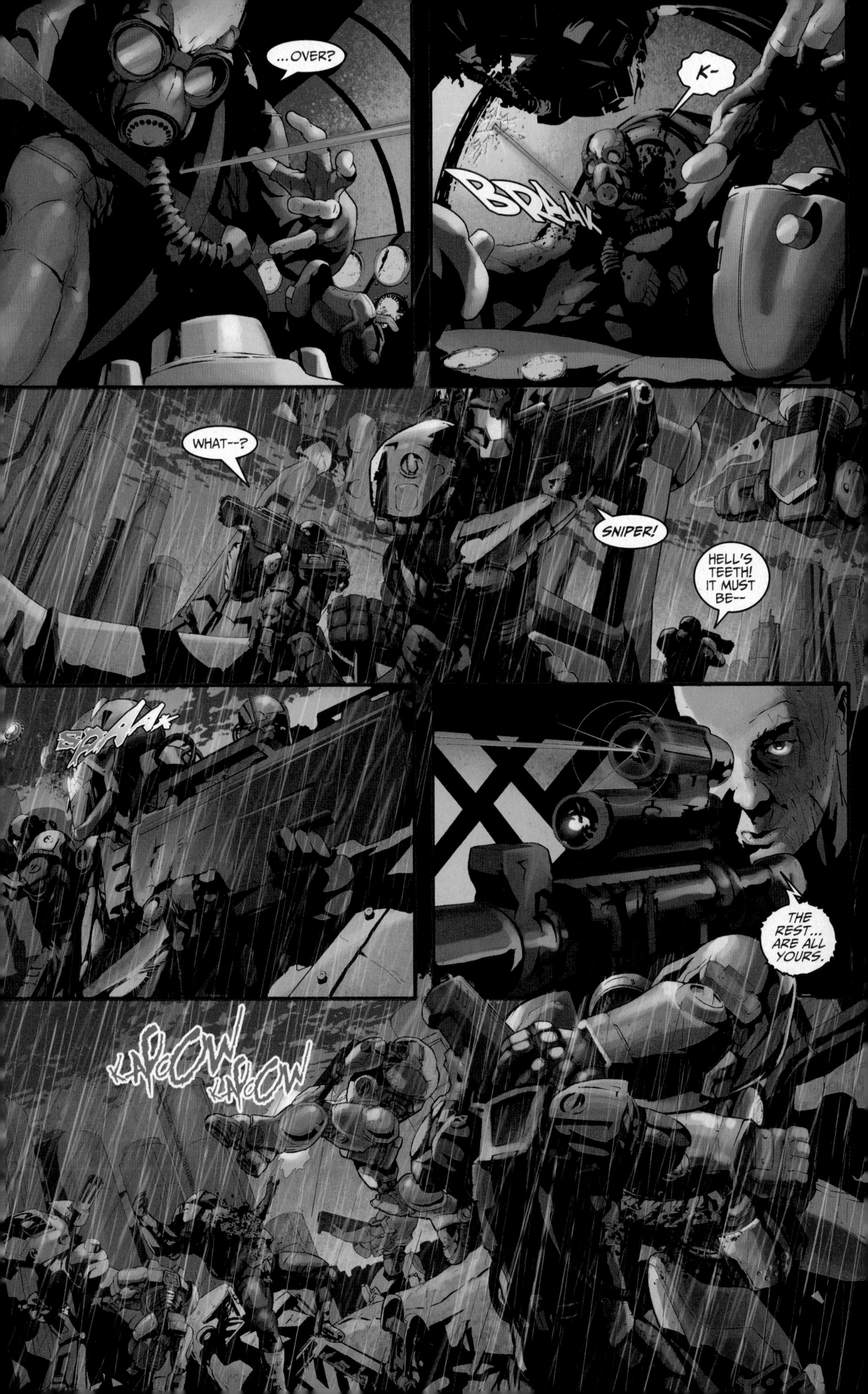
...OVER?
K-
BDRAAK
WHAT--?
SNIPER!
HELL'S TEETH! IT MUST BE--
THE REST... ARE ALL YOURS.
KAPOOW KAPOOW

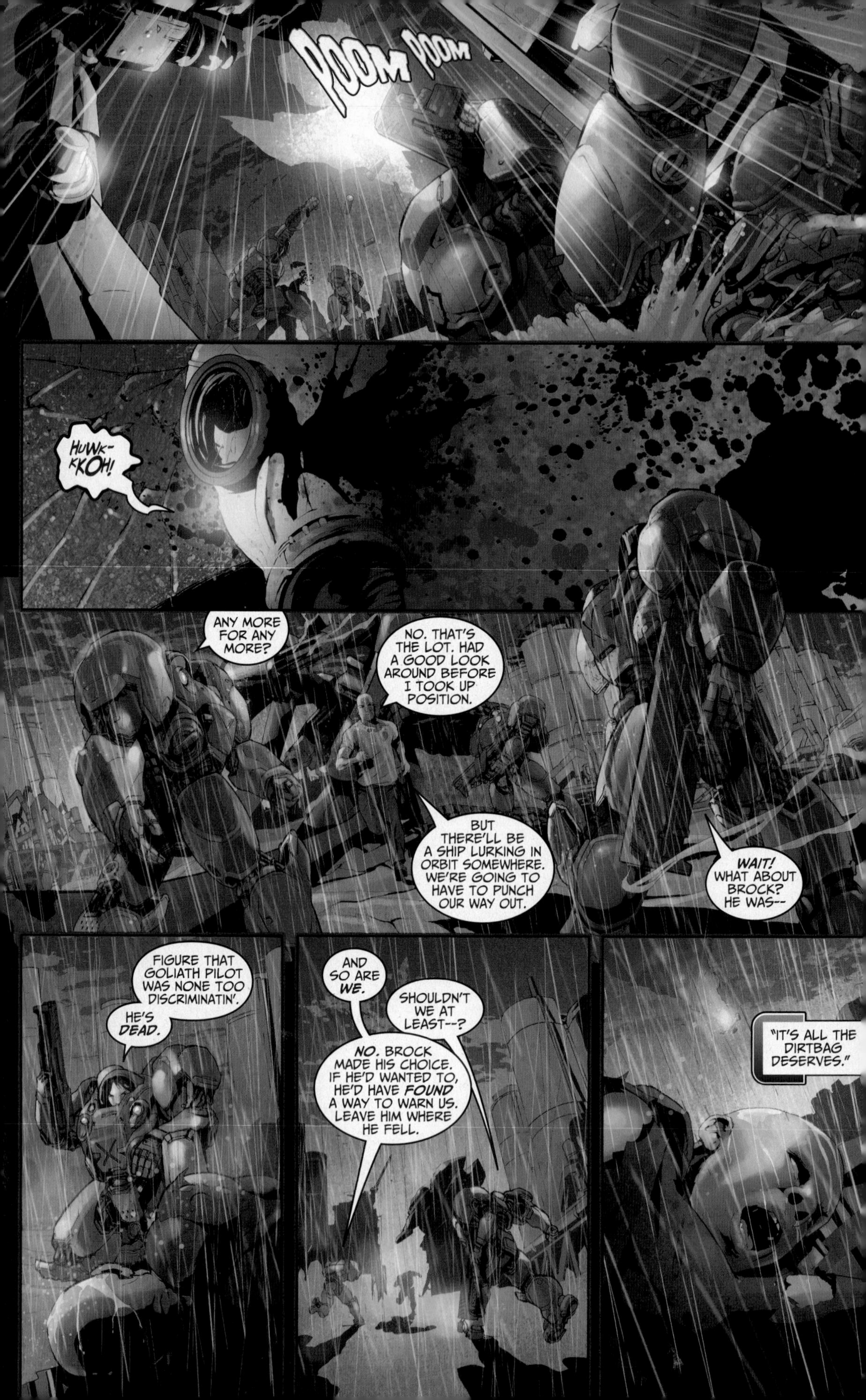
POOM POOM
HUWK-KKOH!
ANY MORE FOR ANY MORE?
NO. THAT'S THE LOT. HAD A GOOD LOOK AROUND BEFORE I TOOK UP POSITION.
BUT THERE'LL BE A SHIP LURKING IN ORBIT SOMEWHERE. WE'RE GOING TO HAVE TO PUNCH OUR WAY OUT.
WAIT! WHAT ABOUT BROCK? HE WAS--
FIGURE THAT GOLIATH PILOT WAS NONE TOO DISCRIMINATIN'.
HE'S DEAD.
AND SO ARE WE.
SHOULDN'T WE AT LEAST--?
NO. BROCK MADE HIS CHOICE. IF HE'D WANTED TO, HE'D HAVE FOUND A WAY TO WARN US. LEAVE HIM WHERE HE FELL.
"IT'S ALL THE DIRTBAG DESERVES."

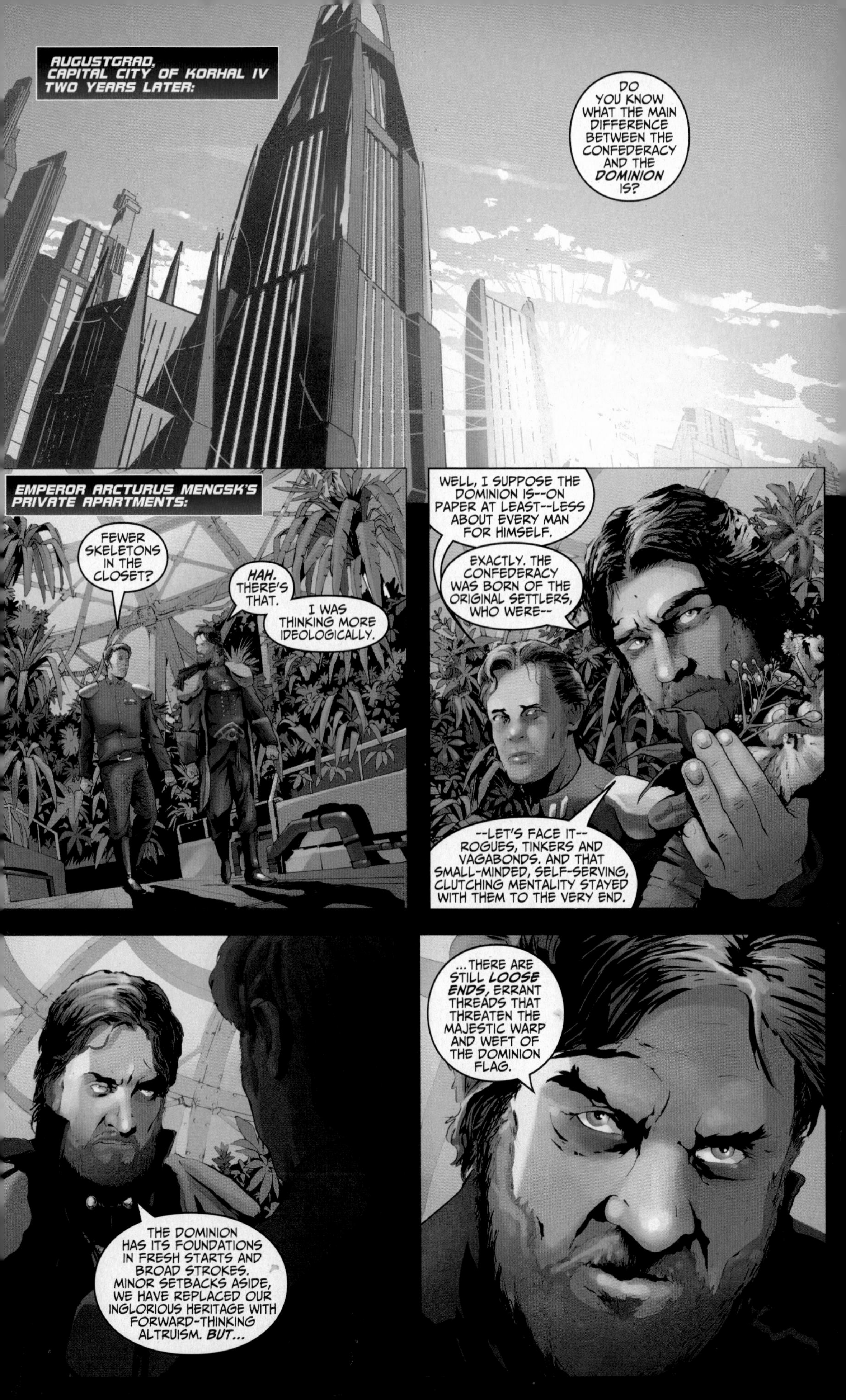
AUGUSTGRAD, CAPITAL CITY OF KORHAL IV TWO YEARS LATER:
DO YOU KNOW WHAT THE MAIN DIFFERENCE BETWEEN THE CONFEDERACY AND THE *DOMINION* IS?
EMPEROR ARCTURUS MENGSK'S PRIVATE APARTMENTS:
FEWER SKELETONS IN THE CLOSET?
HAH. THERE'S THAT.
I WAS THINKING MORE IDEOLOGICALLY.
WELL, I SUPPOSE THE DOMINION IS--ON PAPER AT LEAST--LESS ABOUT EVERY MAN FOR HIMSELF.
EXACTLY. THE CONFEDERACY WAS BORN OF THE ORIGINAL SETTLERS, WHO WERE--
--LET'S FACE IT--ROGUES, TINKERS AND VAGABONDS. AND THAT SMALL-MINDED, SELF-SERVING, CLUTCHING MENTALITY STAYED WITH THEM TO THE VERY END.
THE DOMINION HAS ITS FOUNDATIONS IN FRESH STARTS AND BROAD STROKES. MINOR SETBACKS ASIDE, WE HAVE REPLACED OUR INGLORIOUS HERITAGE WITH FORWARD-THINKING ALTRUISM. *BUT...*
...THERE ARE STILL *LOOSE ENDS,* ERRANT THREADS THAT THREATEN THE MAJESTIC WARP AND WEFT OF THE DOMINION FLAG.

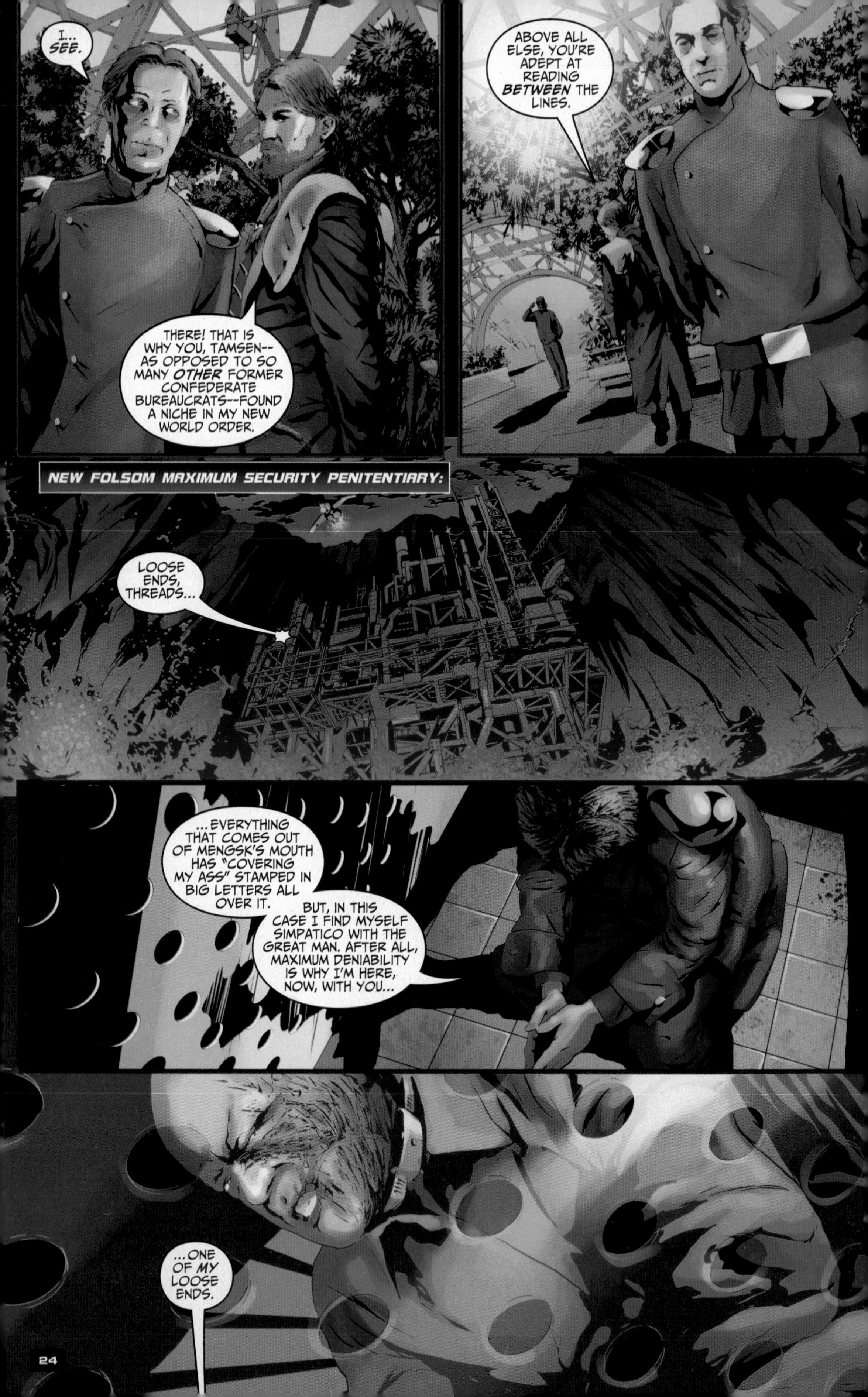
I... SEE.
THERE! THAT IS WHY YOU, TAMSEN-- AS OPPOSED TO SO MANY OTHER FORMER CONFEDERATE BUREAUCRATS--FOUND A NICHE IN MY NEW WORLD ORDER.
ABOVE ALL ELSE, YOU'RE ADEPT AT READING BETWEEN THE LINES.
NEW FOLSOM MAXIMUM SECURITY PENITENTIARY:
LOOSE ENDS, THREADS...
...EVERYTHING THAT COMES OUT OF MENGSK'S MOUTH HAS "COVERING MY ASS" STAMPED IN BIG LETTERS ALL OVER IT.
BUT, IN THIS CASE I FIND MYSELF SIMPATICO WITH THE GREAT MAN. AFTER ALL, MAXIMUM DENIABILITY IS WHY I'M HERE, NOW, WITH YOU...
...ONE OF MY LOOSE ENDS.

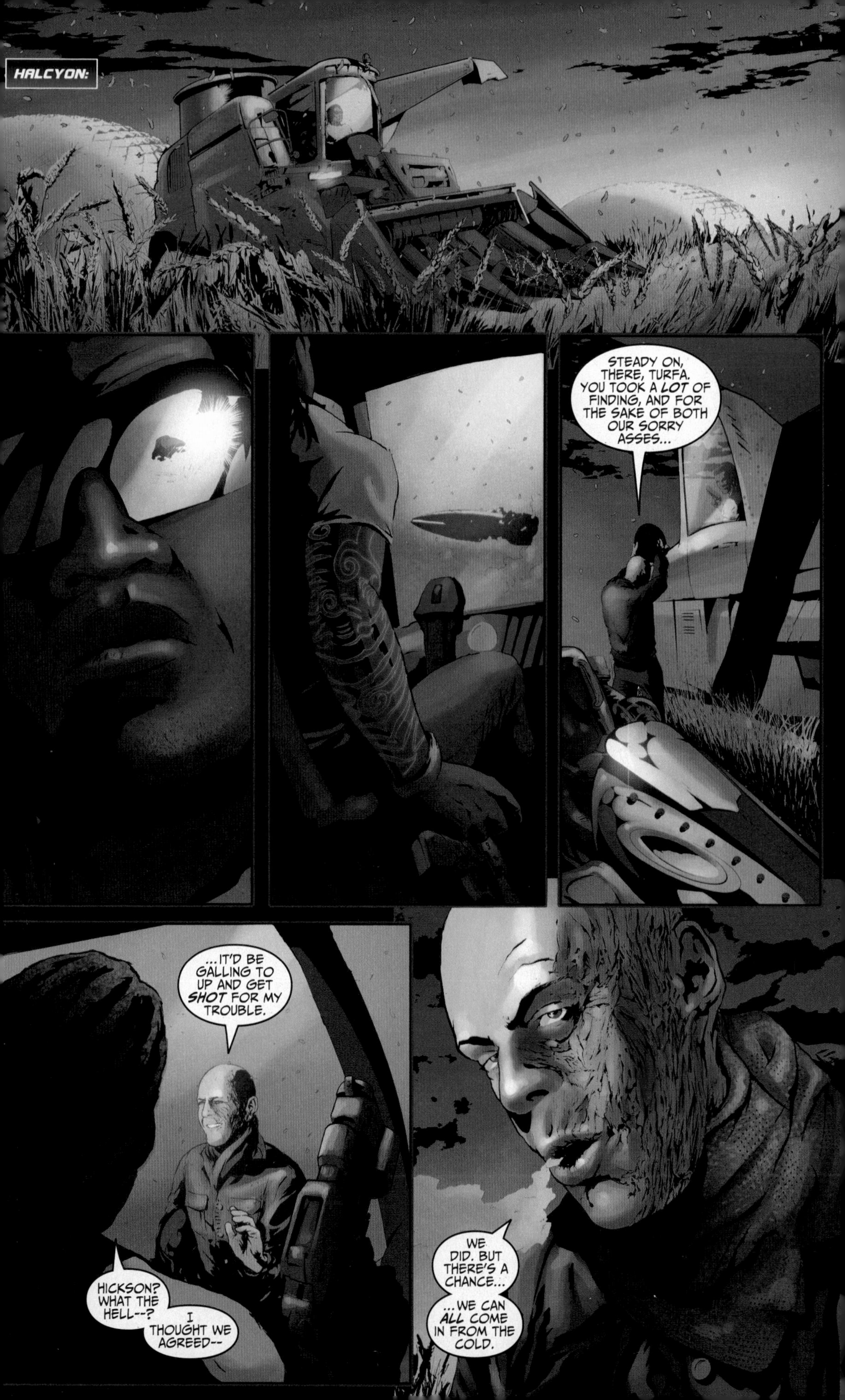
HALCYON:
STEADY ON, THERE, TURFA. YOU TOOK A LOT OF FINDING, AND FOR THE SAKE OF BOTH OUR SORRY ASSES...
...IT'D BE GALLING TO UP AND GET SHOT FOR MY TROUBLE.
HICKSON? WHAT THE HELL--?
I THOUGHT WE AGREED--
WE DID. BUT THERE'S A CHANCE...
...WE CAN ALL COME IN FROM THE COLD.

AND YOU *BELIEVE* HIM?

IT'S A BRAVE NEW WORLD, TURFA. CAULEY NO LONGER HAS HIS OWN DEDICATED AND LABYRINTHINE SUPPORT NETWORK.

MUCH AS HE MIGHT NOT LIKE IT, MENGSK HAS HIM ON A PRETTY TIGHT LEASH.

AND THE DEAL IS *WHAT* EXACTLY?

PUT OUR SQUAD BACK TOGETHER FOR ONE LAST MISSION. DO IT RIGHT AND WE'RE FREE MEN. FULL PARDON, BACK PAY, THE LOT.

ONE *BIG* HAPPY FAMILY, EH. REMEMBER WHAT HAPPENED *LAST* TIME?

I KNOW, I KNOW. THERE'S A LOT TO FORGIVE AND FORGET. WHEN CAULEY BROUGHT IT TO ME, MY FIRST REACTION WAS TO TELL HIM TO STUFF IT.

BUT THE ALTERNATIVE IS TO KEEP SCRAPING AROUND FOR PISS-AWFUL JOBS IN THE ASS END OF NOWHERE. I'M *TIRED*, TURFA...

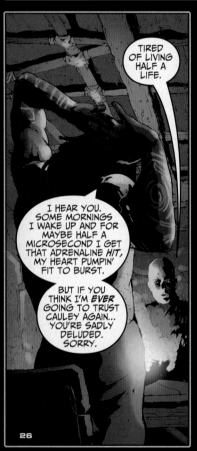

TIRED OF LIVING HALF A LIFE.

I HEAR YOU. SOME MORNINGS I WAKE UP AND FOR MAYBE HALF A MICROSECOND I GET THAT ADRENALINE *HIT*, MY HEART PUMPIN' FIT TO BURST.

BUT IF YOU THINK I'M *EVER* GOING TO TRUST CAULEY AGAIN... YOU'RE SADLY DELUDED. SORRY.

UM. JUST OUTTA CURIOSITY, WHAT'S THE JOB?

STANDARD. LOCATE AND ELIMINATE.

THE MARK?

EX-CONFEDERATE MARSHAL, RENEGADE, AND ALL ROUND THORN IN MENGSK'S BUTT.

JIM RAYNOR.

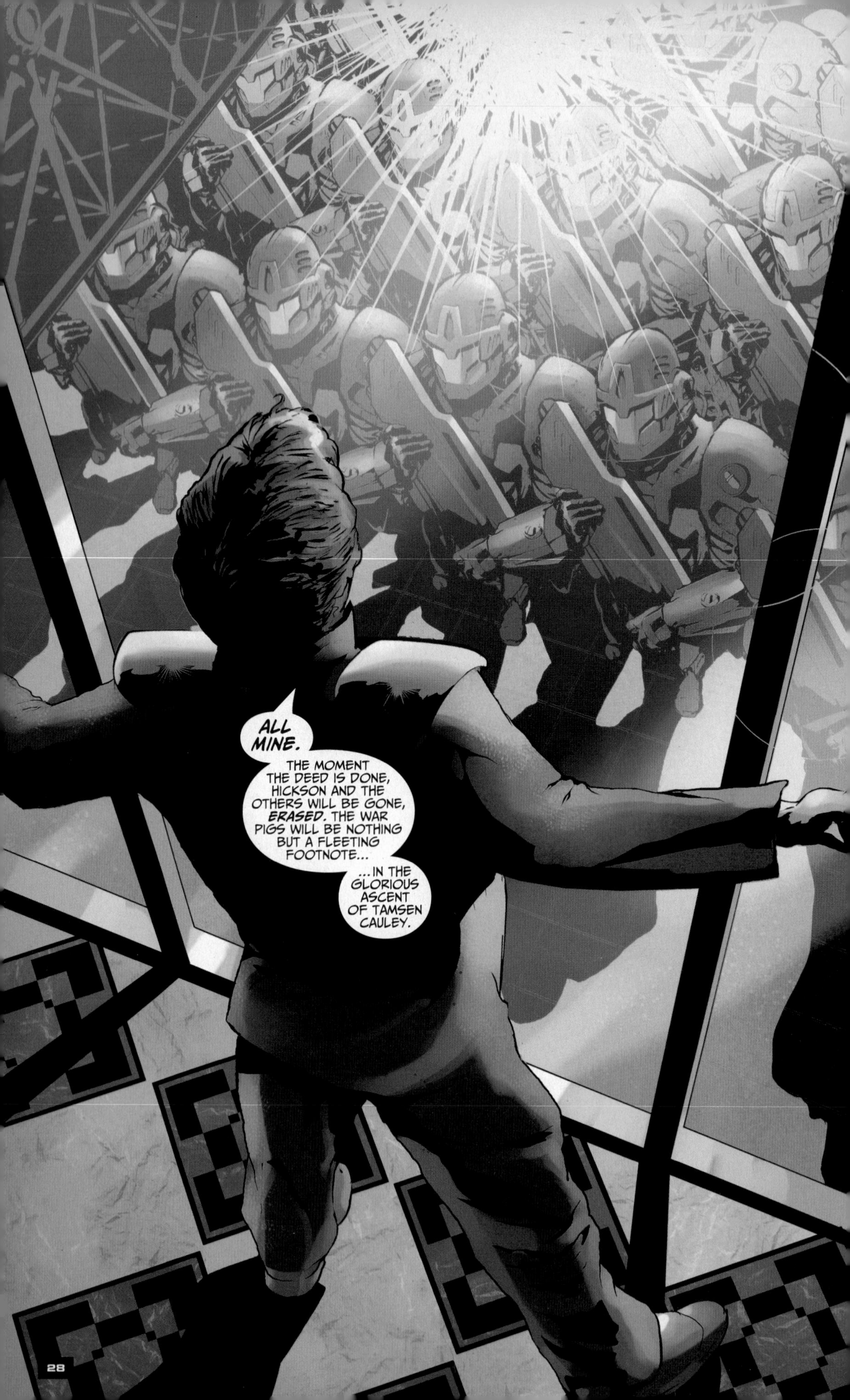
ALL MINE.
THE MOMENT THE DEED IS DONE, HICKSON AND THE OTHERS WILL BE GONE, ERASED. THE WAR PIGS WILL BE NOTHING BUT A FLEETING FOOTNOTE...
...IN THE GLORIOUS ASCENT OF TAMSEN CAULEY.

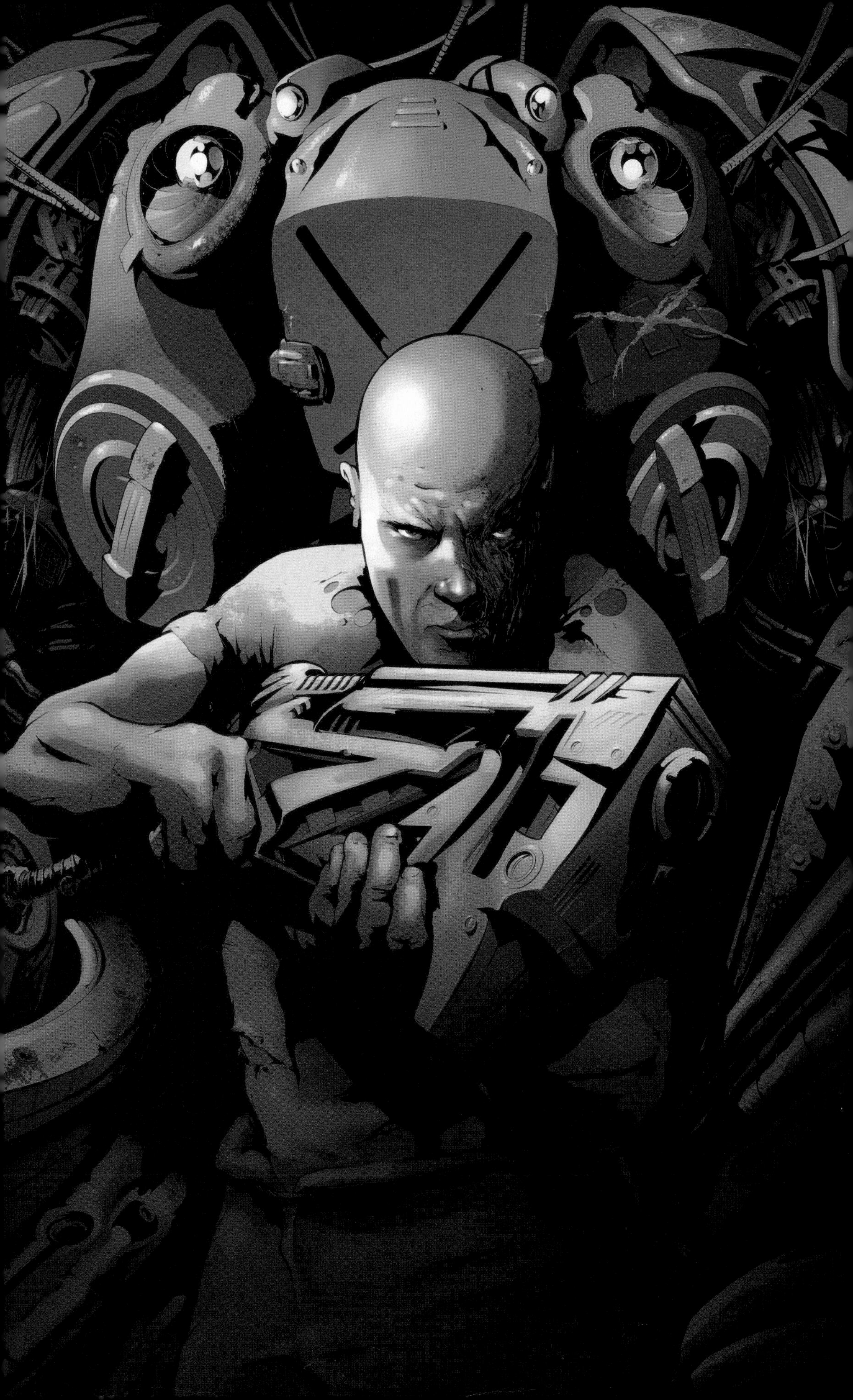

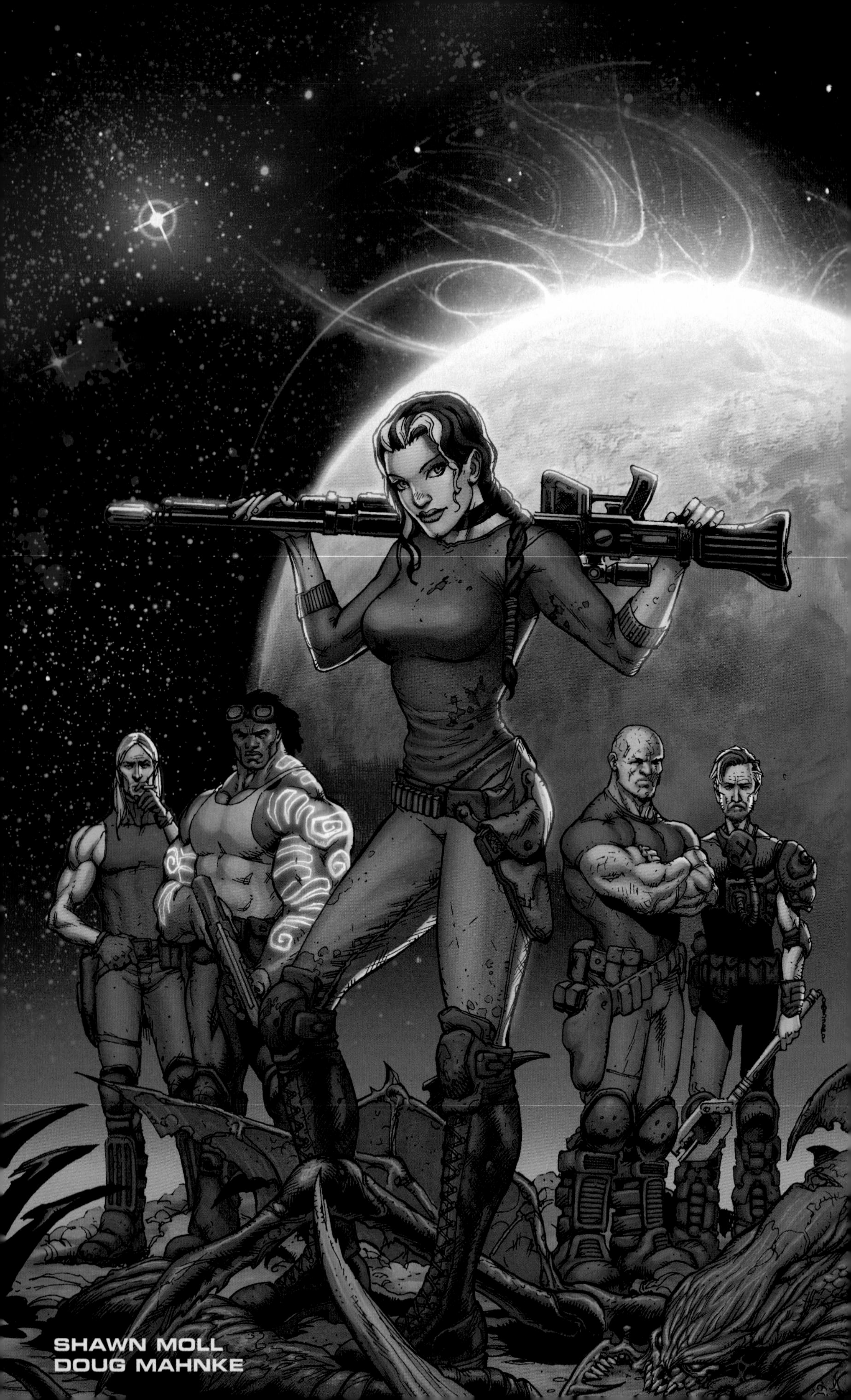
SHAWN MOLL
DOUG MAHNKE

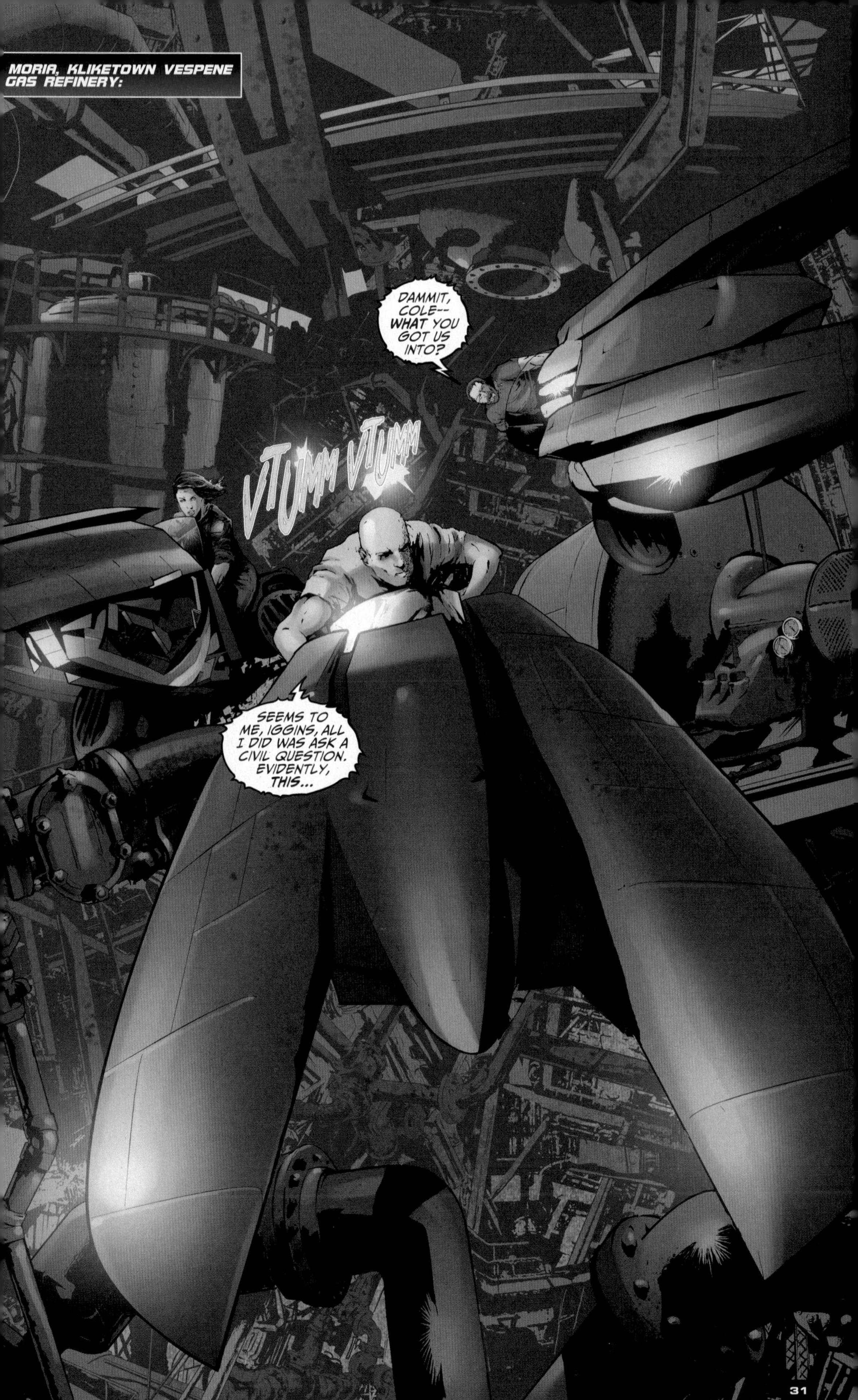

MORIA, KLIKETOWN VESPENE GAS REFINERY:
DAMMIT, COLE-- WHAT YOU GOT US INTO?
VTUMM VTUMM
SEEMS TO ME, IGGINS, ALL I DID WAS ASK A CIVIL QUESTION. EVIDENTLY, THIS...

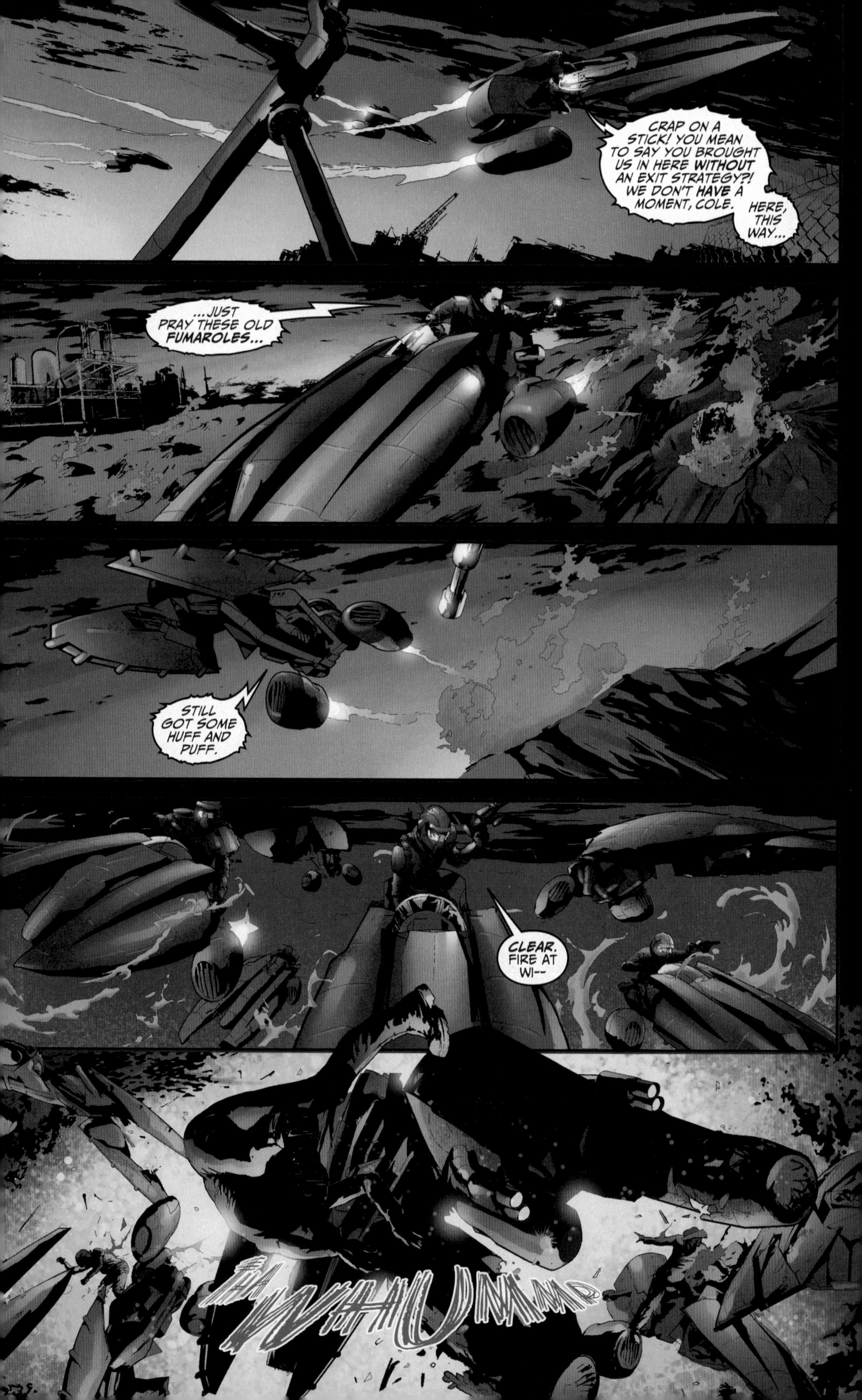

CRAP ON A STICK! YOU MEAN TO SAY YOU BROUGHT US IN HERE WITHOUT AN EXIT STRATEGY?! WE DON'T HAVE A MOMENT, COLE.
HERE, THIS WAY...
...JUST PRAY THESE OLD FUMAROLES...
STILL GOT SOME HUFF AND PUFF.
CLEAR. FIRE AT WI--
THWHUMMP

NICELY DONE, NUURA.

HEY...

WE WERE LUCKY. THAT'S ALL. AND LUCK IS THE LAST RECOURSE OF THE SOON-TO-BE-DEPARTED. YOUR WORDS, COLE...

...WHERE'S THE SLUGGIN' GENERAL LEE?

kDAK *kDAK*

kDAK

VATHUUUMM.

C'MON-- C'MON! HAD TO DUST OFF AT THE DOUBLE AND WE CAN'T HANG AROUND.

LISTEN UP...

...WE'LL BE COMING IN TOO FAST FOR BRAKES TO DO MUCH GOOD...

...SO PREPARE TO BAIL.

POOR BABY. SEE WHAT HAPPENS WHEN I LEAVE YOU?

UNIDENTIFIED VEHICLES

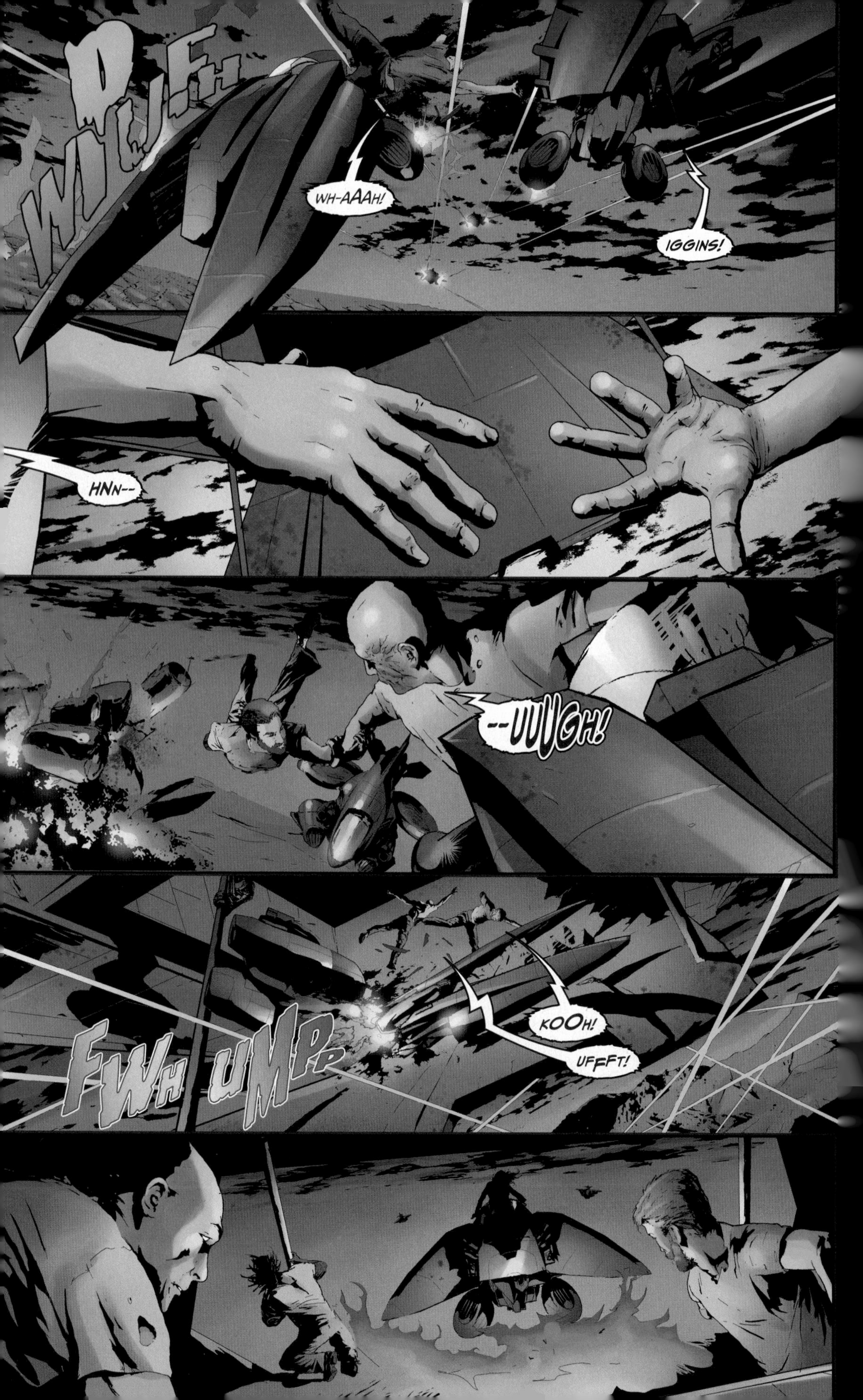
WHUFH
WH-AAAH!
IGGINS!
HNn--
--UUUGH!
KOOH!
UFFFT!
FWHUMP

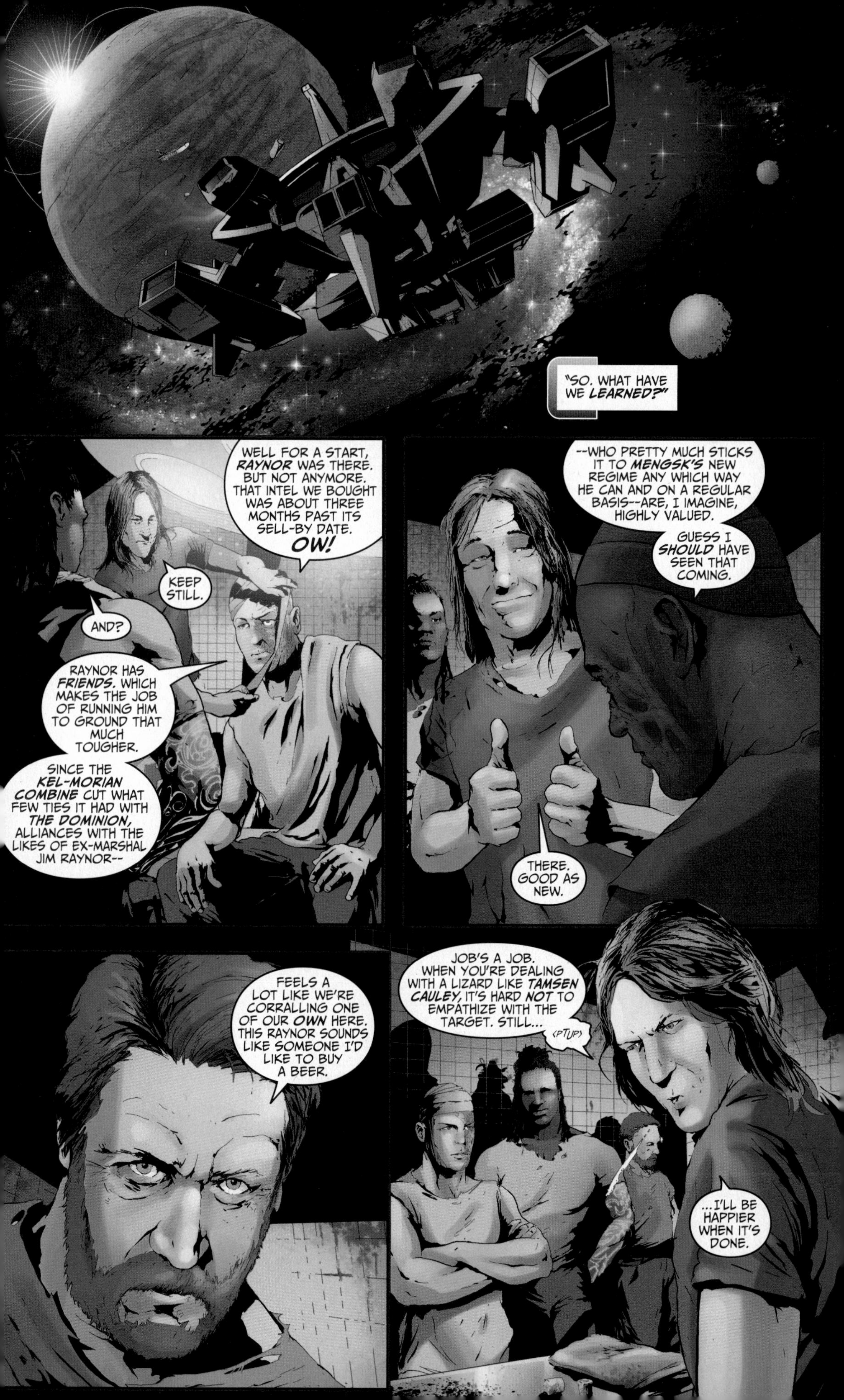

"SO. WHAT HAVE WE LEARNED?"
WELL FOR A START, RAYNOR WAS THERE. BUT NOT ANYMORE. THAT INTEL WE BOUGHT WAS ABOUT THREE MONTHS PAST ITS SELL-BY DATE. OW!
KEEP STILL.
AND?
RAYNOR HAS FRIENDS. WHICH MAKES THE JOB OF RUNNING HIM TO GROUND THAT MUCH TOUGHER.
SINCE THE KEL-MORIAN COMBINE CUT WHAT FEW TIES IT HAD WITH THE DOMINION, ALLIANCES WITH THE LIKES OF EX-MARSHAL JIM RAYNOR--
--WHO PRETTY MUCH STICKS IT TO MENGSK'S NEW REGIME ANY WHICH WAY HE CAN AND ON A REGULAR BASIS--ARE, I IMAGINE, HIGHLY VALUED.
GUESS I SHOULD HAVE SEEN THAT COMING.
THERE. GOOD AS NEW.
FEELS A LOT LIKE WE'RE CORRALLING ONE OF OUR OWN HERE. THIS RAYNOR SOUNDS LIKE SOMEONE I'D LIKE TO BUY A BEER.
JOB'S A JOB. WHEN YOU'RE DEALING WITH A LIZARD LIKE TAMSEN CAULEY, IT'S HARD NOT TO EMPATHIZE WITH THE TARGET. STILL...
<PTUP>
...I'LL BE HAPPIER WHEN IT'S DONE.

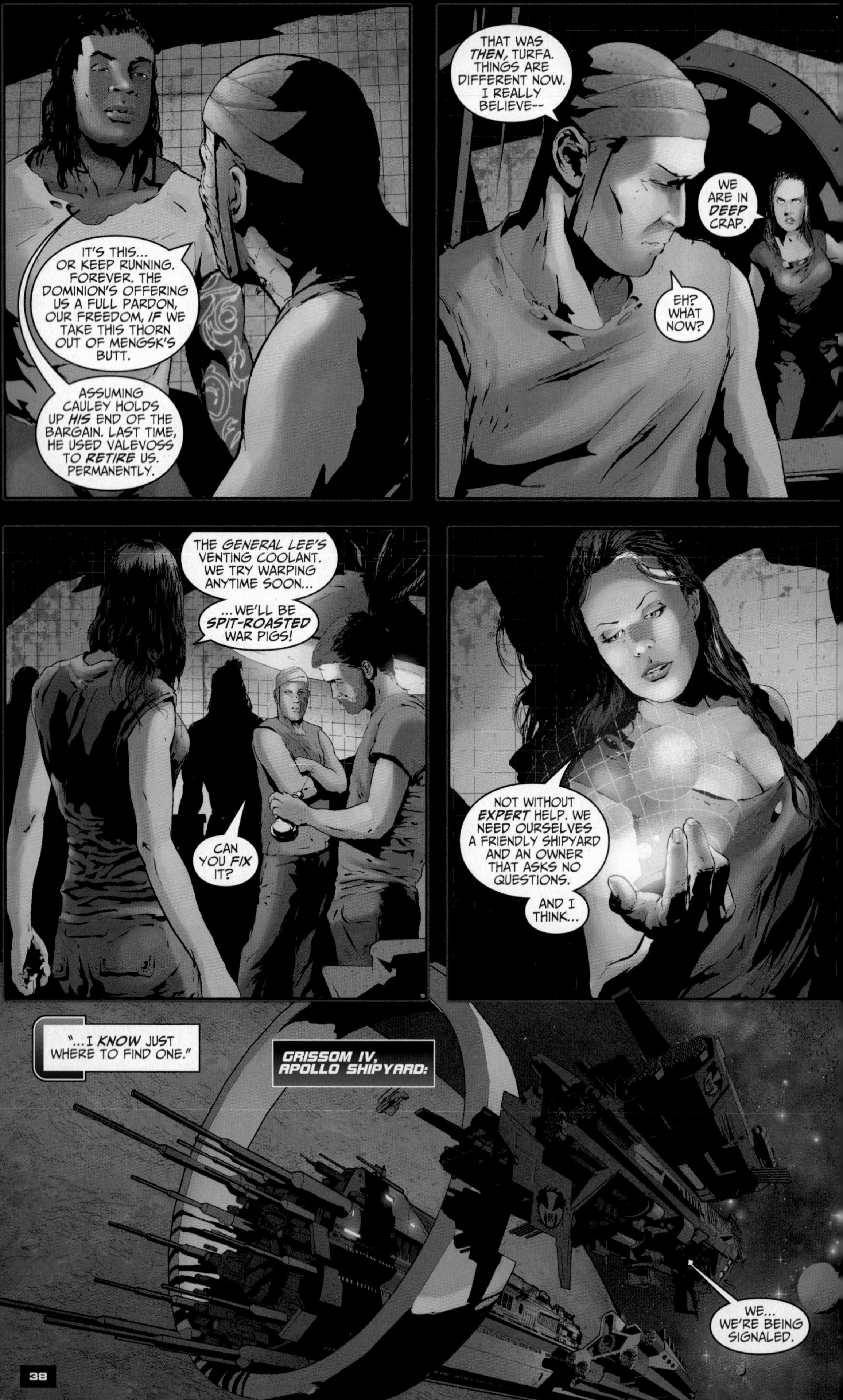
IT'S THIS... OR KEEP RUNNING. FOREVER. THE DOMINION'S OFFERING US A FULL PARDON, OUR FREEDOM, IF WE TAKE THIS THORN OUT OF MENGSK'S BUTT.
ASSUMING CAULEY HOLDS UP HIS END OF THE BARGAIN. LAST TIME, HE USED VALEVOSS TO RETIRE US. PERMANENTLY.
THAT WAS THEN, TURFA. THINGS ARE DIFFERENT NOW. I REALLY BELIEVE--
WE ARE IN DEEP CRAP.
EH? WHAT NOW?
THE GENERAL LEE'S VENTING COOLANT. WE TRY WARPING ANYTIME SOON...
...WE'LL BE SPIT-ROASTED WAR PIGS!
CAN YOU FIX IT?
NOT WITHOUT EXPERT HELP. WE NEED OURSELVES A FRIENDLY SHIPYARD AND AN OWNER THAT ASKS NO QUESTIONS.
AND I THINK...
"...I KNOW JUST WHERE TO FIND ONE."
GRISSOM IV, APOLLO SHIPYARD:
WE... WE'RE BEING SIGNALED.

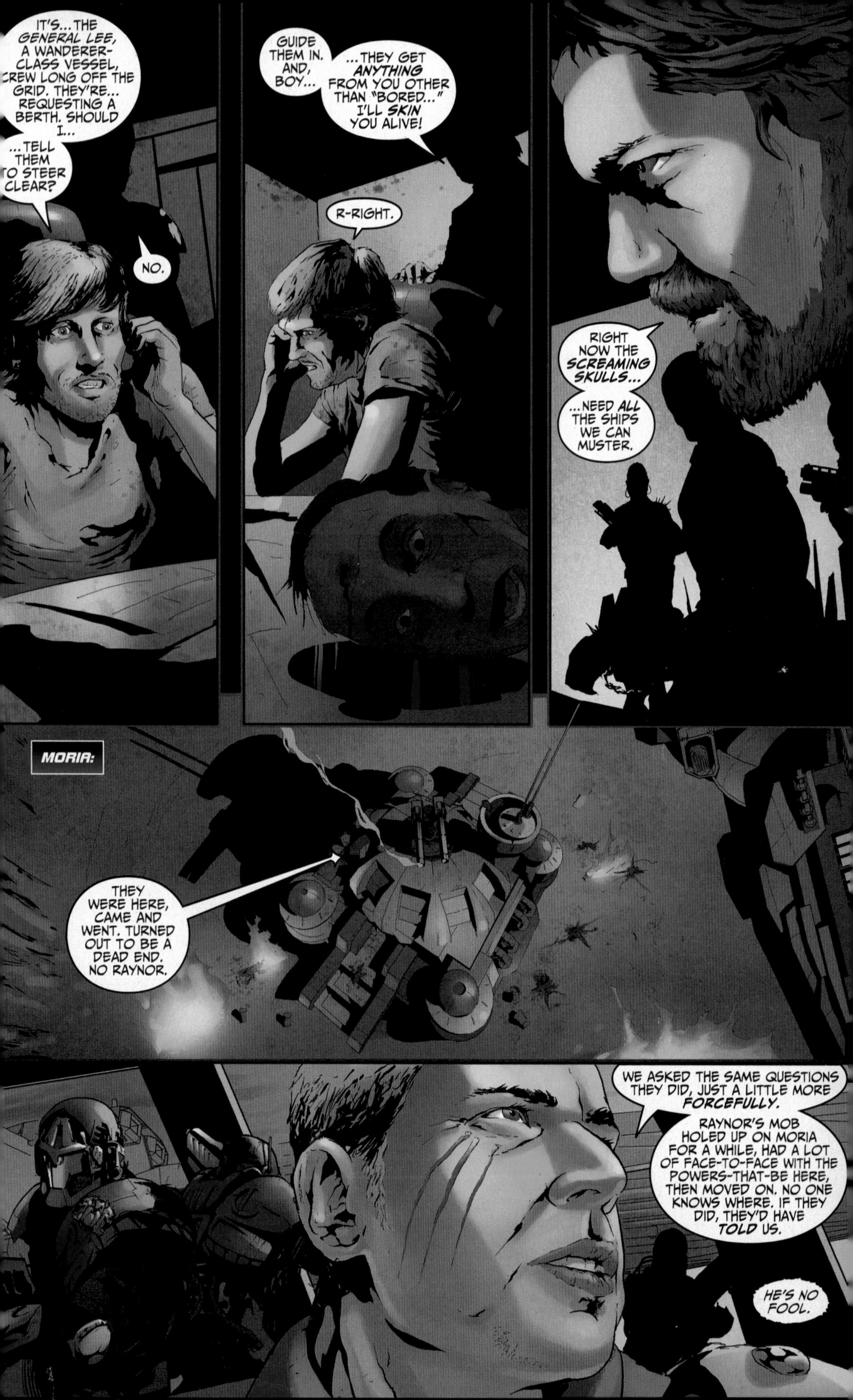

IT'S...THE *GENERAL LEE,* A WANDERER-CLASS VESSEL, CREW LONG OFF THE GRID. THEY'RE... REQUESTING A BERTH. SHOULD I...
...TELL THEM TO STEER CLEAR?
NO.
GUIDE THEM IN. AND, BOY...
...THEY GET ***ANYTHING*** FROM YOU OTHER THAN "BORED..." I'LL ***SKIN*** YOU ALIVE!
R-RIGHT.
RIGHT NOW THE ***SCREAMING SKULLS...***
...NEED ***ALL*** THE SHIPS WE CAN MUSTER.
MORIA:
THEY WERE HERE, CAME AND WENT. TURNED OUT TO BE A DEAD END. NO RAYNOR.
WE ASKED THE SAME QUESTIONS THEY DID, JUST A LITTLE MORE ***FORCEFULLY.***
RAYNOR'S MOB HOLED UP ON MORIA FOR A WHILE, HAD A LOT OF FACE-TO-FACE WITH THE POWERS-THAT-BE HERE, THEN MOVED ON. NO ONE KNOWS WHERE. IF THEY DID, THEY'D HAVE ***TOLD*** US.
HE'S NO FOOL.

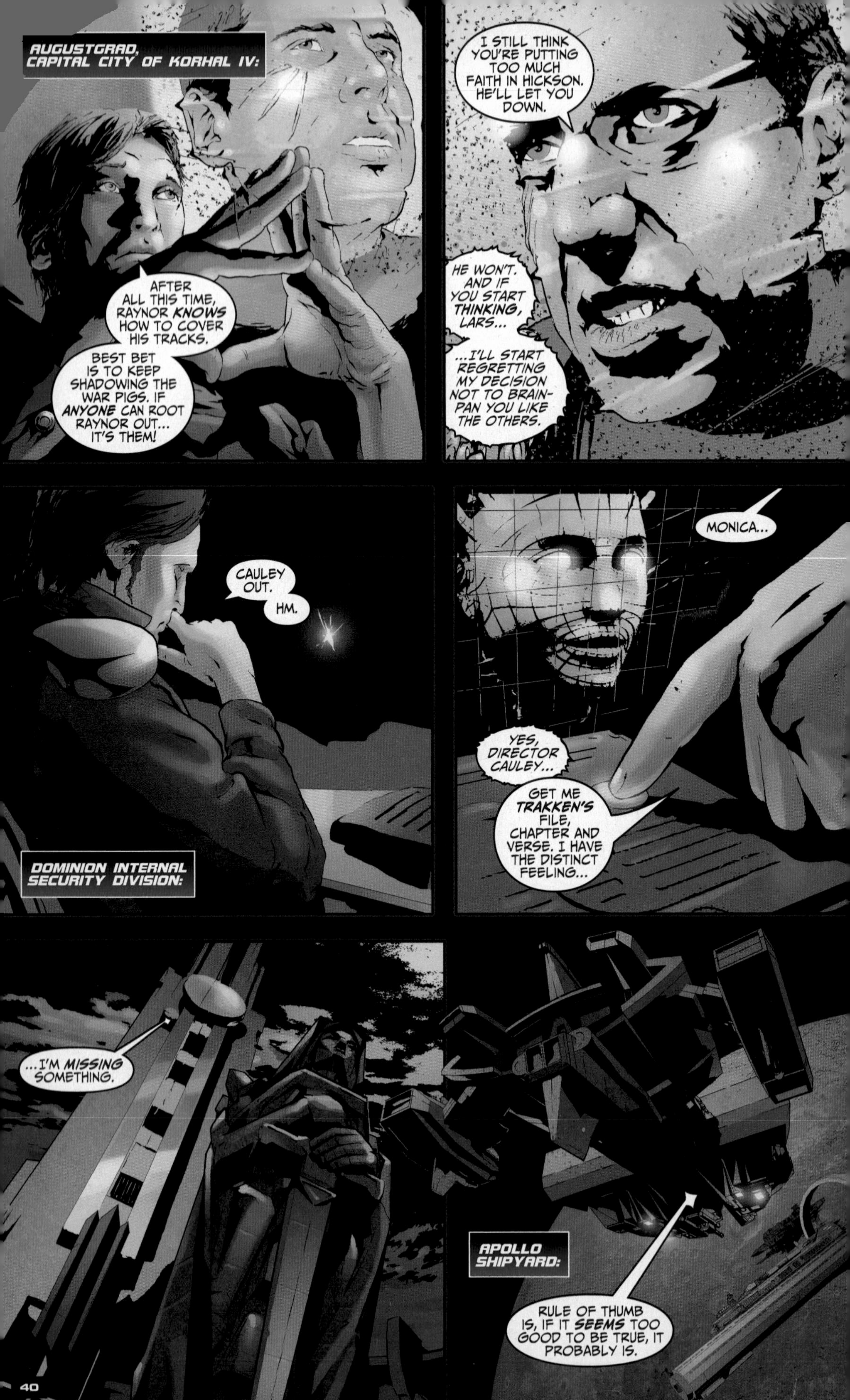
AUGUSTGRAD, CAPITAL CITY OF KORHAL IV:
AFTER ALL THIS TIME, RAYNOR KNOWS HOW TO COVER HIS TRACKS.
BEST BET IS TO KEEP SHADOWING THE WAR PIGS. IF ANYONE CAN ROOT RAYNOR OUT... IT'S THEM!
I STILL THINK YOU'RE PUTTING TOO MUCH FAITH IN HICKSON. HE'LL LET YOU DOWN.
HE WON'T. AND IF YOU START THINKING, LARS...
...I'LL START REGRETTING MY DECISION NOT TO BRAIN-PAN YOU LIKE THE OTHERS.
CAULEY OUT.
HM.
DOMINION INTERNAL SECURITY DIVISION:
MONICA...
YES, DIRECTOR CAULEY...
GET ME TRAKKEN'S FILE, CHAPTER AND VERSE. I HAVE THE DISTINCT FEELING...
...I'M MISSING SOMETHING.
APOLLO SHIPYARD:
RULE OF THUMB IS, IF IT SEEMS TOO GOOD TO BE TRUE, IT PROBABLY IS.

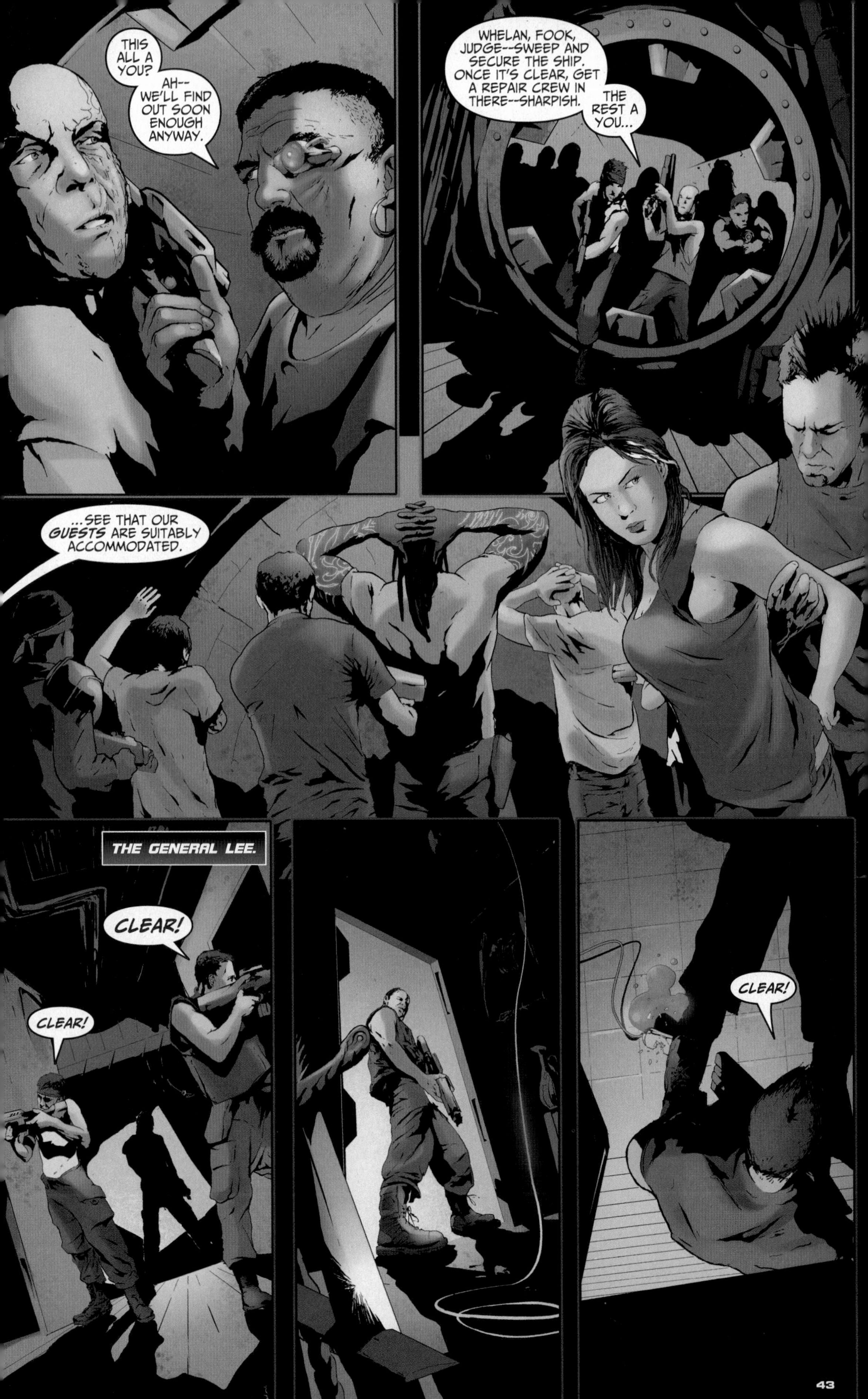
THIS ALL A YOU?
AH-- WE'LL FIND OUT SOON ENOUGH ANYWAY.
WHELAN, FOOK, JUDGE--SWEEP AND SECURE THE SHIP. ONCE IT'S CLEAR, GET A REPAIR CREW IN THERE--SHARPISH.
THE REST A YOU...
...SEE THAT OUR *GUESTS* ARE SUITABLY ACCOMMODATED.
THE GENERAL LEE.
CLEAR!
CLEAR!
CLEAR!

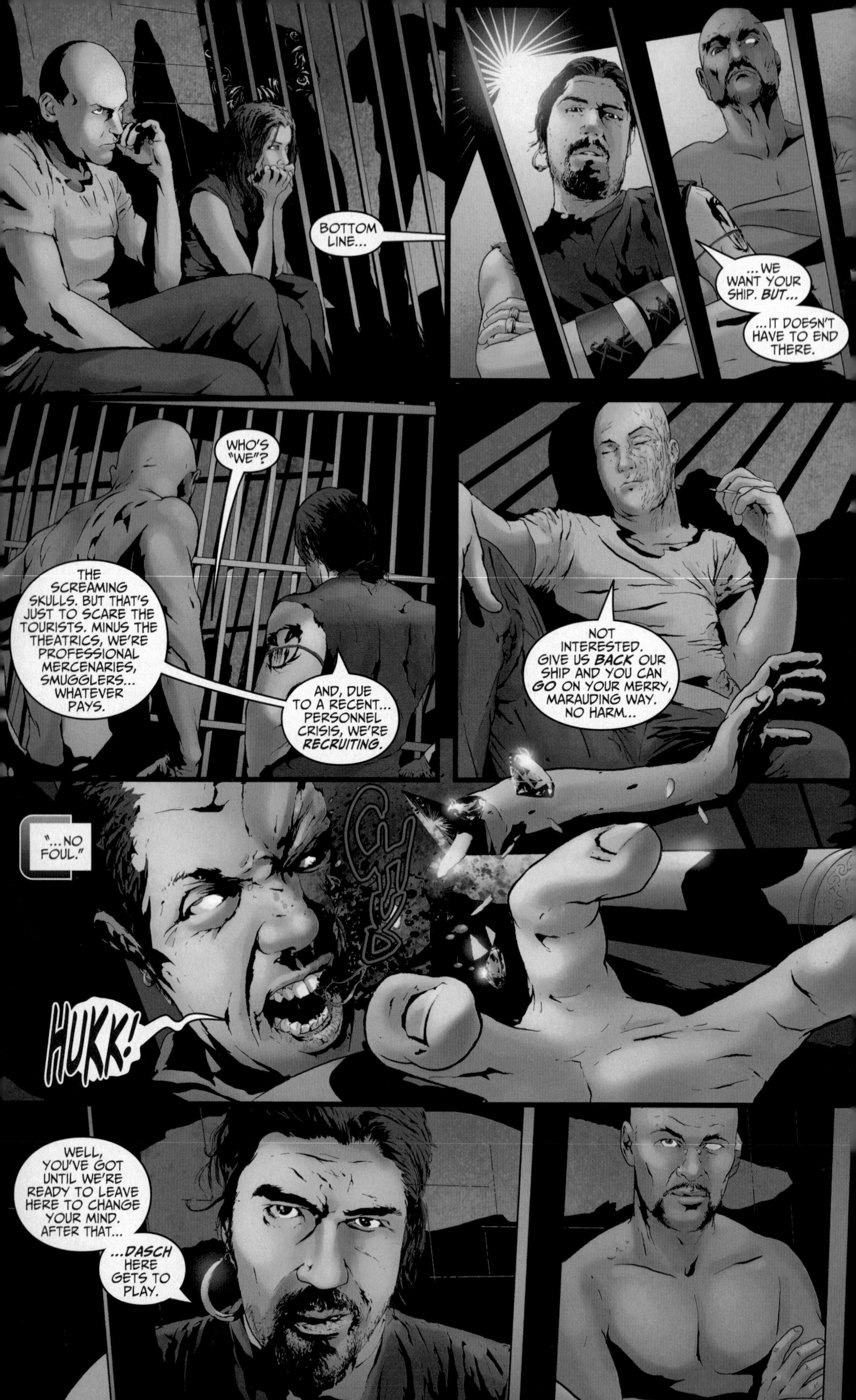
BOTTOM LINE...
...WE WANT YOUR SHIP. BUT...
...IT DOESN'T HAVE TO END THERE.
WHO'S "WE"?
THE SCREAMING SKULLS. BUT THAT'S JUST TO SCARE THE TOURISTS. MINUS THE THEATRICS, WE'RE PROFESSIONAL MERCENARIES, SMUGGLERS... WHATEVER PAYS.
AND, DUE TO A RECENT... PERSONNEL CRISIS, WE'RE RECRUITING.
NOT INTERESTED. GIVE US BACK OUR SHIP AND YOU CAN GO ON YOUR MERRY, MARAUDING WAY. NO HARM...
"...NO FOUL."
HUKK!
WELL, YOU'VE GOT UNTIL WE'RE READY TO LEAVE HERE TO CHANGE YOUR MIND. AFTER THAT...
...DASCH HERE GETS TO PLAY.

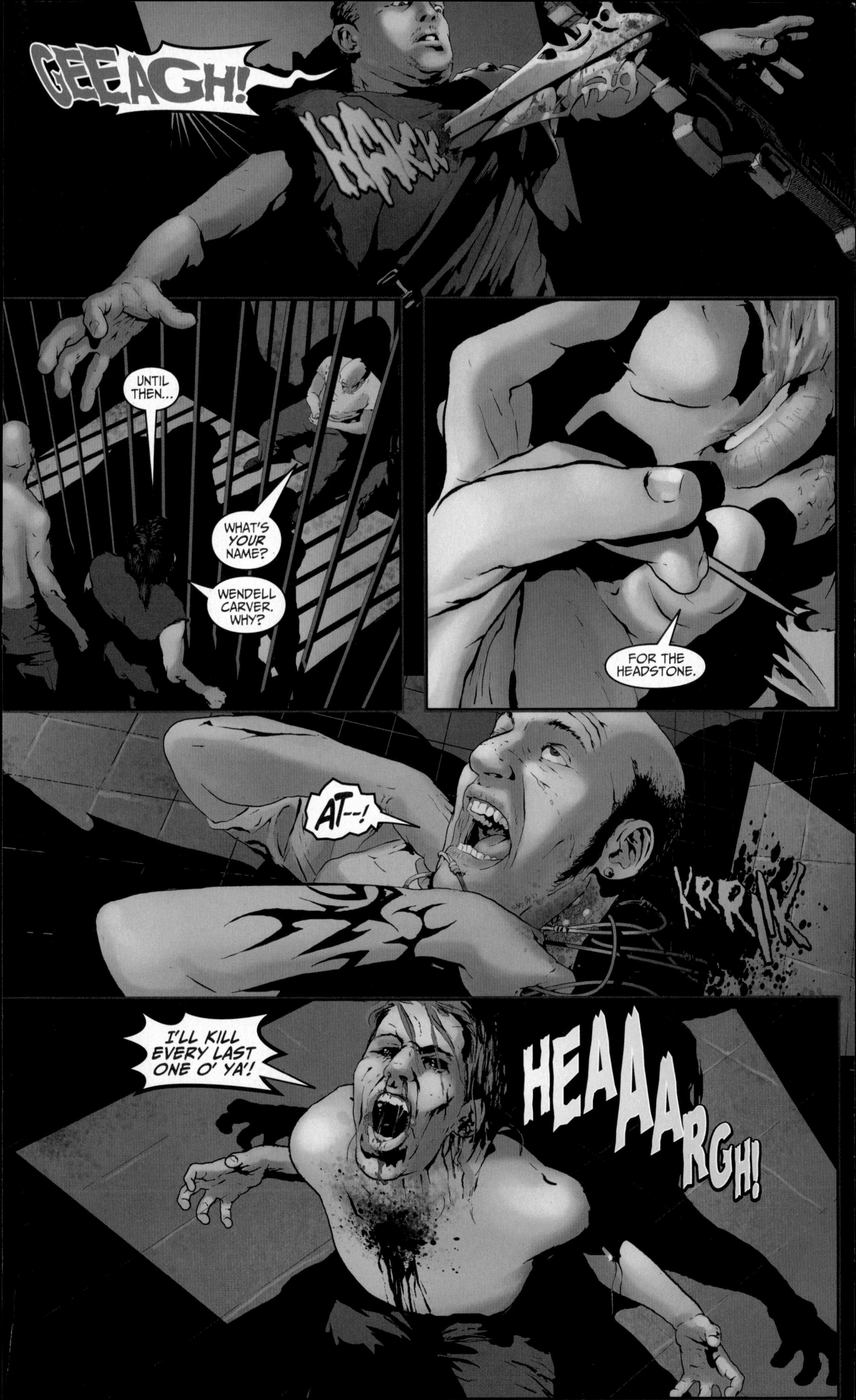
GEEAGH!
HAKK
UNTIL THEN...
WHAT'S YOUR NAME?
WENDELL CARVER. WHY?
FOR THE HEADSTONE.
AT--!
KRRIK
I'LL KILL EVERY LAST ONE O' YA'!
HEAAARGH!

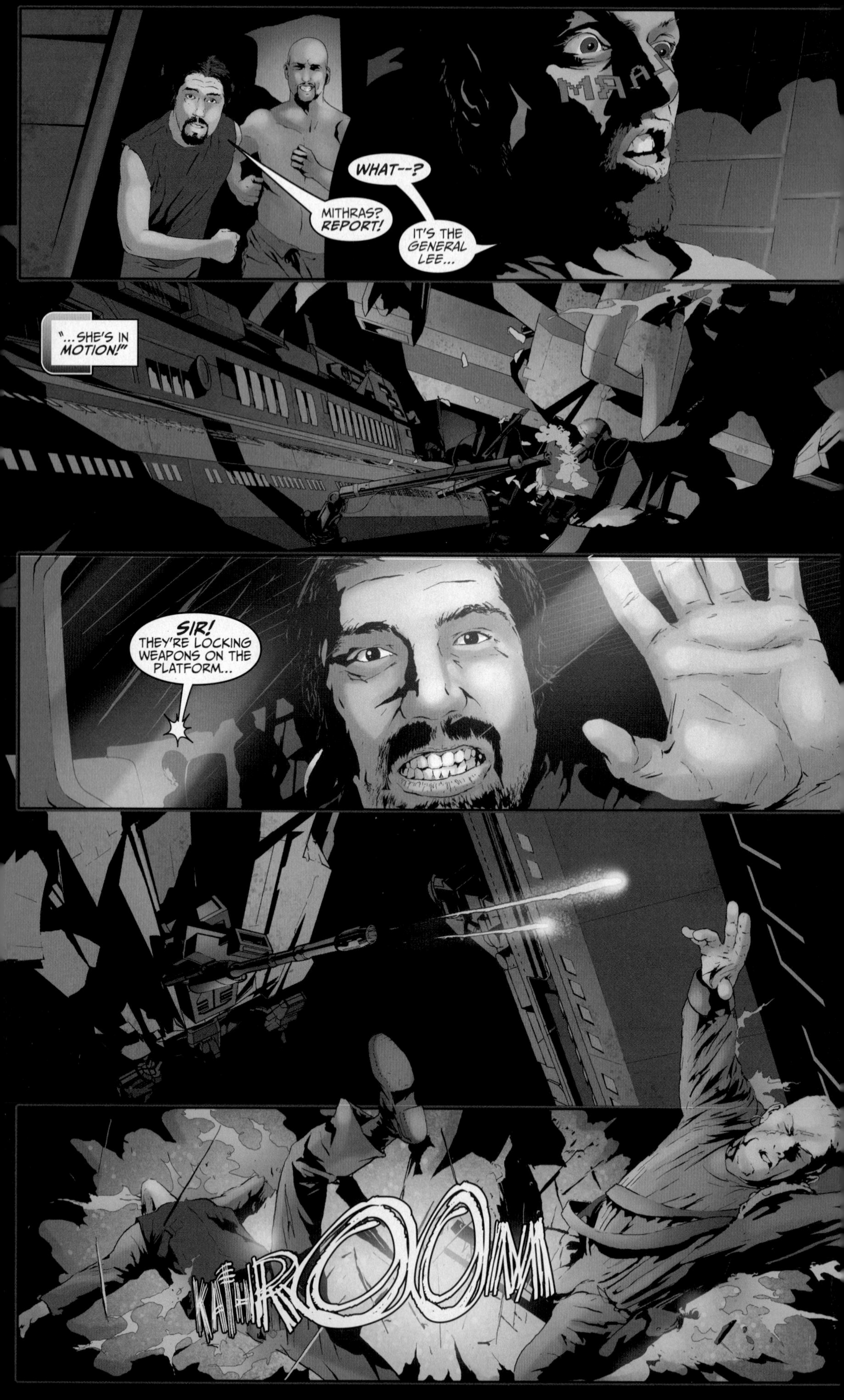

MITHRAS? REPORT!
WHAT--?
IT'S THE GENERAL LEE...
"...SHE'S IN MOTION!"
SIR! THEY'RE LOCKING WEAPONS ON THE PLATFORM...
KATHROOOM

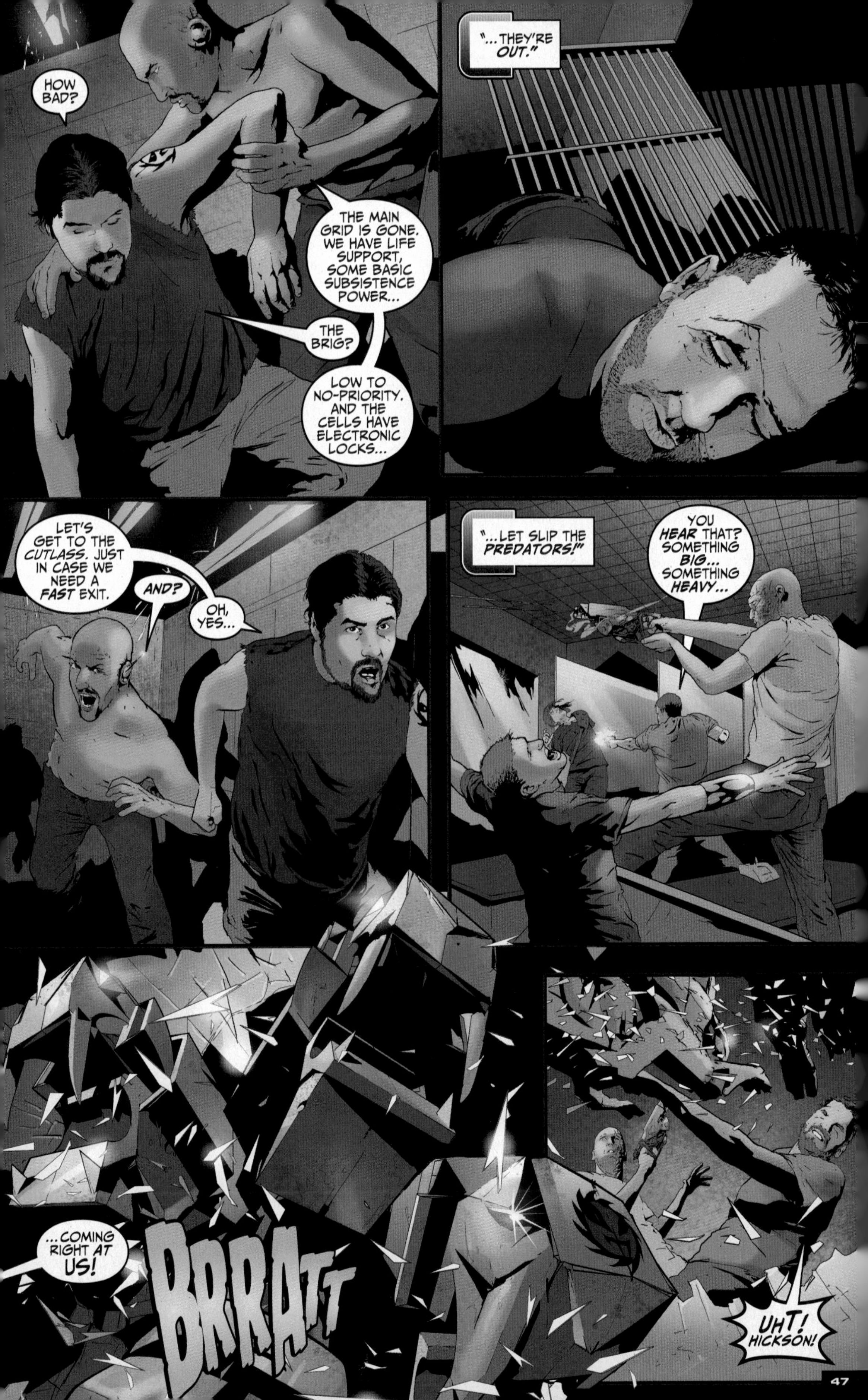
HOW BAD?
THE MAIN GRID IS GONE. WE HAVE LIFE SUPPORT, SOME BASIC SUBSISTENCE POWER...
THE BRIG?
LOW TO NO-PRIORITY. AND THE CELLS HAVE ELECTRONIC LOCKS...
"...THEY'RE OUT."
LET'S GET TO THE CUTLASS. JUST IN CASE WE NEED A FAST EXIT.
AND?
OH, YES...
"...LET SLIP THE PREDATORS!"
YOU HEAR THAT? SOMETHING BIG... SOMETHING HEAVY...
...COMING RIGHT AT US!
BRRATT
UHT! HICKSON!

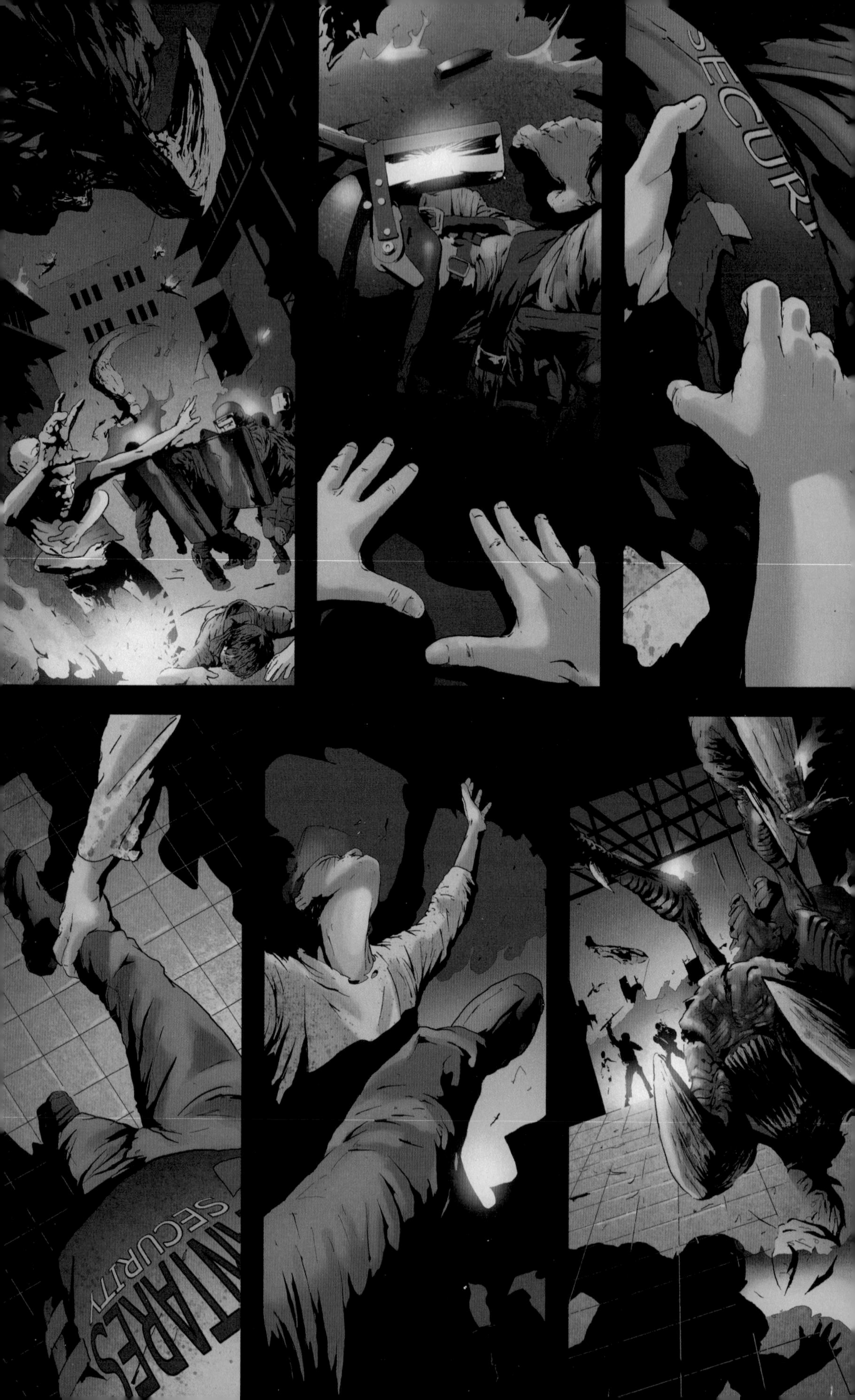
SECURI
SECURITY

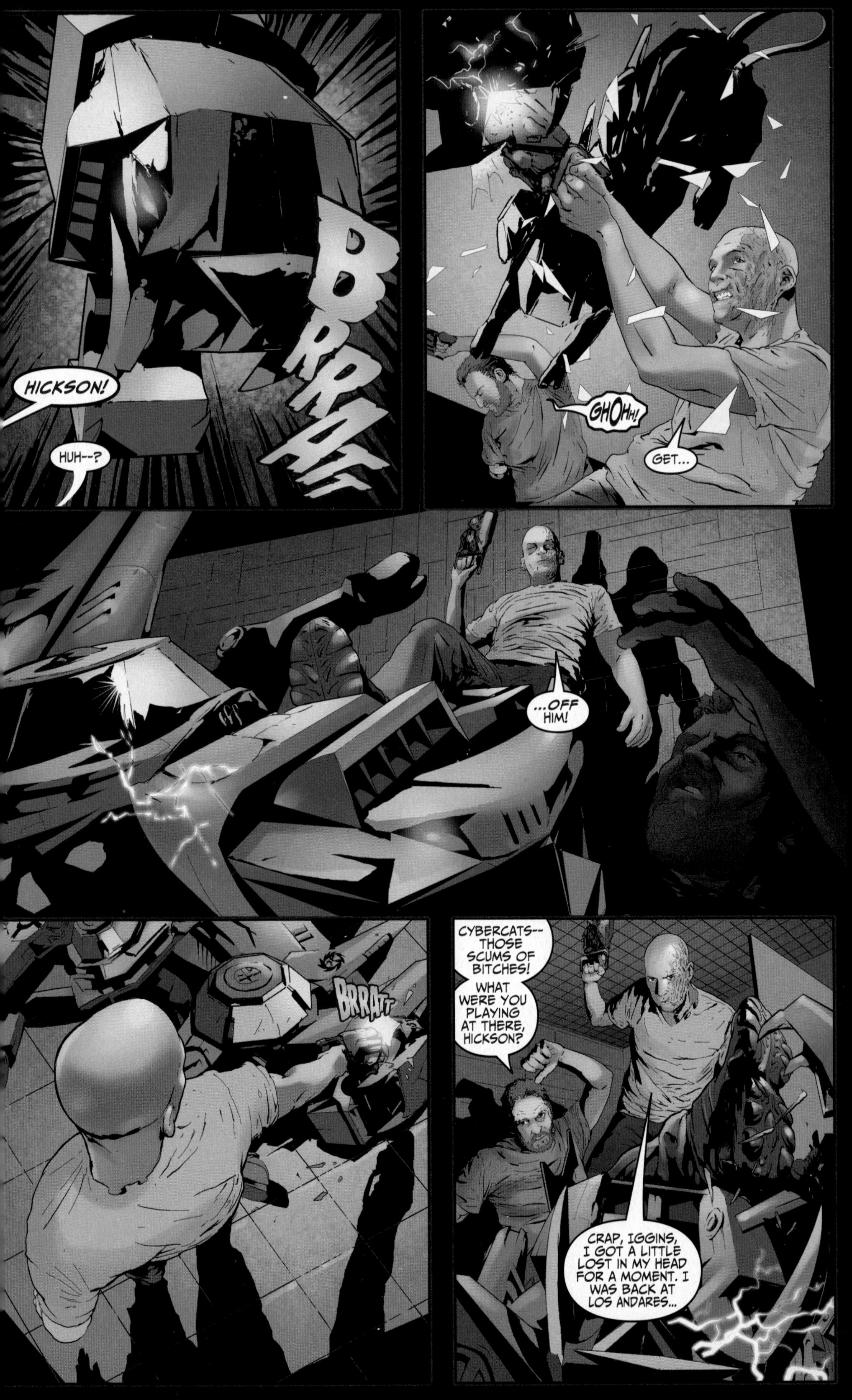
HICKSON!
HUH--?
BRRRAAT
GHOHH!
GET...
...OFF HIM!
BRRATT
CYBERCATS-- THOSE SCUMS OF BITCHES!
WHAT WERE YOU PLAYING AT THERE, HICKSON?
CRAP, IGGINS, I GOT A LITTLE LOST IN MY HEAD FOR A MOMENT. I WAS BACK AT LOS ANDARES...

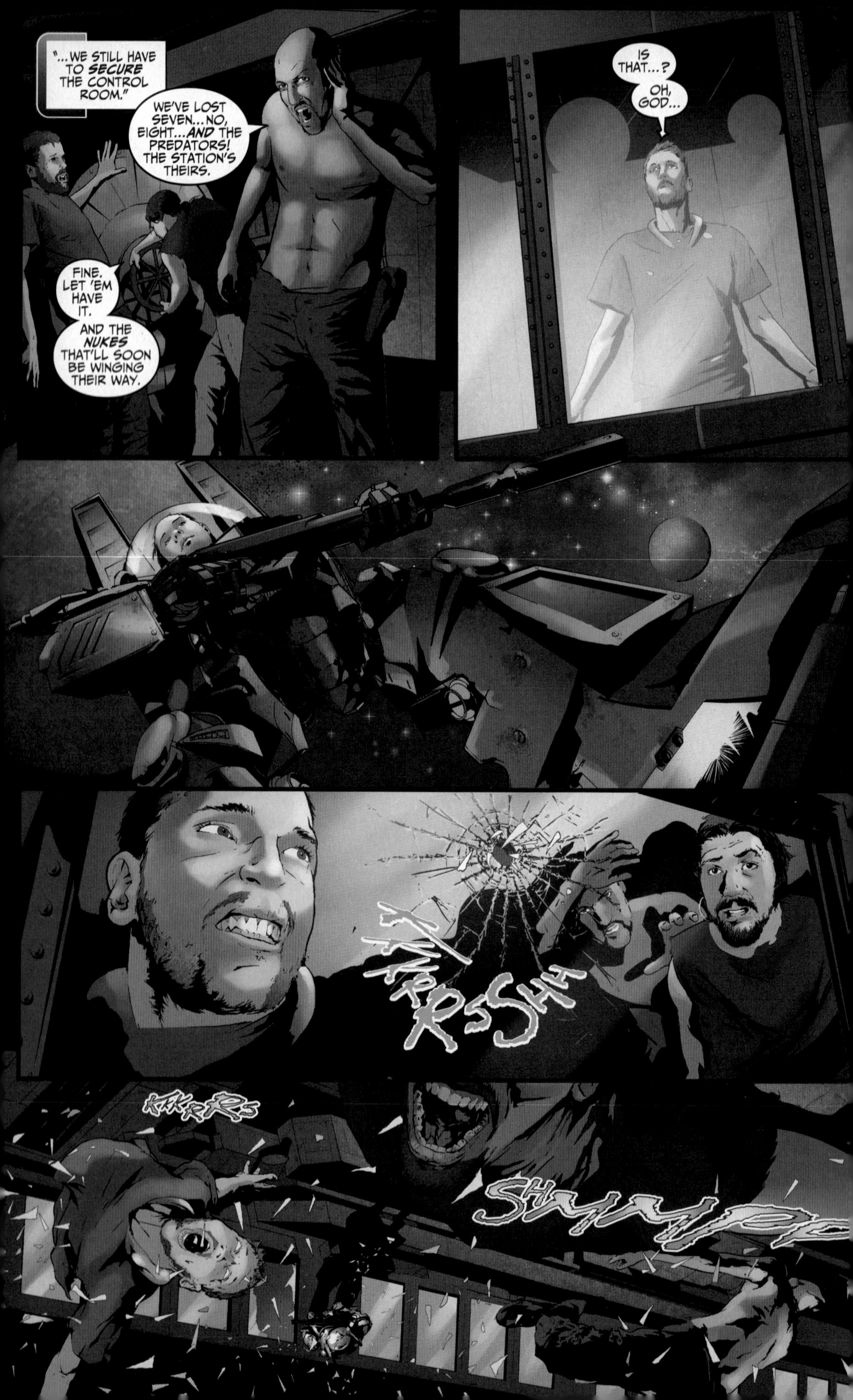
"...WE STILL HAVE TO *SECURE* THE CONTROL ROOM."
WE'VE LOST SEVEN...NO, EIGHT...*AND* THE PREDATORS! THE STATION'S THEIRS.
FINE. LET 'EM HAVE IT.
AND THE *NUKES* THAT'LL SOON BE WINGING THEIR WAY.
IS THAT...?
OH, GOD...

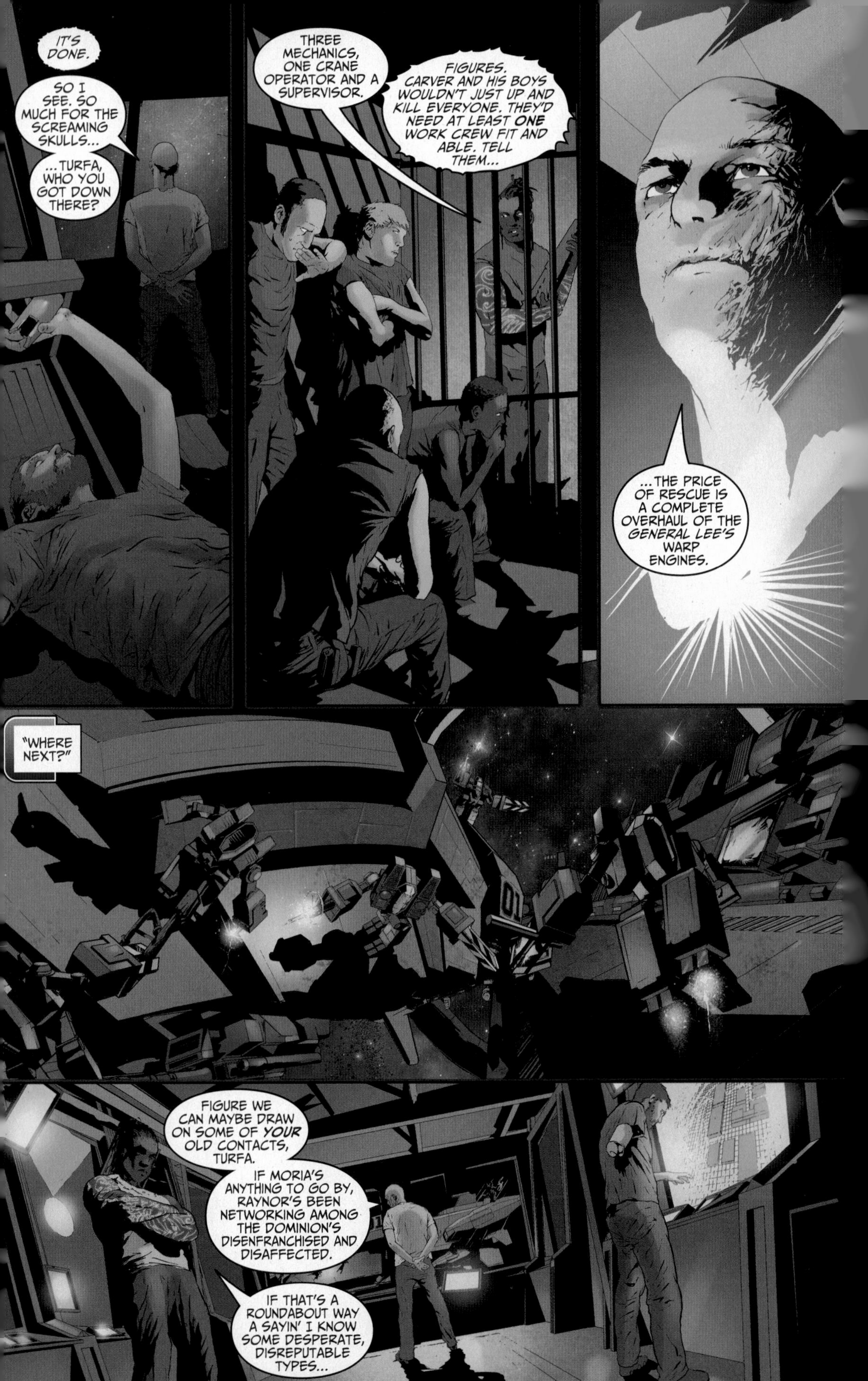
IT'S DONE.
SO I SEE. SO MUCH FOR THE SCREAMING SKULLS...
...TURFA, WHO YOU GOT DOWN THERE?
THREE MECHANICS, ONE CRANE OPERATOR AND A SUPERVISOR.
FIGURES. CARVER AND HIS BOYS WOULDN'T JUST UP AND KILL EVERYONE. THEY'D NEED AT LEAST ONE WORK CREW FIT AND ABLE. TELL THEM...
...THE PRICE OF RESCUE IS A COMPLETE OVERHAUL OF THE GENERAL LEE'S WARP ENGINES.
"WHERE NEXT?"
01
FIGURE WE CAN MAYBE DRAW ON SOME OF YOUR OLD CONTACTS, TURFA.
IF MORIA'S ANYTHING TO GO BY, RAYNOR'S BEEN NETWORKING AMONG THE DOMINION'S DISENFRANCHISED AND DISAFFECTED.
IF THAT'S A ROUNDABOUT WAY A SAYIN' I KNOW SOME DESPERATE, DISREPUTABLE TYPES...

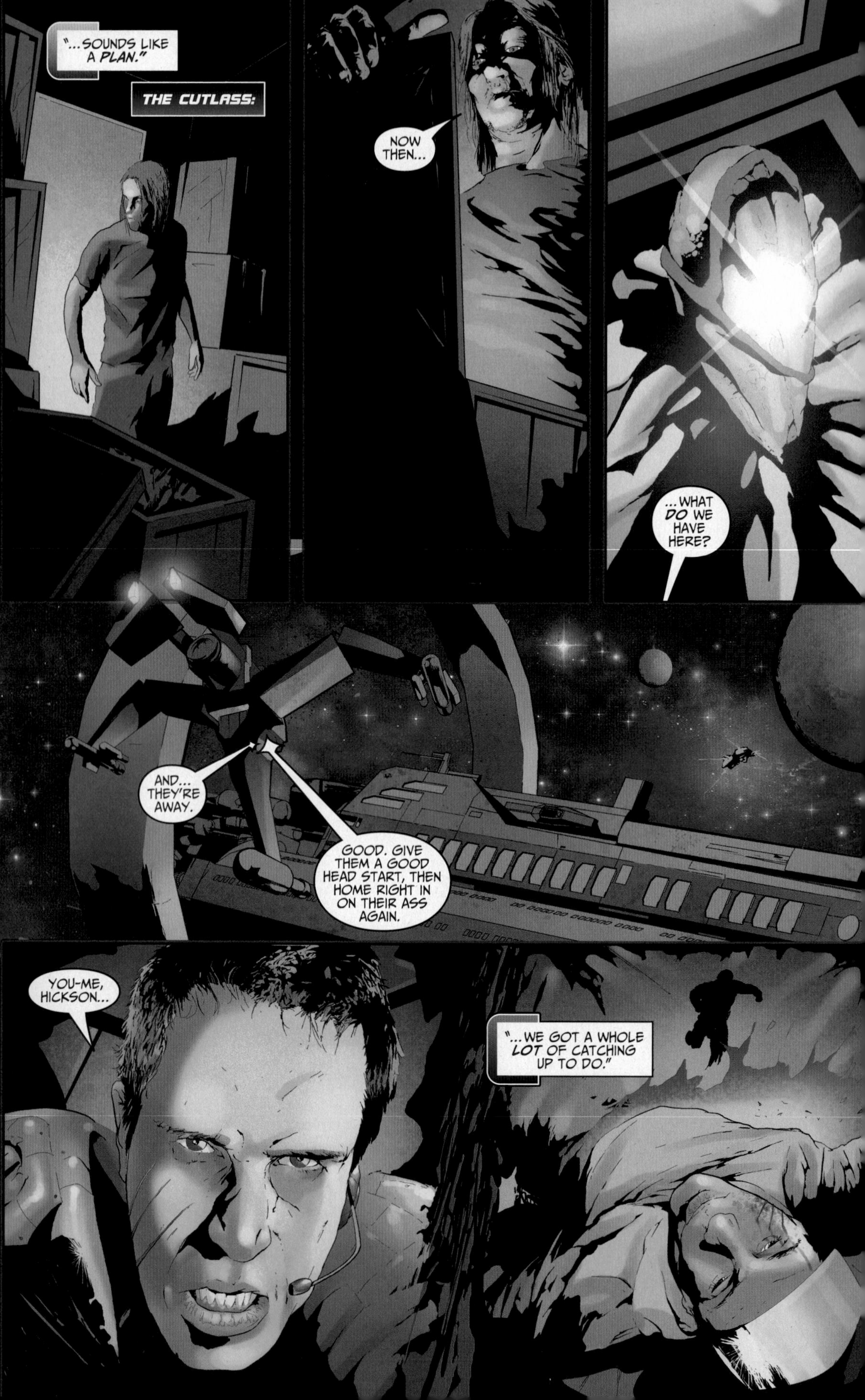
"...SOUNDS LIKE A PLAN."
THE CUTLASS:
NOW THEN...
...WHAT DO WE HAVE HERE?
AND... THEY'RE AWAY.
GOOD. GIVE THEM A GOOD HEAD START, THEN HOME RIGHT IN ON THEIR ASS AGAIN.
YOU-ME, HICKSON...
"...WE GOT A WHOLE LOT OF CATCHING UP TO DO."

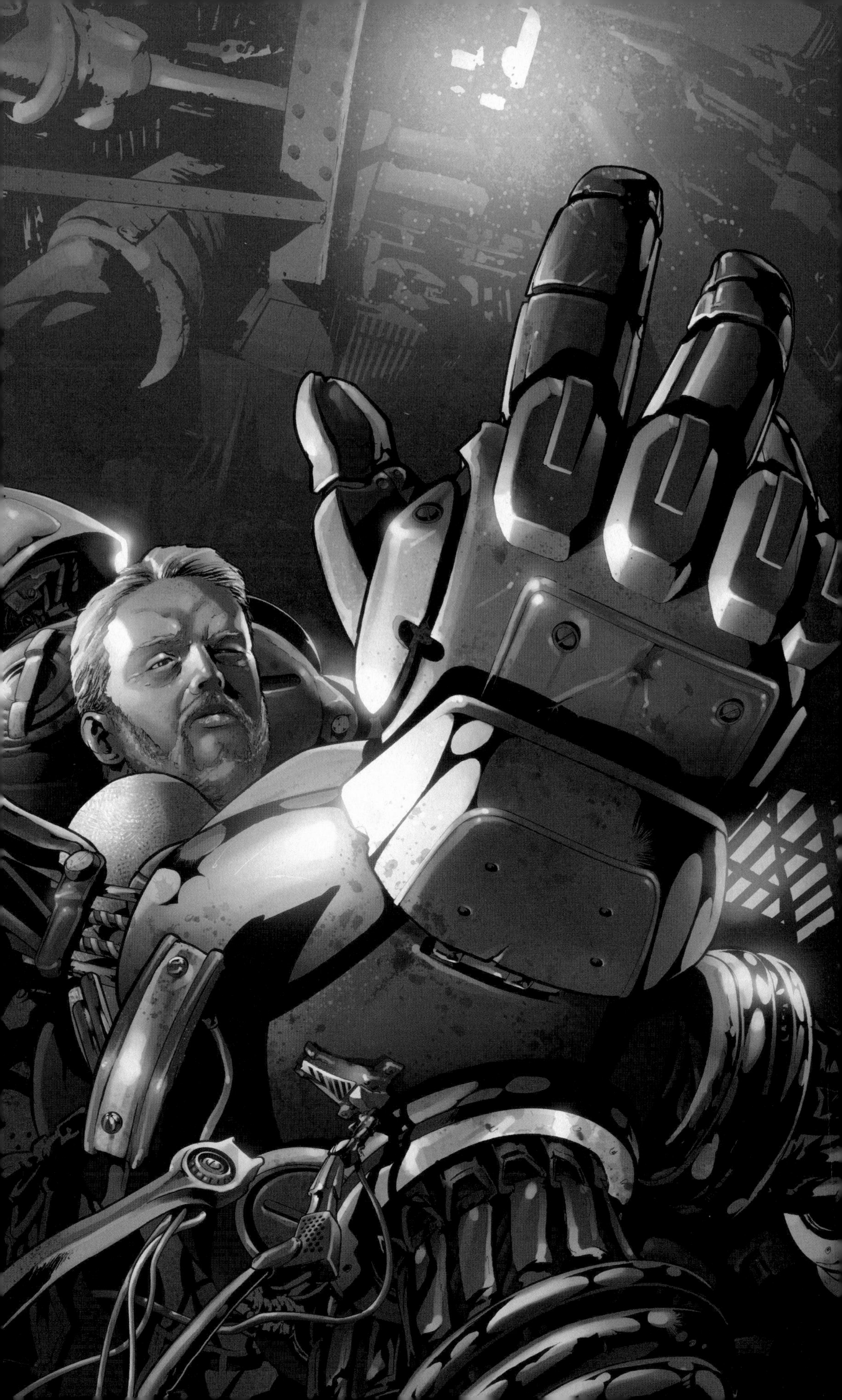

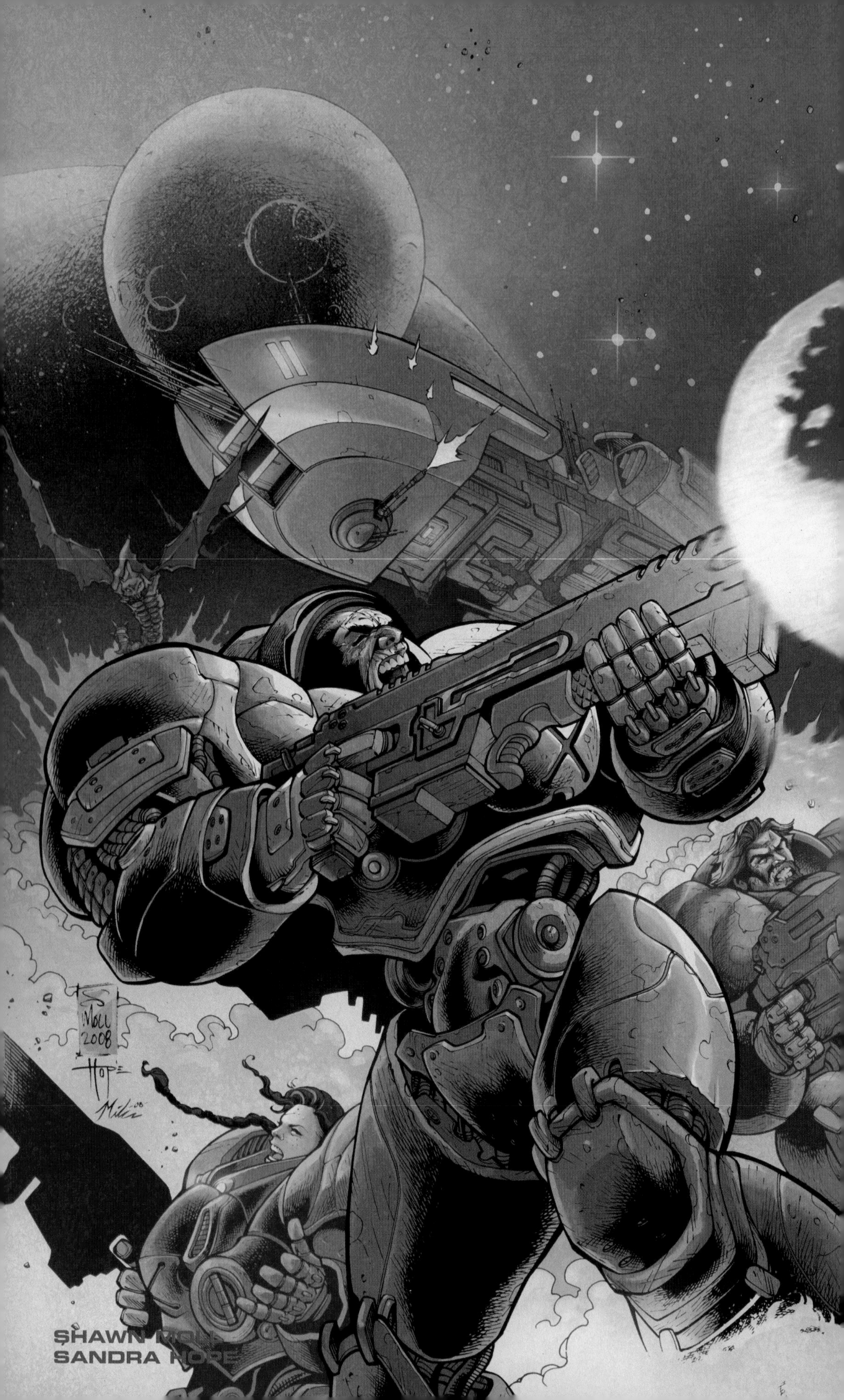
SHAWN MOLL
SANDRA HOPE

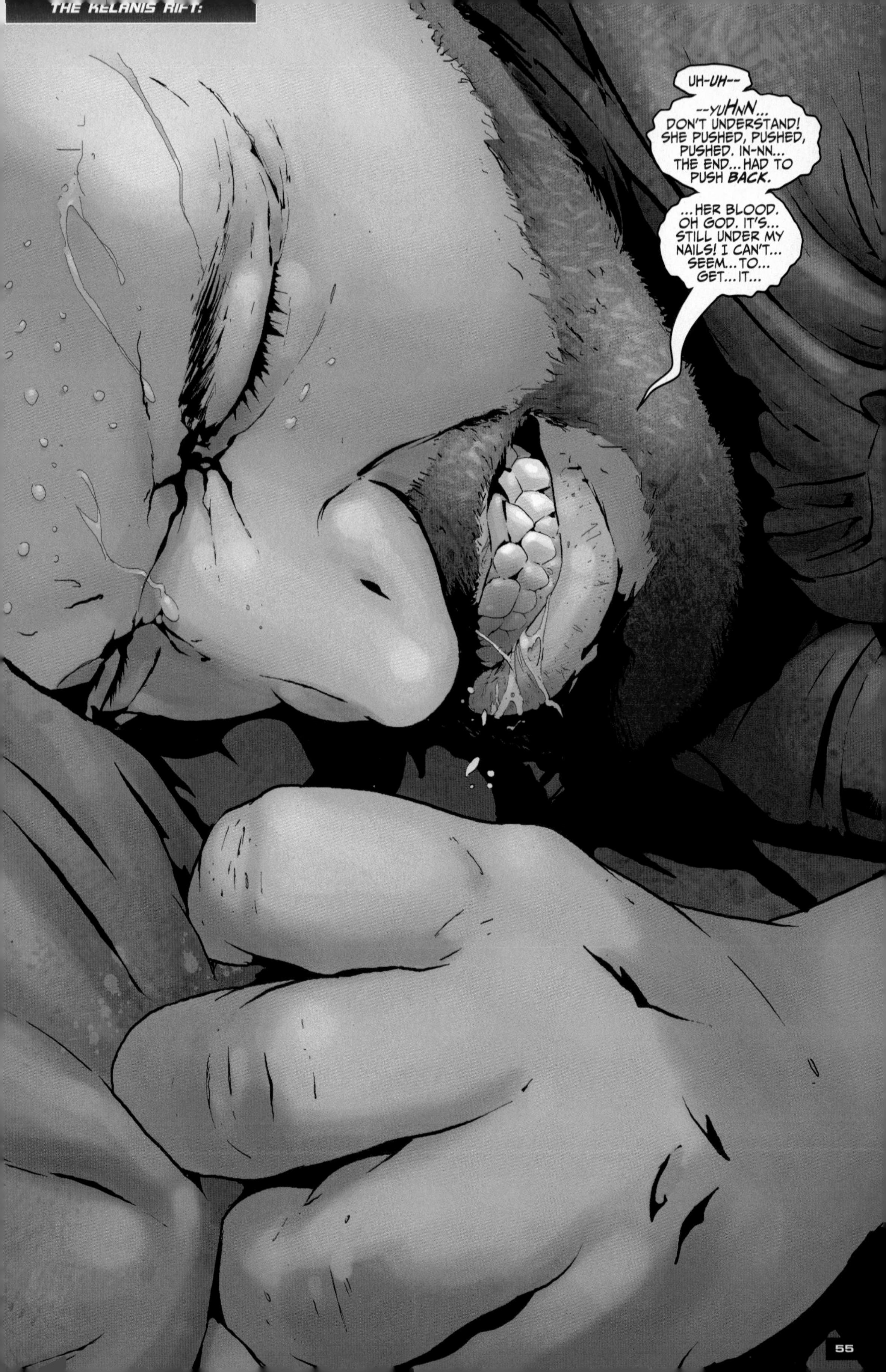
UH-UH--
--YUHNN... DON'T UNDERSTAND! SHE PUSHED, PUSHED, PUSHED. IN-NN... THE END...HAD TO PUSH BACK.
...HER BLOOD. OH GOD. IT'S... STILL UNDER MY NAILS! I CAN'T... SEEM...TO... GET...IT...

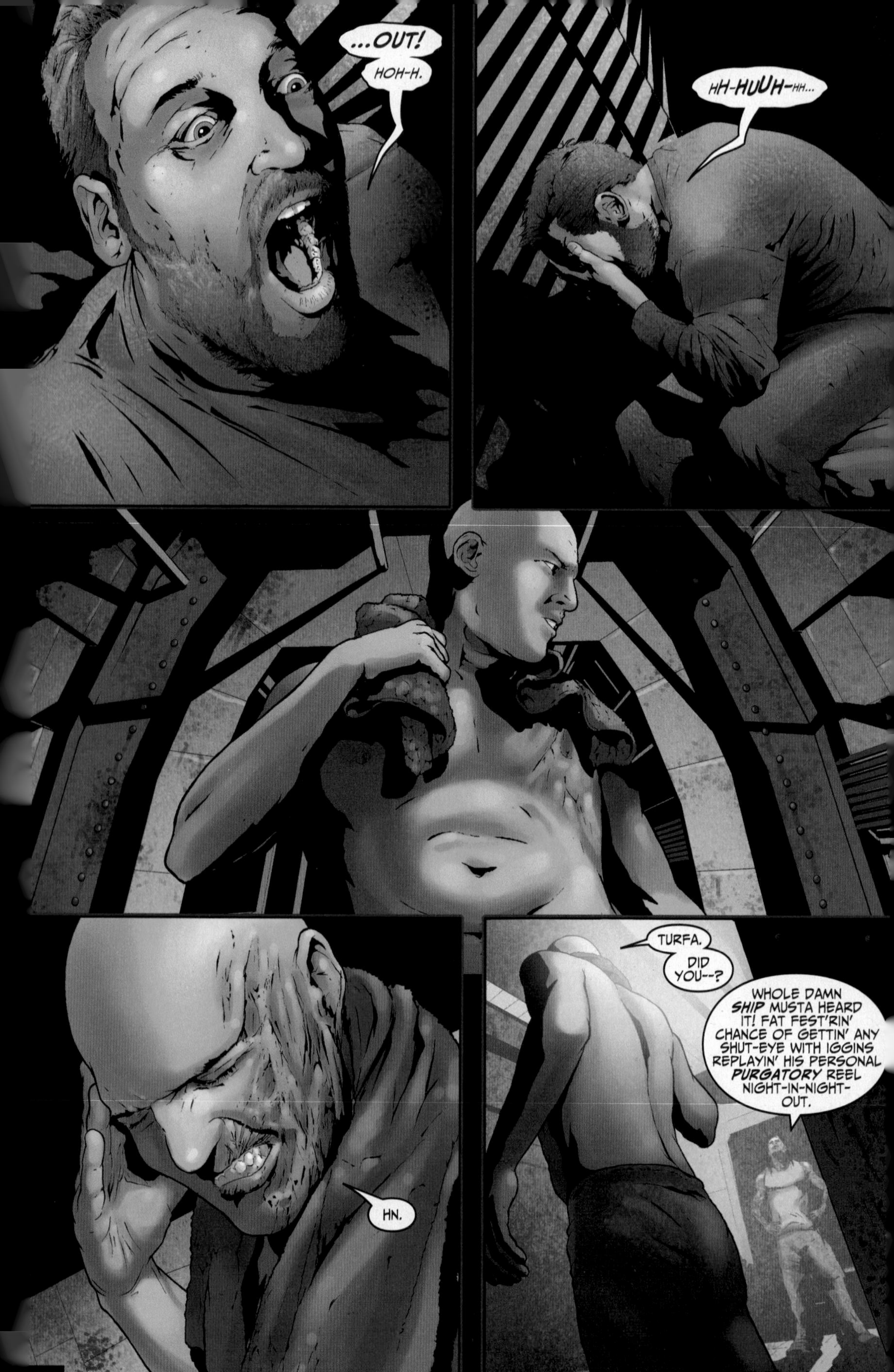
...OUT!
HOH-H.
HH-HUUH-HH...
HN.
TURFA.
DID YOU--?
WHOLE DAMN SHIP MUSTA HEARD IT! FAT FEST'RIN' CHANCE OF GETTIN' ANY SHUT-EYE WITH IGGINS REPLAYIN' HIS PERSONAL PURGATORY REEL NIGHT-IN-NIGHT-OUT.

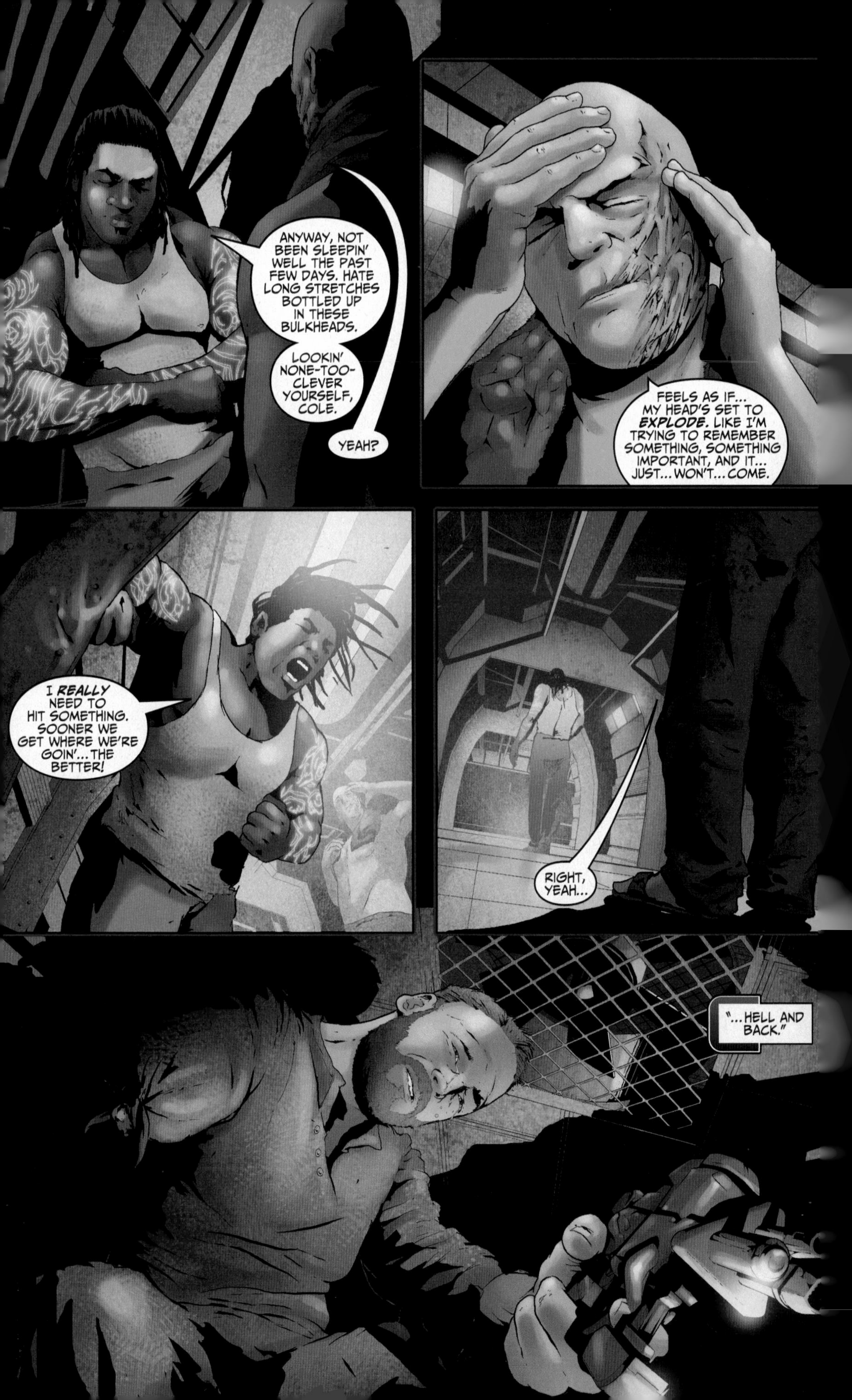
ANYWAY, NOT BEEN SLEEPIN' WELL THE PAST FEW DAYS. HATE LONG STRETCHES BOTTLED UP IN THESE BULKHEADS.
LOOKIN' NONE-TOO-CLEVER YOURSELF, COLE.
YEAH?
FEELS AS IF... MY HEAD'S SET TO EXPLODE. LIKE I'M TRYING TO REMEMBER SOMETHING, SOMETHING IMPORTANT, AND IT... JUST... WON'T... COME.
I REALLY NEED TO HIT SOMETHING. SOONER WE GET WHERE WE'RE GOIN'... THE BETTER!
RIGHT, YEAH...
"...HELL AND BACK."

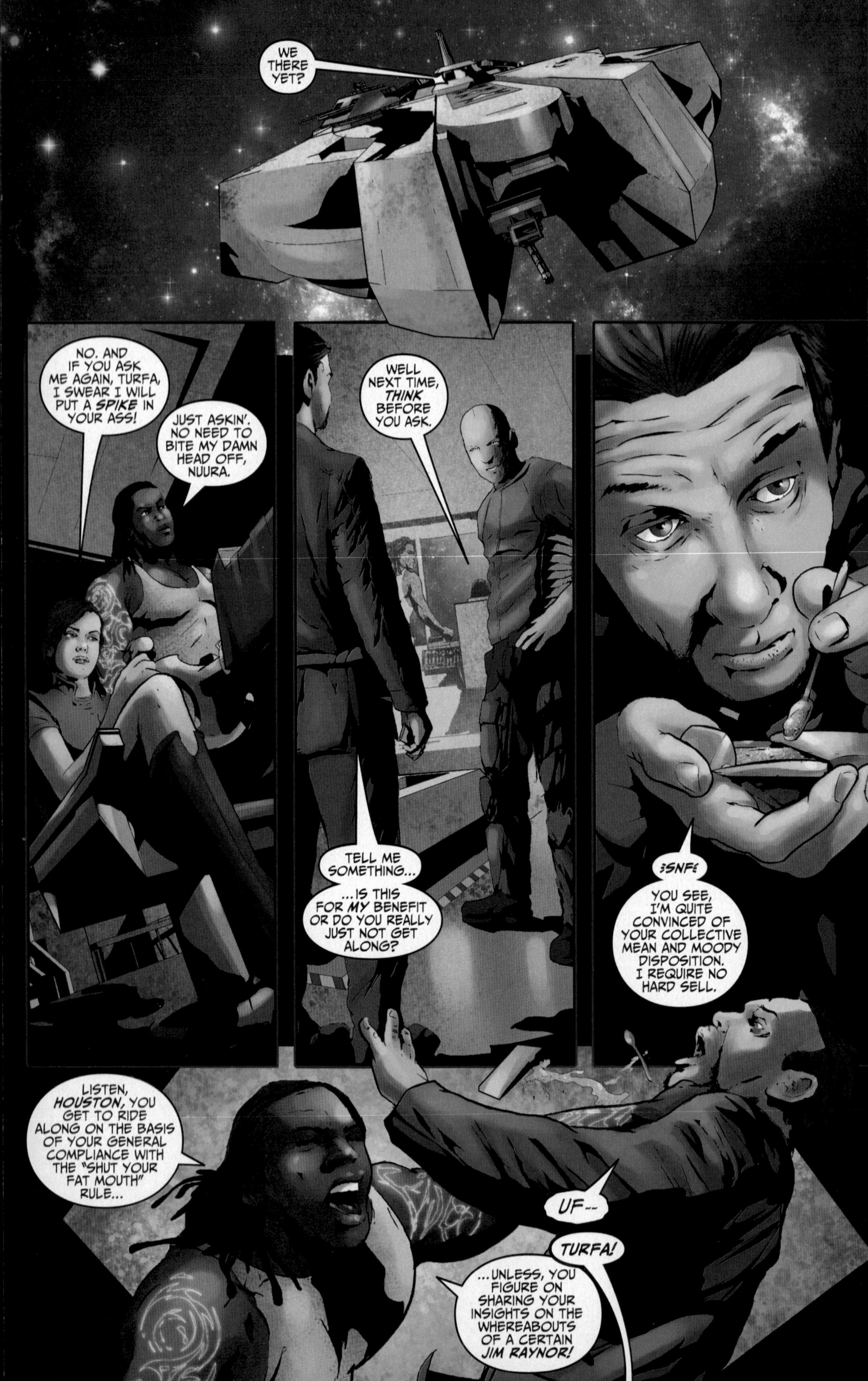
WE THERE YET?
NO. AND IF YOU ASK ME AGAIN, TURFA, I SWEAR I WILL PUT A SPIKE IN YOUR ASS!
JUST ASKIN'. NO NEED TO BITE MY DAMN HEAD OFF, NUURA.
WELL NEXT TIME, THINK BEFORE YOU ASK.
TELL ME SOMETHING...
...IS THIS FOR MY BENEFIT OR DO YOU REALLY JUST NOT GET ALONG?
SNF
YOU SEE, I'M QUITE CONVINCED OF YOUR COLLECTIVE MEAN AND MOODY DISPOSITION. I REQUIRE NO HARD SELL.
LISTEN, HOUSTON, YOU GET TO RIDE ALONG ON THE BASIS OF YOUR GENERAL COMPLIANCE WITH THE "SHUT YOUR FAT MOUTH" RULE...
UF--
TURFA!
...UNLESS, YOU FIGURE ON SHARING YOUR INSIGHTS ON THE WHEREABOUTS OF A CERTAIN JIM RAYNOR!

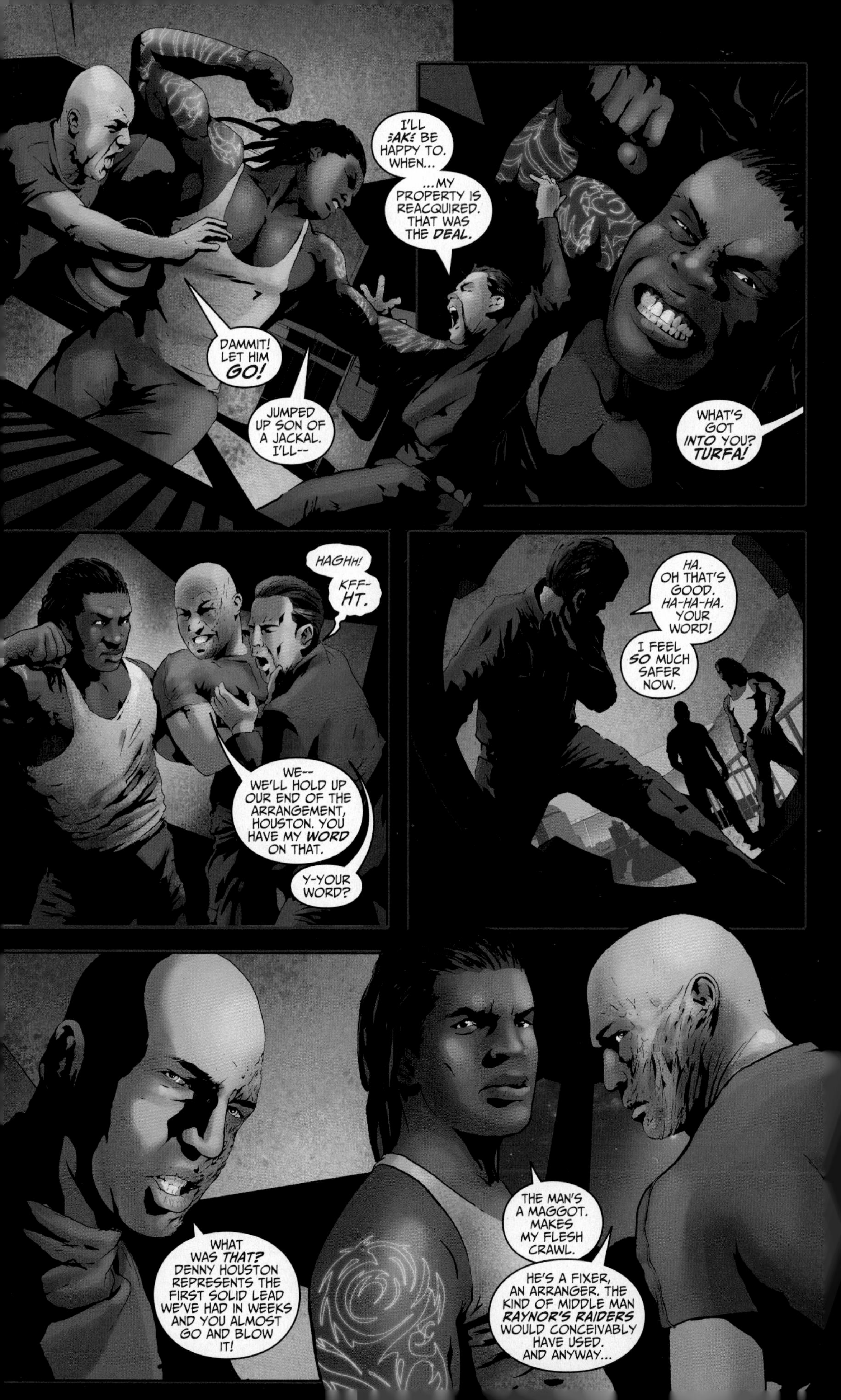

DAMMIT! LET HIM GO!
JUMPED UP SON OF A JACKAL. I'LL--
I'LL AK BE HAPPY TO. WHEN...
...MY PROPERTY IS REACQUIRED. THAT WAS THE DEAL.
WHAT'S GOT INTO YOU? TURFA!
HAGHH!
KFF-HT.
WE-- WE'LL HOLD UP OUR END OF THE ARRANGEMENT, HOUSTON. YOU HAVE MY WORD ON THAT.
Y-YOUR WORD?
HA. OH THAT'S GOOD. HA-HA-HA. YOUR WORD!
I FEEL SO MUCH SAFER NOW.
WHAT WAS THAT? DENNY HOUSTON REPRESENTS THE FIRST SOLID LEAD WE'VE HAD IN WEEKS AND YOU ALMOST GO AND BLOW IT!
THE MAN'S A MAGGOT. MAKES MY FLESH CRAWL.
HE'S A FIXER, AN ARRANGER. THE KIND OF MIDDLE MAN RAYNOR'S RAIDERS WOULD CONCEIVABLY HAVE USED. AND ANYWAY...

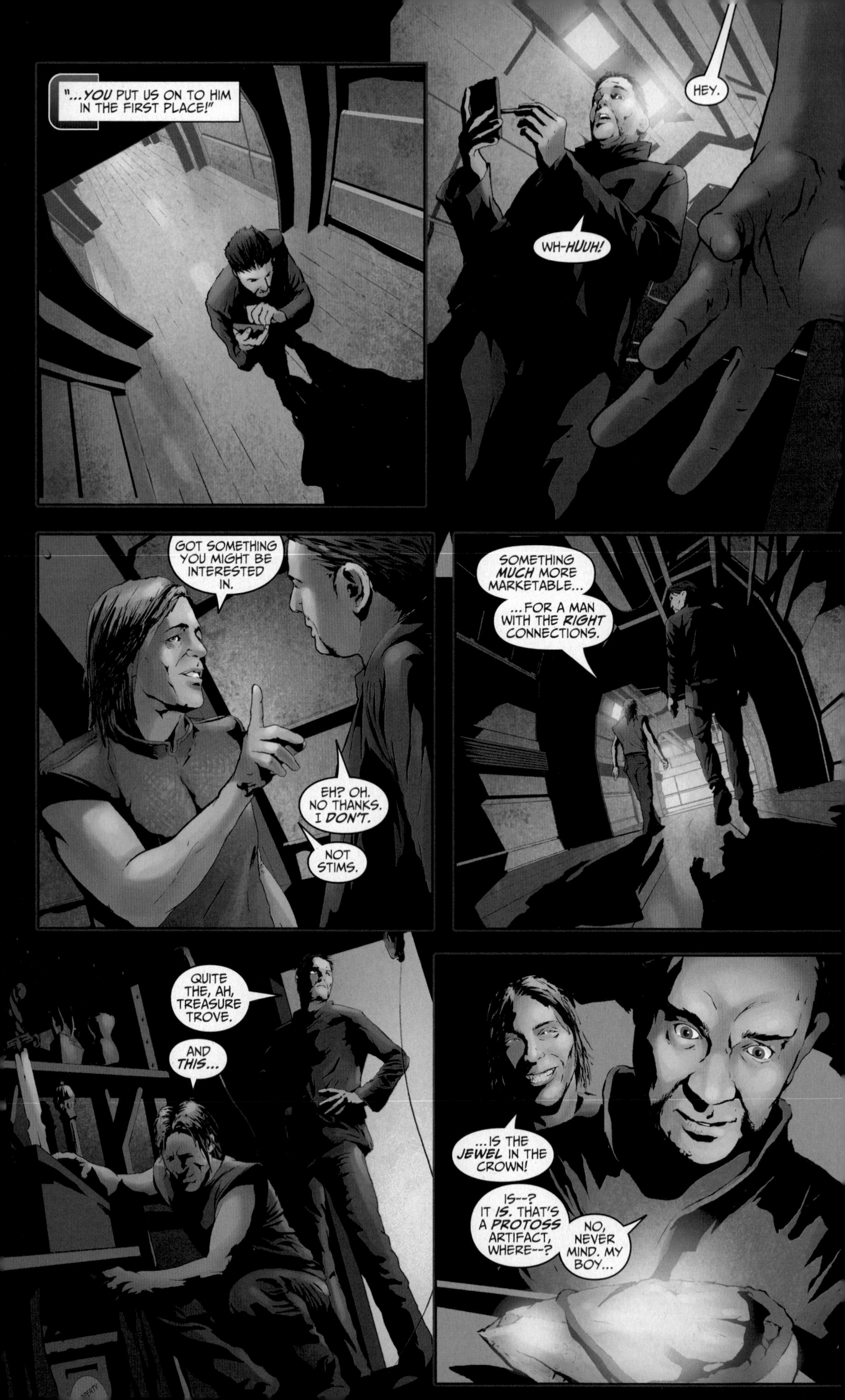
"...YOU PUT US ON TO HIM IN THE FIRST PLACE!"
HEY.
WH-HUUH!
GOT SOMETHING YOU MIGHT BE INTERESTED IN.
EH? OH. NO THANKS. I DON'T.
NOT STIMS.
SOMETHING MUCH MORE MARKETABLE...
...FOR A MAN WITH THE RIGHT CONNECTIONS.
QUITE THE, AH, TREASURE TROVE.
AND THIS...
...IS THE JEWEL IN THE CROWN!
IS--? IT IS. THAT'S A PROTOSS ARTIFACT, WHERE--?
NO, NEVER MIND. MY BOY...

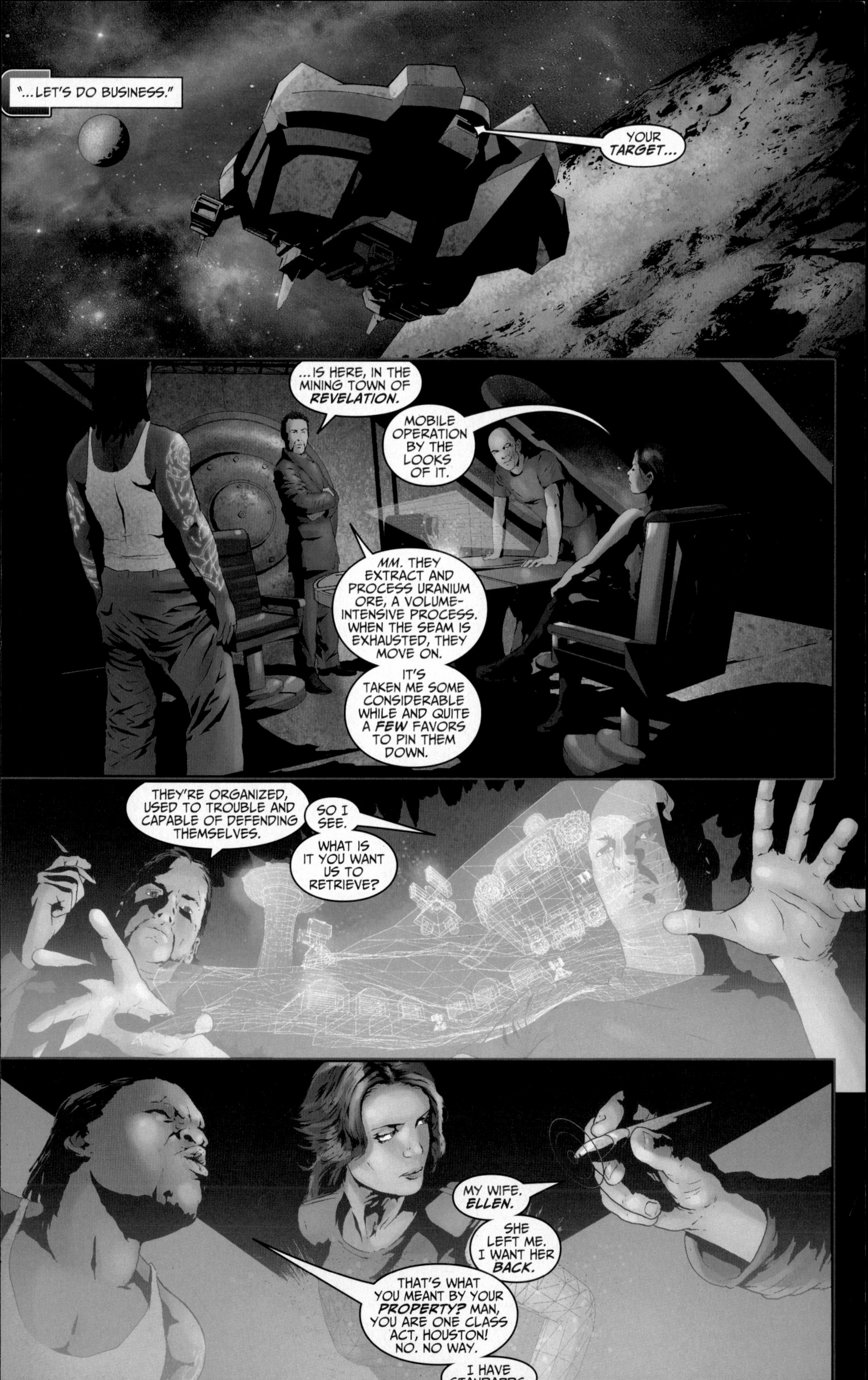
"...LET'S DO BUSINESS."
YOUR TARGET...
...IS HERE, IN THE MINING TOWN OF REVELATION.
MOBILE OPERATION BY THE LOOKS OF IT.
MM. THEY EXTRACT AND PROCESS URANIUM ORE, A VOLUME-INTENSIVE PROCESS. WHEN THE SEAM IS EXHAUSTED, THEY MOVE ON.
IT'S TAKEN ME SOME CONSIDERABLE WHILE AND QUITE A FEW FAVORS TO PIN THEM DOWN.
THEY'RE ORGANIZED, USED TO TROUBLE AND CAPABLE OF DEFENDING THEMSELVES.
SO I SEE.
WHAT IS IT YOU WANT US TO RETRIEVE?
MY WIFE. ELLEN.
SHE LEFT ME. I WANT HER BACK.
THAT'S WHAT YOU MEANT BY YOUR PROPERTY? MAN, YOU ARE ONE CLASS ACT, HOUSTON! NO. NO WAY.
I HAVE STANDARDS.

VERY WELL. RAYNOR IS WITH THE *ZERG*.

I DON'T.

LISTEN, HOUSTON. I'LL GO GET YOUR WIFE, EVEN THOUGH MY SYMPATHIES ARE WITH HER, BUT *ONLY* IF YOU GIVE US SOMETHING NOW-- ON ACCOUNT.

WHAT? IS THAT EVEN POSSIBLE?

QUITE.

"I ASKED *HIM* THE SAME QUESTION..."

IT'S RISKY, BUT THE THING WITH THE ZERG IS THEY'RE ALL ABOUT FOCUS. THERE ARE WAYS AND MEANS TO WORK AROUND THEM IF YOU KEEP A VERY LOW PROFILE AND ABSOLUTELY DO *NOT* PISS THEM OFF.

IT ALMOST SOUNDS LIKE YOU *ADMIRE* THEM.

WHAT YOU SEE IS WHAT YOU GET. I ADMIRE *THAT*.

THAT'S... JUST *CRAZY* ENOUGH TO BE TRUE!

BUT *WHERE?* THERE ARE A HUNDRED ZERG-INFESTED WORLDS, MORE!

I'LL GIVE YOU RAYNOR'S *EXACT* LOCATION...

"...*AFTER* YOU GET ELLEN BACK FOR ME."

JOTUN:

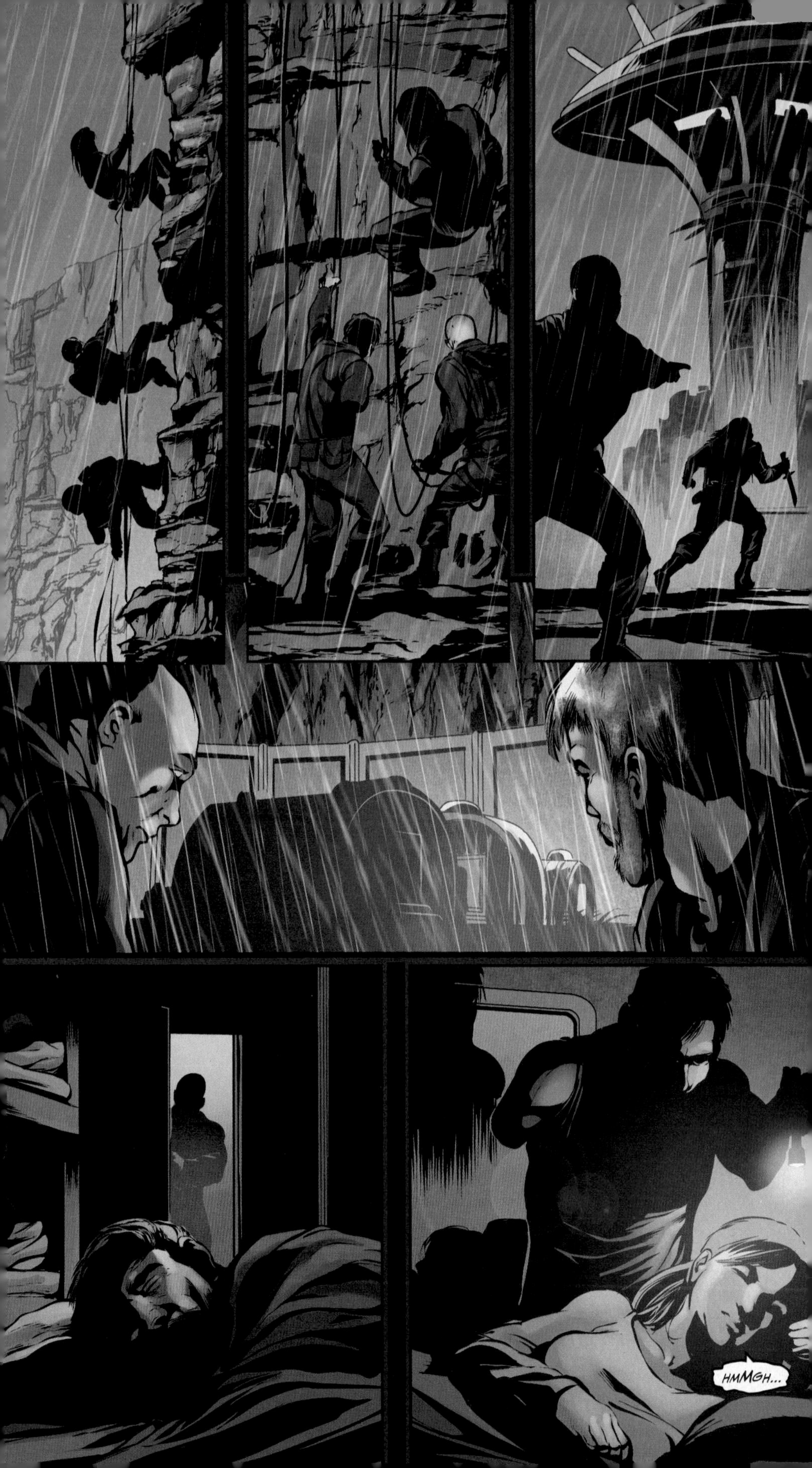
HMMGH...

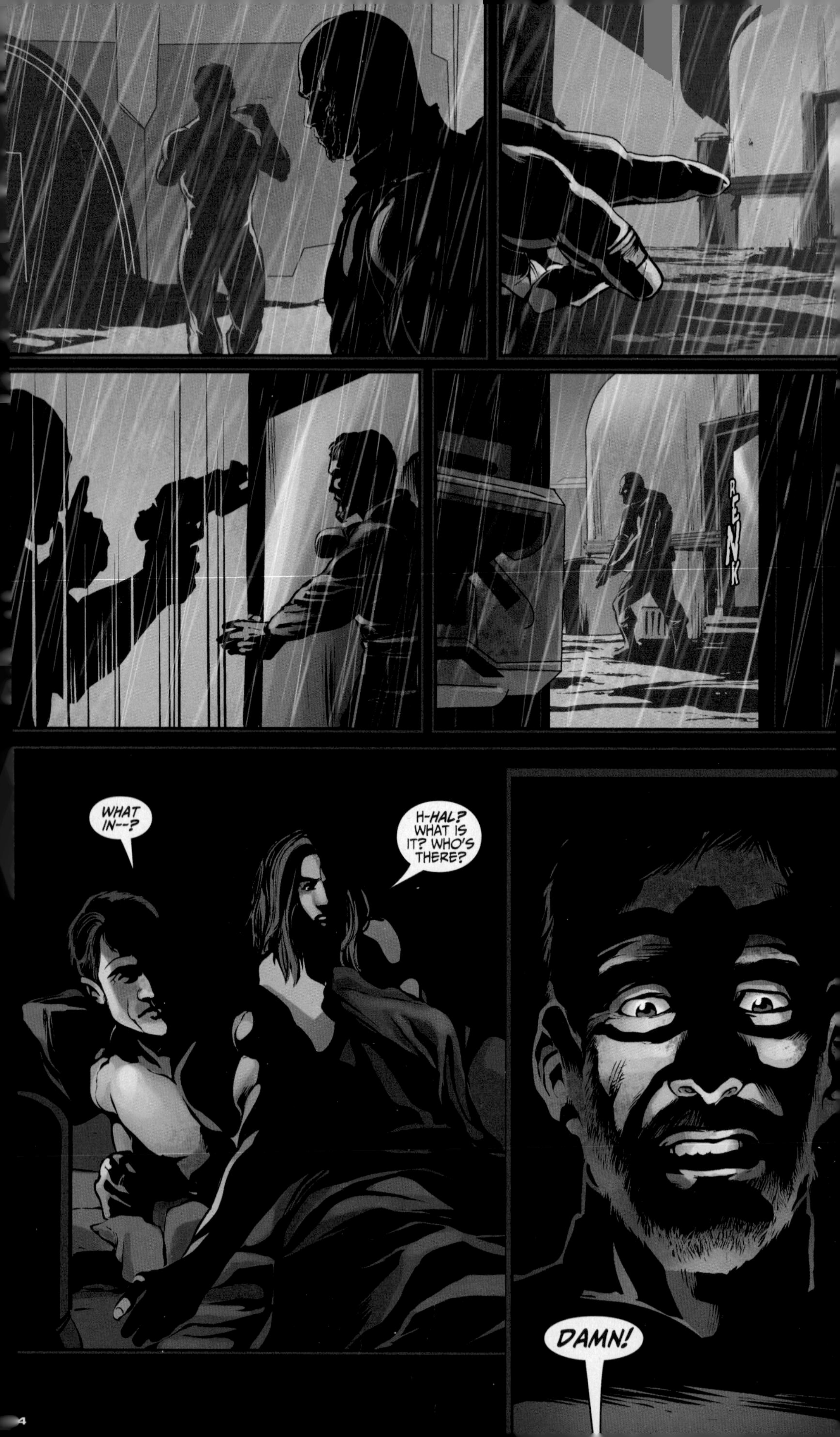

REENK
WHAT IN--?
H-HAL? WHAT IS IT? WHO'S THERE?
DAMN!

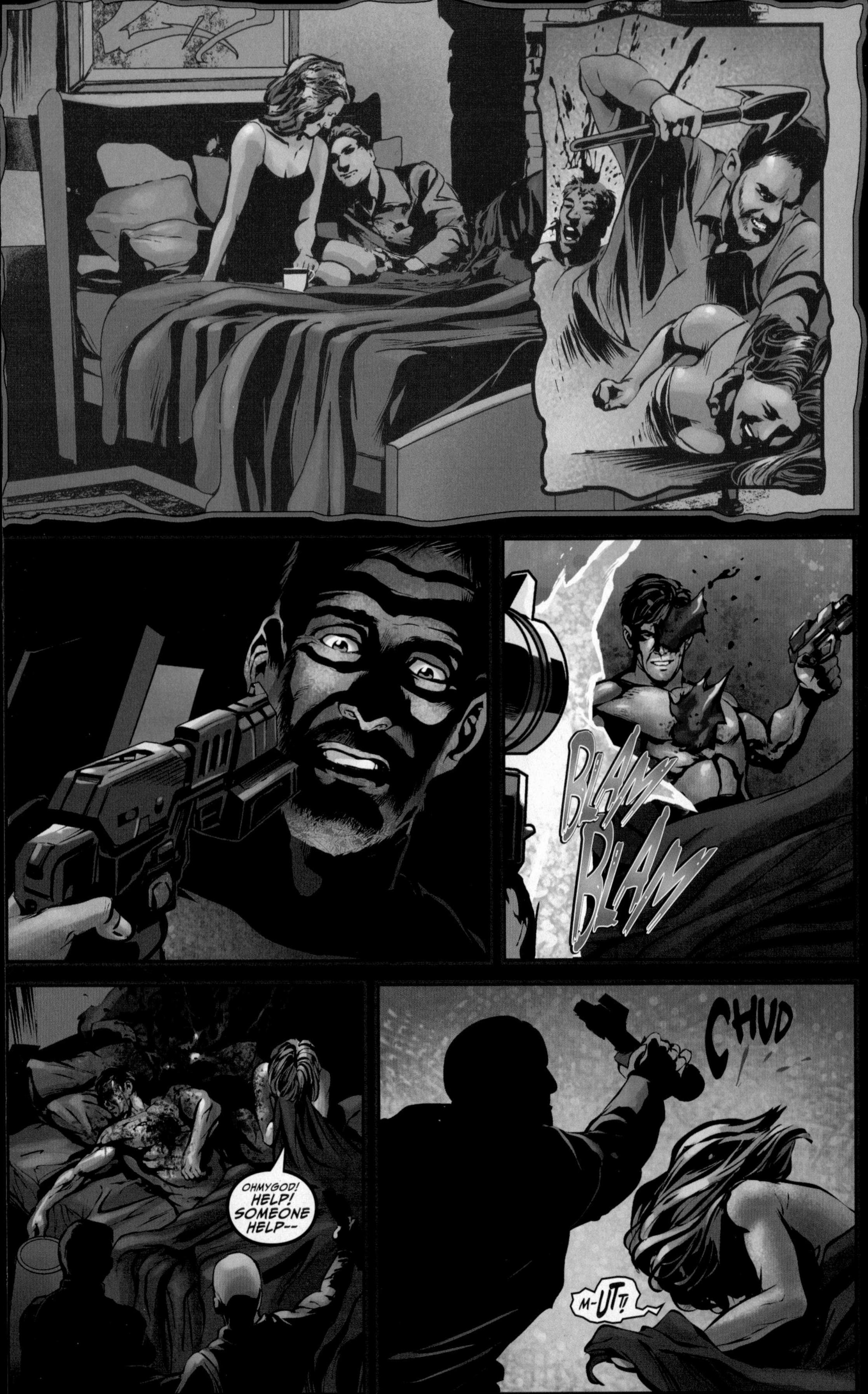
BLAM
BLAM
OHMYGOD! HELP! SOMEONE HELP--
CHUD
M-UTT!

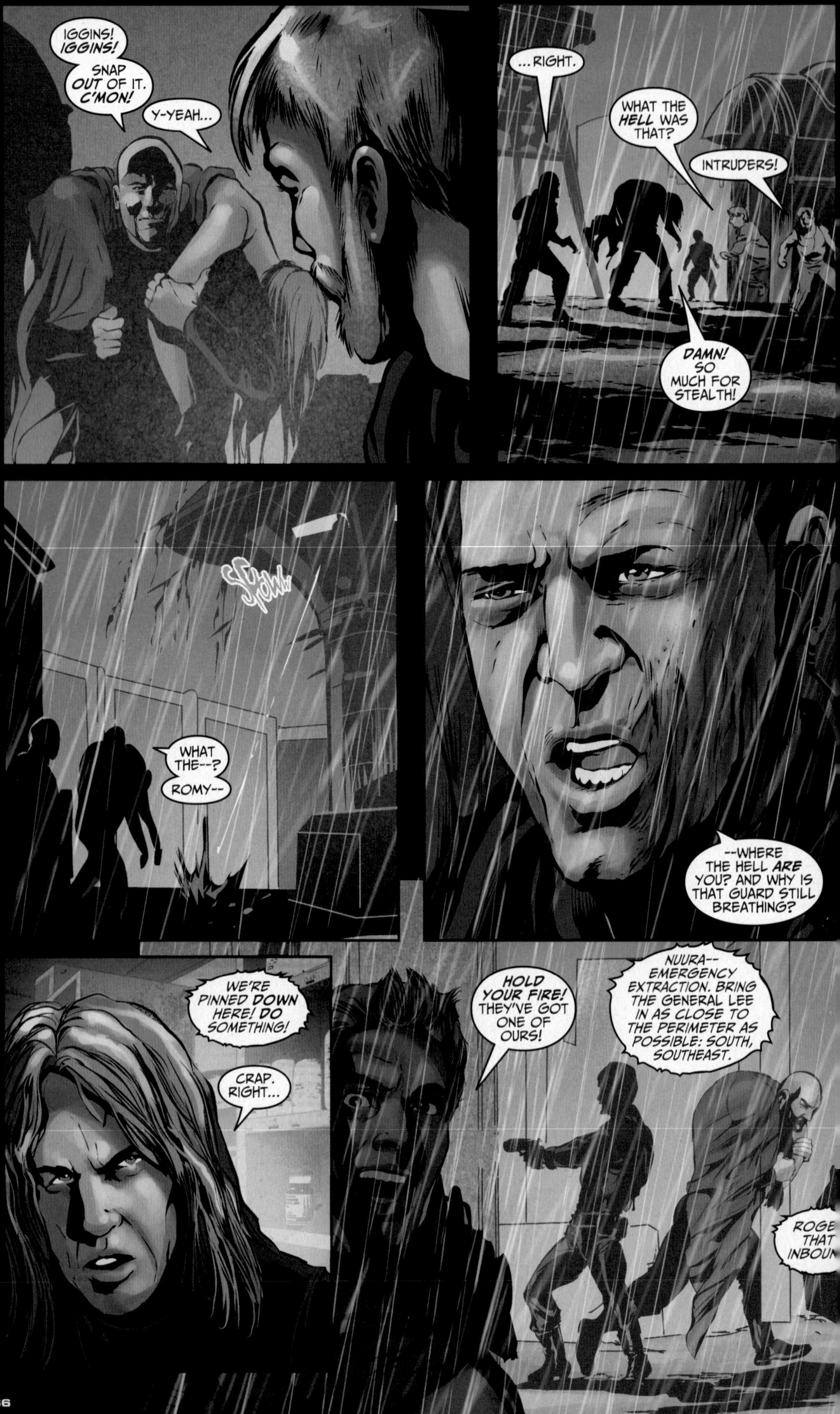
IGGINS! IGGINS!
SNAP OUT OF IT. C'MON!
Y-YEAH...
...RIGHT.
WHAT THE HELL WAS THAT?
INTRUDERS!
DAMN! SO MUCH FOR STEALTH!
WHAT THE--?
ROMY--
--WHERE THE HELL ARE YOU? AND WHY IS THAT GUARD STILL BREATHING?
WE'RE PINNED DOWN HERE! DO SOMETHING!
CRAP. RIGHT...
HOLD YOUR FIRE! THEY'VE GOT ONE OF OURS!
NUURA-- EMERGENCY EXTRACTION. BRING THE GENERAL LEE IN AS CLOSE TO THE PERIMETER AS POSSIBLE: SOUTH, SOUTHEAST.
ROGE THAT INBOUN

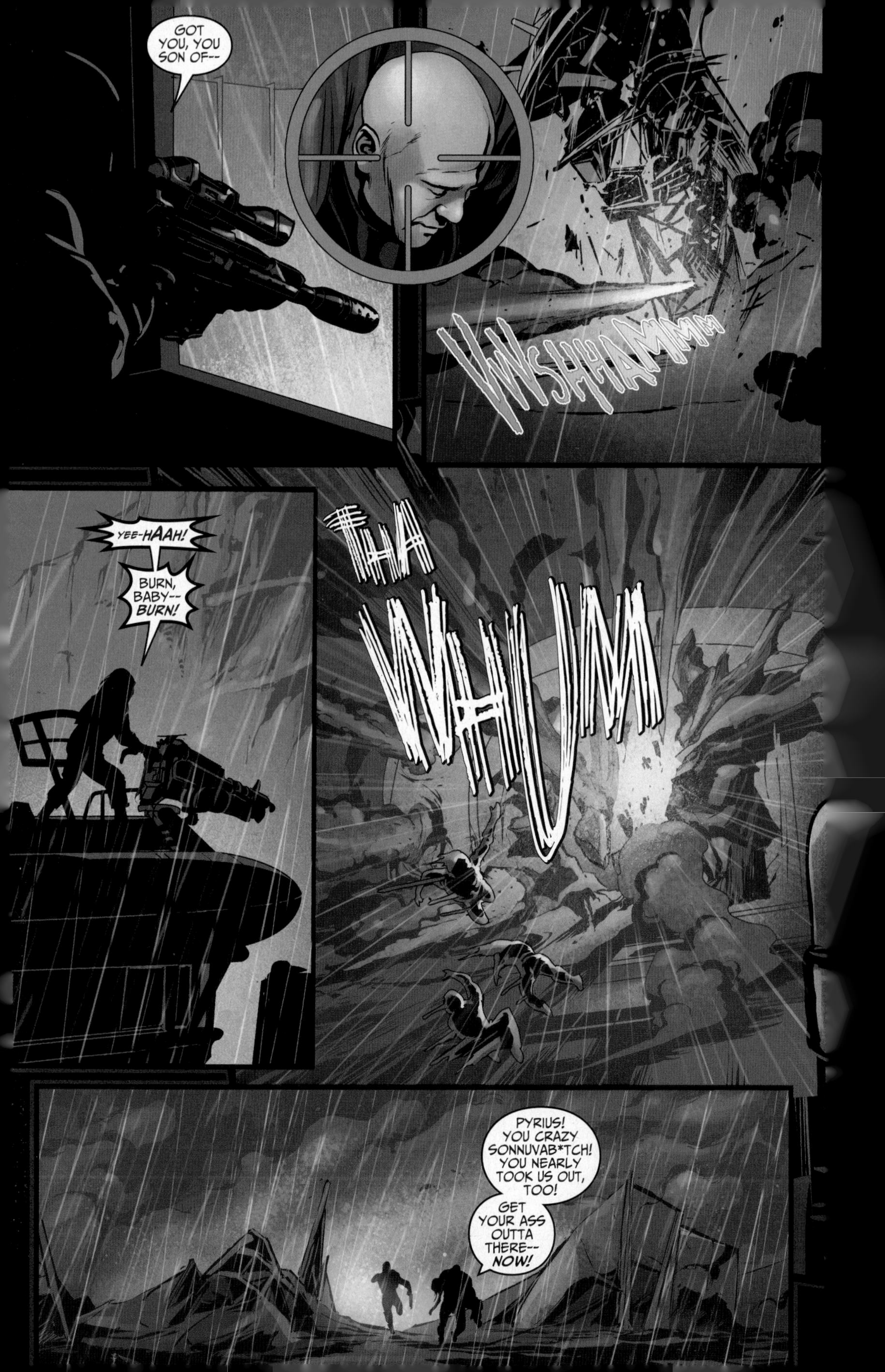
GOT YOU, YOU SON OF--
VVVSHHAMMMM
YEE-HAAH!
BURN, BABY-- BURN!
THA
VVHHUMM
PYRIUS! YOU CRAZY SONNUVAB*TCH! YOU NEARLY TOOK US OUT, TOO!
GET YOUR ASS OUTTA THERE-- NOW!

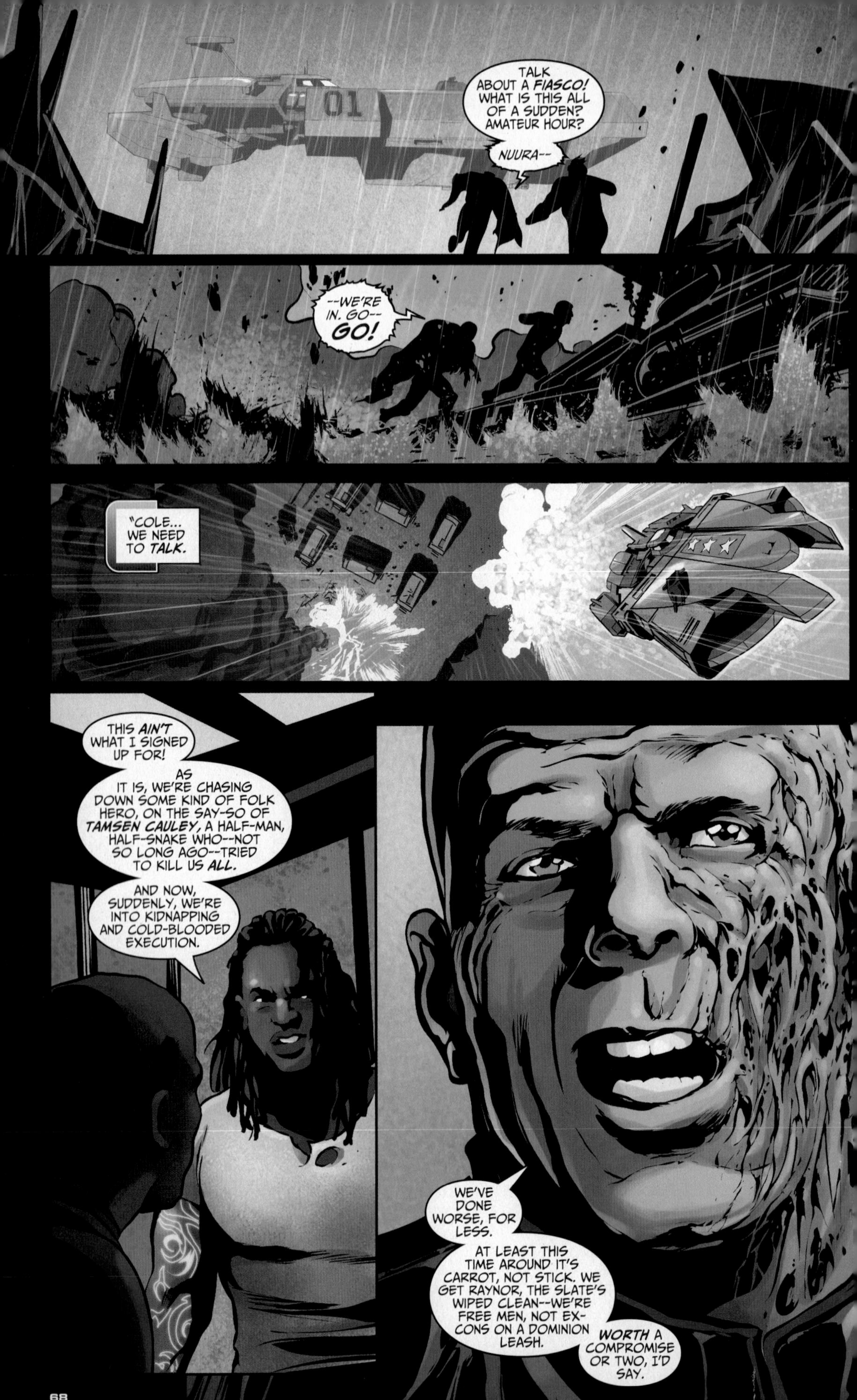
TALK ABOUT A *FIASCO!* WHAT IS THIS ALL OF A SUDDEN? AMATEUR HOUR?
NUURA--
--WE'RE IN. GO-- **GO!**
"COLE... WE NEED TO *TALK.*
THIS *AIN'T* WHAT I SIGNED UP FOR!
AS IT IS, WE'RE CHASING DOWN SOME KIND OF FOLK HERO, ON THE SAY-SO OF *TAMSEN CAULEY,* A HALF-MAN, HALF-SNAKE WHO--NOT SO LONG AGO--TRIED TO KILL US *ALL.*
AND NOW, SUDDENLY, WE'RE INTO KIDNAPPING AND COLD-BLOODED EXECUTION.
WE'VE DONE WORSE, FOR LESS.
AT LEAST THIS TIME AROUND IT'S CARROT, NOT STICK. WE GET RAYNOR, THE SLATE'S WIPED CLEAN--WE'RE FREE MEN, NOT EX-CONS ON A DOMINION LEASH.
WORTH A COMPROMISE OR TWO, I'D SAY.

NUURA'S RIGHT--YOU'VE *CHANGED,* COLE. I'M STARTING TO WONDER WHAT CAULEY OFFERED YOU...AND IF THE REST OF US ARE ANY PART OF THAT DEAL!

BACK. OFF. BEFORE I--

ENOUGH! WHAT'S *HAPPENING* TO US?

IGGINS HAS GONE ALL CREEPY-SCHIZO, NUURA'S UP AND LOCKED HERSELF IN ON THE FLIGHT DECK, AND YOU TWO ARE AT EACH OTHER'S THROATS!

WE'RE *WAR PIGS,* REMEMBER?

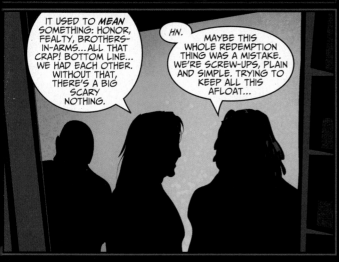

IT USED TO *MEAN* SOMETHING: HONOR, FEALTY, BROTHERS-IN-ARMS...ALL THAT CRAP! BOTTOM LINE... WE HAD EACH OTHER. WITHOUT THAT, THERE'S A BIG SCARY NOTHING.

HN. MAYBE THIS WHOLE REDEMPTION THING WAS A MISTAKE. WE'RE SCREW-UPS, PLAIN AND SIMPLE. TRYING TO KEEP ALL THIS AFLOAT...

...JUST SETS US UP FOR A BIGGER FALL.

MH-HH...

IT'S OKAY, ELLEN. YOU'RE BACK WITH ME NOW. BACK WHERE YOU *BELONG...*

WH--? *NO!* NONONO!

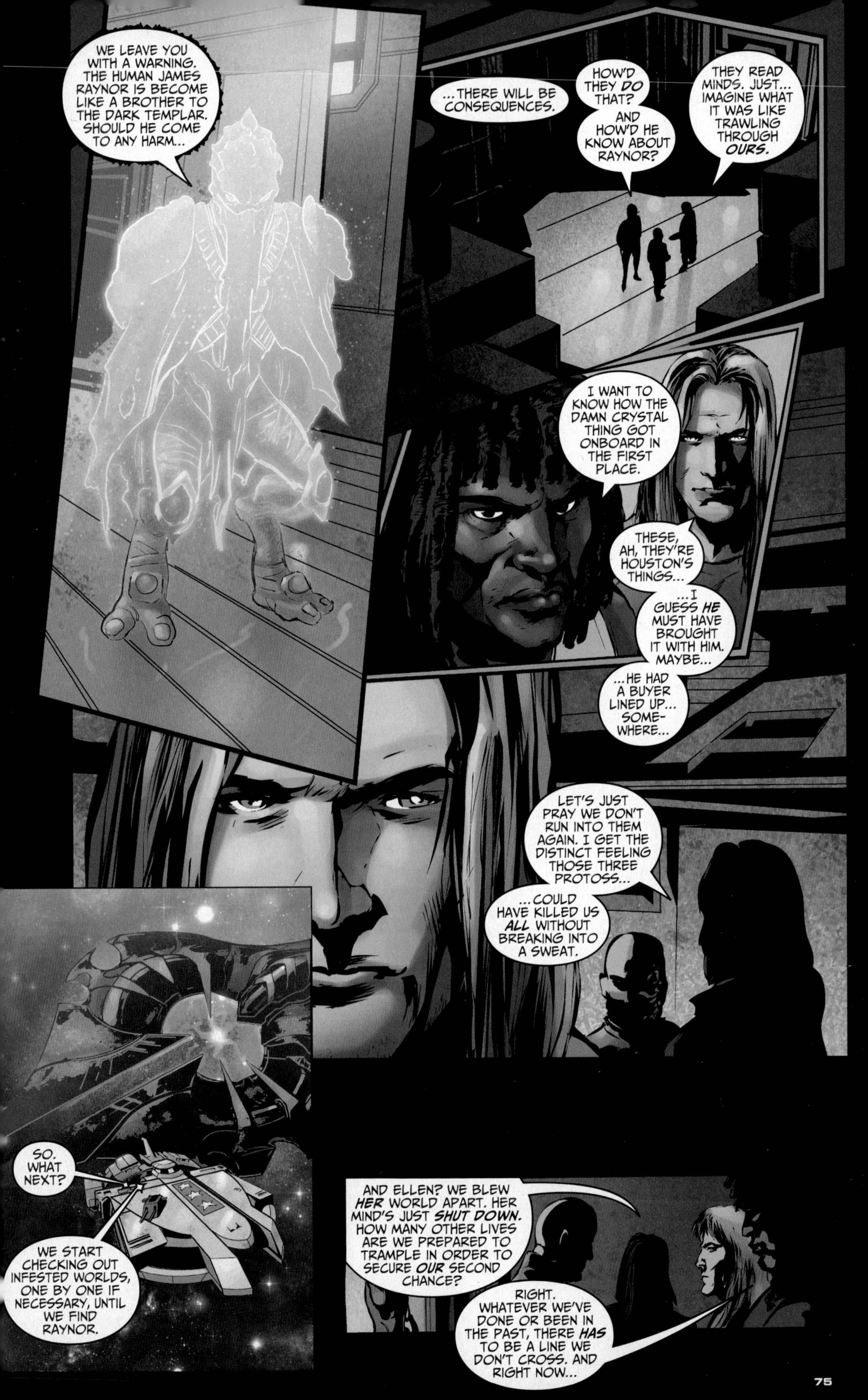
WE LEAVE YOU WITH A WARNING. THE HUMAN JAMES RAYNOR IS BECOME LIKE A BROTHER TO THE DARK TEMPLAR. SHOULD HE COME TO ANY HARM...
...THERE WILL BE CONSEQUENCES.
HOW'D THEY DO THAT?
AND HOW'D HE KNOW ABOUT RAYNOR?
THEY READ MINDS. JUST... IMAGINE WHAT IT WAS LIKE TRAWLING THROUGH OURS.
I WANT TO KNOW HOW THE DAMN CRYSTAL THING GOT ONBOARD IN THE FIRST PLACE.
THESE, AH, THEY'RE HOUSTON'S THINGS...
...I GUESS HE MUST HAVE BROUGHT IT WITH HIM. MAYBE...
...HE HAD A BUYER LINED UP... SOME-WHERE...
LET'S JUST PRAY WE DON'T RUN INTO THEM AGAIN. I GET THE DISTINCT FEELING THOSE THREE PROTOSS...
...COULD HAVE KILLED US ALL WITHOUT BREAKING INTO A SWEAT.
SO. WHAT NEXT?
WE START CHECKING OUT INFESTED WORLDS, ONE BY ONE IF NECESSARY, UNTIL WE FIND RAYNOR.
AND ELLEN? WE BLEW HER WORLD APART. HER MIND'S JUST SHUT DOWN. HOW MANY OTHER LIVES ARE WE PREPARED TO TRAMPLE IN ORDER TO SECURE OUR SECOND CHANCE?
RIGHT. WHATEVER WE'VE DONE OR BEEN IN THE PAST, THERE HAS TO BE A LINE WE DON'T CROSS. AND RIGHT NOW...

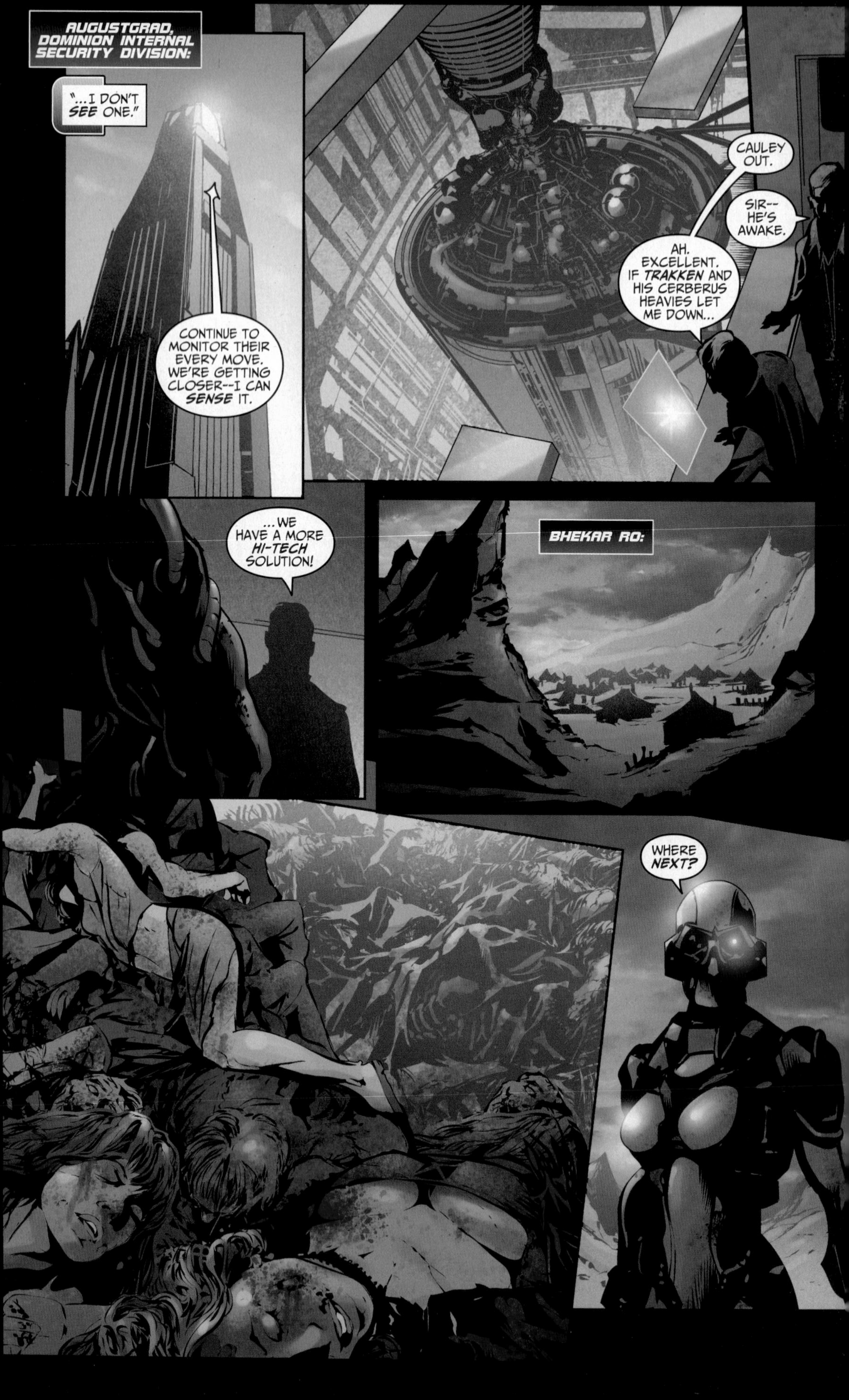
AUGUSTGRAD, DOMINION INTERNAL SECURITY DIVISION:
"...I DON'T SEE ONE."
CONTINUE TO MONITOR THEIR EVERY MOVE. WE'RE GETTING CLOSER--I CAN SENSE IT.
CAULEY OUT.
SIR-- HE'S AWAKE.
AH. EXCELLENT. IF TRAKKEN AND HIS CERBERUS HEAVIES LET ME DOWN...
...WE HAVE A MORE HI-TECH SOLUTION!
BHEKAR RO:
WHERE NEXT?

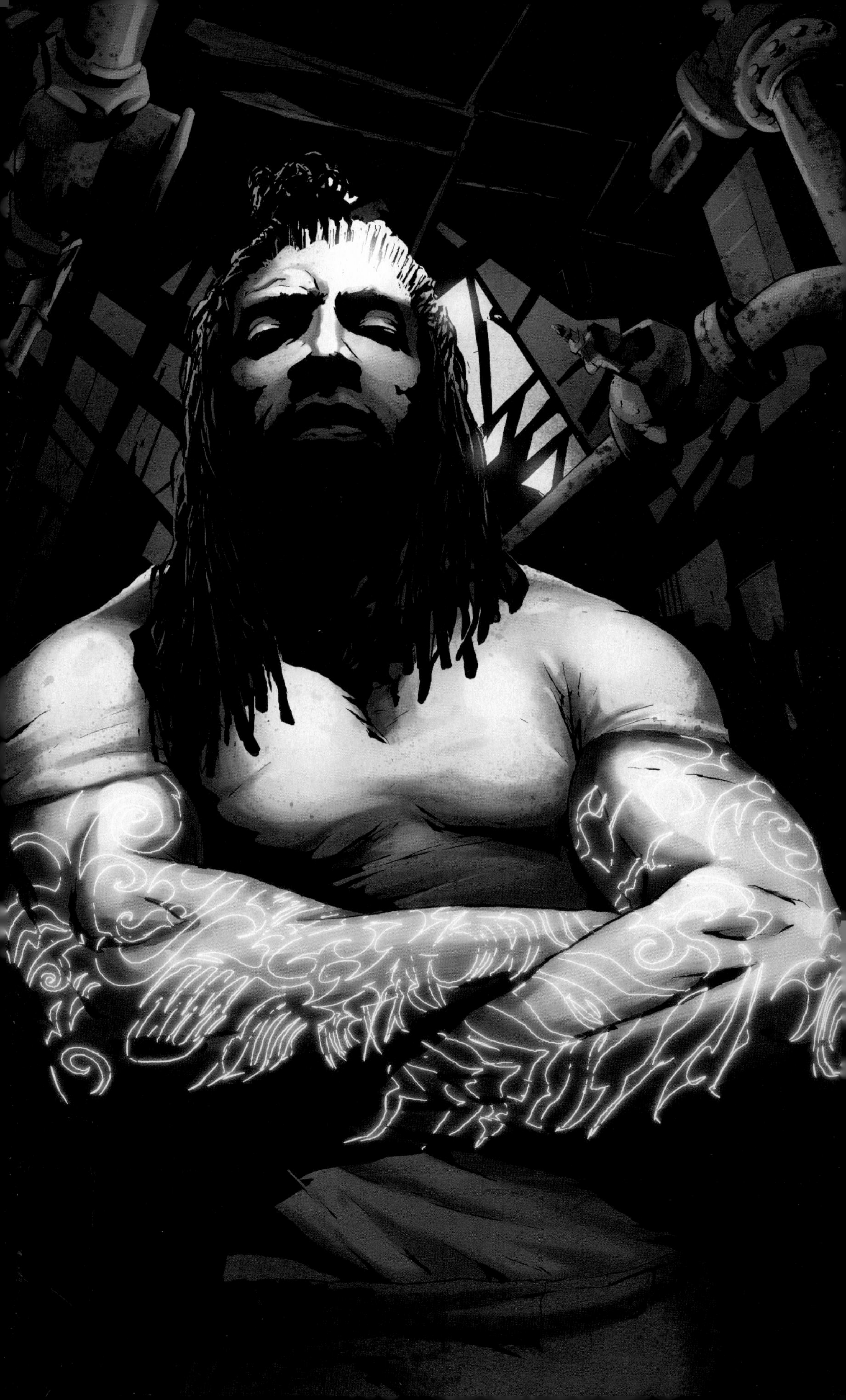

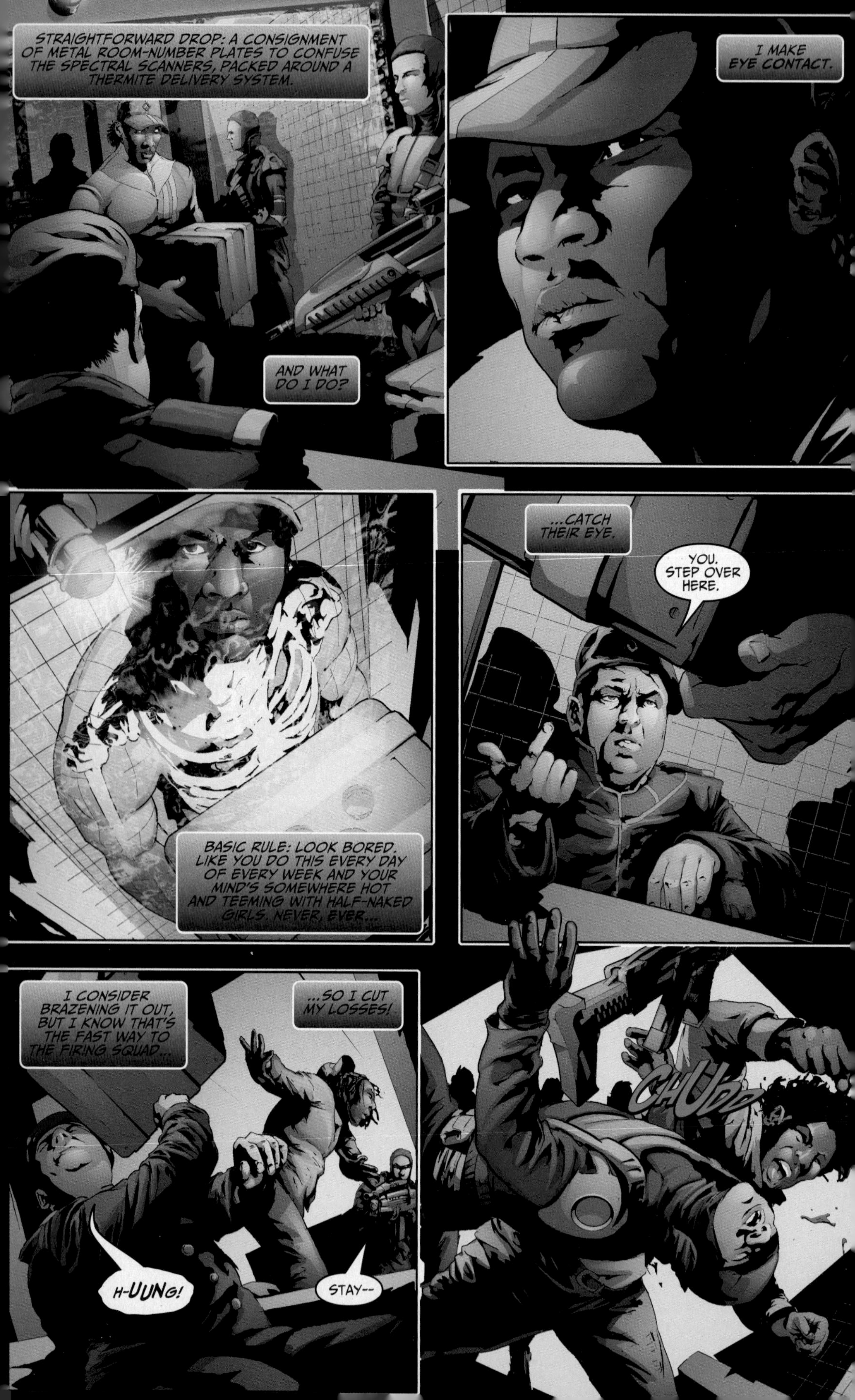
STRAIGHTFORWARD DROP: A CONSIGNMENT OF METAL ROOM-NUMBER PLATES TO CONFUSE THE SPECTRAL SCANNERS, PACKED AROUND A THERMITE DELIVERY SYSTEM.
AND WHAT DO I DO?
I MAKE EYE CONTACT.
BASIC RULE: LOOK BORED. LIKE YOU DO THIS EVERY DAY OF EVERY WEEK AND YOUR MIND'S SOMEWHERE HOT AND TEEMING WITH HALF-NAKED GIRLS. NEVER, EVER...
...CATCH THEIR EYE.
YOU. STEP OVER HERE.
I CONSIDER BRAZENING IT OUT, BUT I KNOW THAT'S THE FAST WAY TO THE FIRING SQUAD...
...SO I CUT MY LOSSES!
H-UUNG!
STAY--
CHUDD

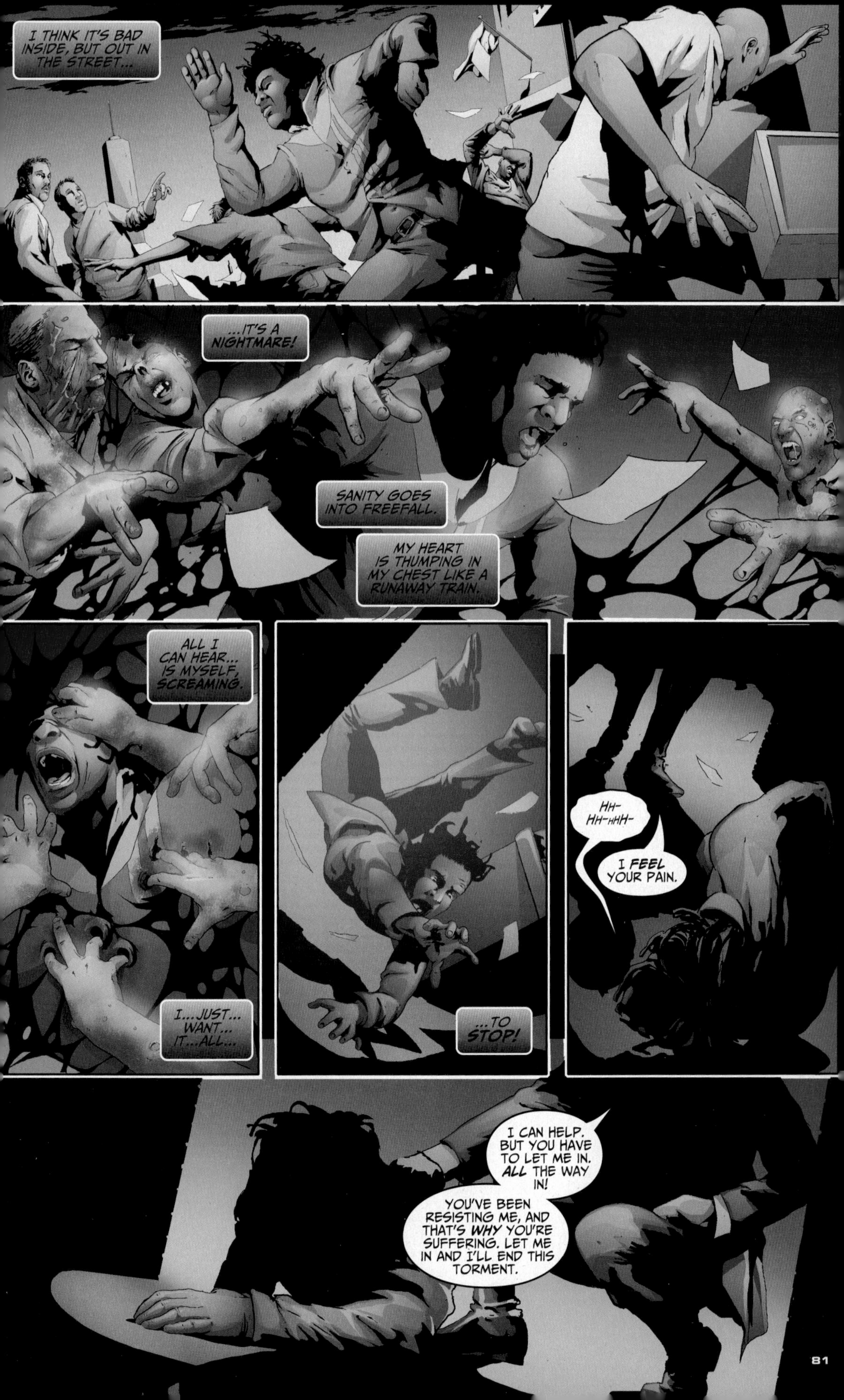
I THINK IT'S BAD INSIDE, BUT OUT IN THE STREET...
...IT'S A NIGHTMARE!
SANITY GOES INTO FREEFALL.
MY HEART IS THUMPING IN MY CHEST LIKE A RUNAWAY TRAIN.
ALL I CAN HEAR... IS MYSELF, SCREAMING.
I...JUST... WANT... IT...ALL...
...TO STOP!
HH-HH-HHH-
I FEEL YOUR PAIN.
I CAN HELP. BUT YOU HAVE TO LET ME IN. ALL THE WAY IN!
YOU'VE BEEN RESISTING ME, AND THAT'S WHY YOU'RE SUFFERING. LET ME IN AND I'LL END THIS TORMENT.

Y-YOU. I *KNOW* YOU.

BECAUSE WE'VE BEEN TOGETHER NOW FOR FOUR DAYS... OH YES, AND NIGHTS. ALL I WANT IS A FEW NAMES, A LOCATION OR TWO, AND I'LL BE GONE.

I'M JUST LIKE YOU, TURFA, TALENT-FOR-HIRE MAKING A LIVING ANY WAY I CAN. *DON'T* FIGHT ME...

YOU'VE... BEEN... IN...MY... HEAD!

TURFA? WHAT ARE YOU DOING? TURFA?

WHY... AREN'T YOU BROKEN? CRYING FOR OBLIVION? *WHY?*

YOU...*VIOLATED* ME. YOU TURNED MY LIFE INTO A LIVING HELL, AND FOR WHAT? INFORMATION? I'M NOT BROKEN...

...I'M MAD AS HELL!

I DON'T RUSH. HE TAKES LONG MINUTES TO DIE.

MY HANDS NEVER TREMBLE.

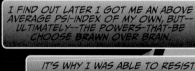

I FIND OUT LATER I GOT ME AN ABOVE AVERAGE PSI-INDEX OF MY OWN, BUT-- ULTIMATELY--THE POWERS-THAT-BE CHOOSE BRAWN OVER BRAIN.

IT'S WHY I WAS ABLE TO RESIST THE TELEPATH'S PROBES, WHY I WAS ABLE TO FIGHT BACK. BUT STILL...

...IT LEAVES *SCARS*, ONES THAT WILL NEVER GO AWAY. EVER.

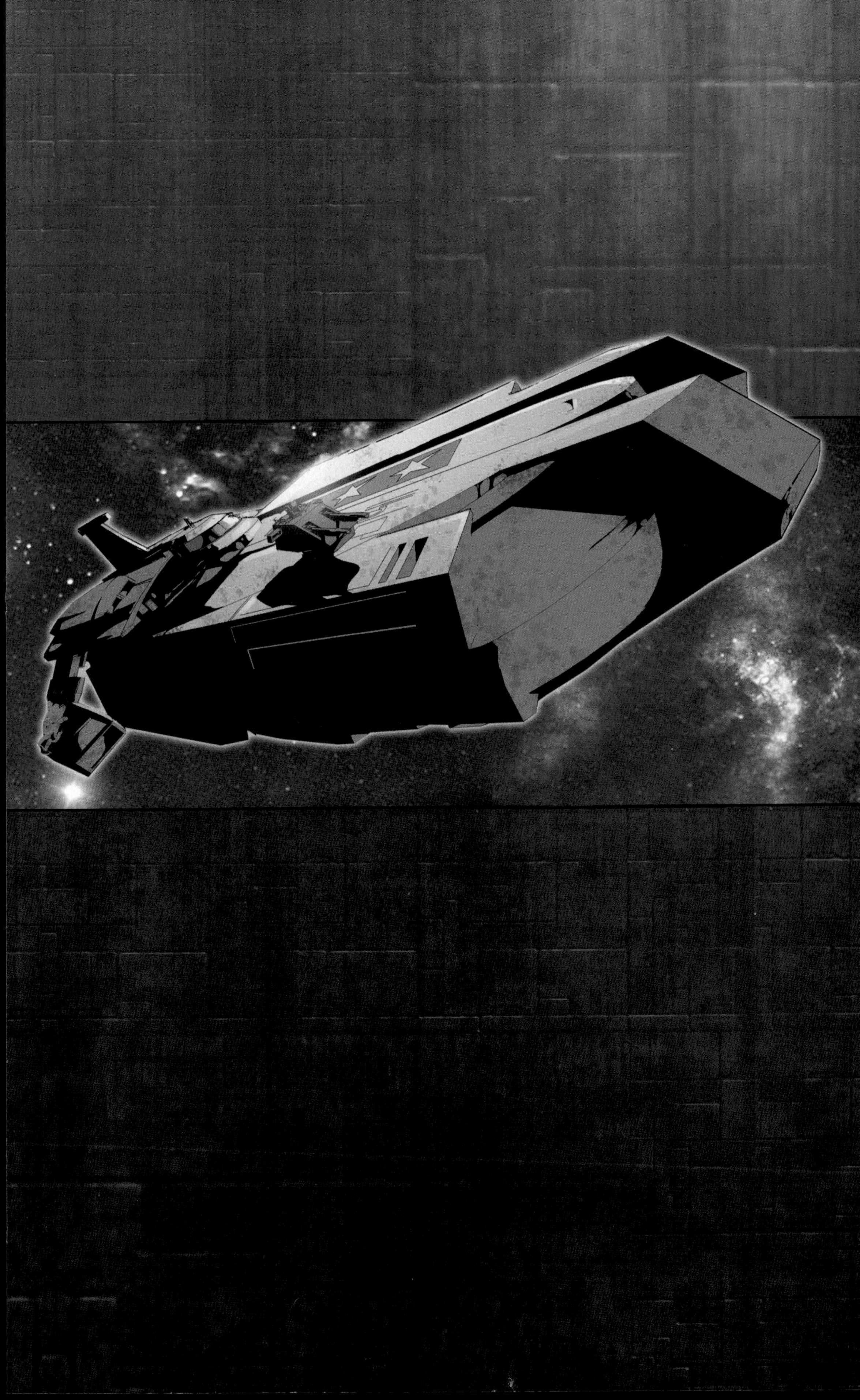

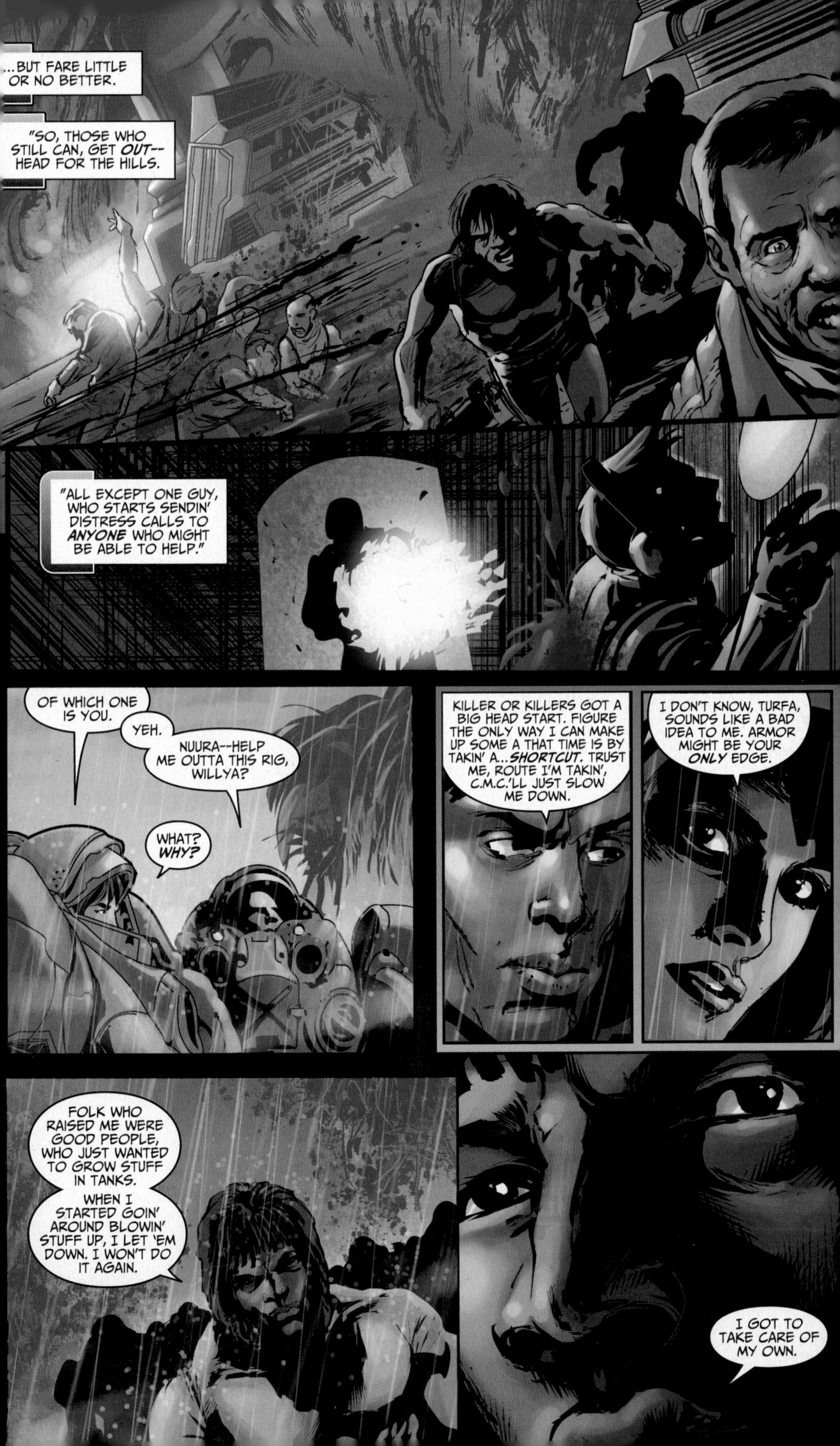
...BUT FARE LITTLE OR NO BETTER.
"SO, THOSE WHO STILL CAN, GET OUT--HEAD FOR THE HILLS.
"ALL EXCEPT ONE GUY, WHO STARTS SENDIN' DISTRESS CALLS TO ANYONE WHO MIGHT BE ABLE TO HELP."
OF WHICH ONE IS YOU.
YEH.
NUURA--HELP ME OUTTA THIS RIG, WILLYA?
WHAT? WHY?
KILLER OR KILLERS GOT A BIG HEAD START. FIGURE THE ONLY WAY I CAN MAKE UP SOME A THAT TIME IS BY TAKIN' A...SHORTCUT. TRUST ME, ROUTE I'M TAKIN', C.M.C.'LL JUST SLOW ME DOWN.
I DON'T KNOW, TURFA, SOUNDS LIKE A BAD IDEA TO ME. ARMOR MIGHT BE YOUR ONLY EDGE.
FOLK WHO RAISED ME WERE GOOD PEOPLE, WHO JUST WANTED TO GROW STUFF IN TANKS.
WHEN I STARTED GOIN' AROUND BLOWIN' STUFF UP, I LET 'EM DOWN. I WON'T DO IT AGAIN.
I GOT TO TAKE CARE OF MY OWN.

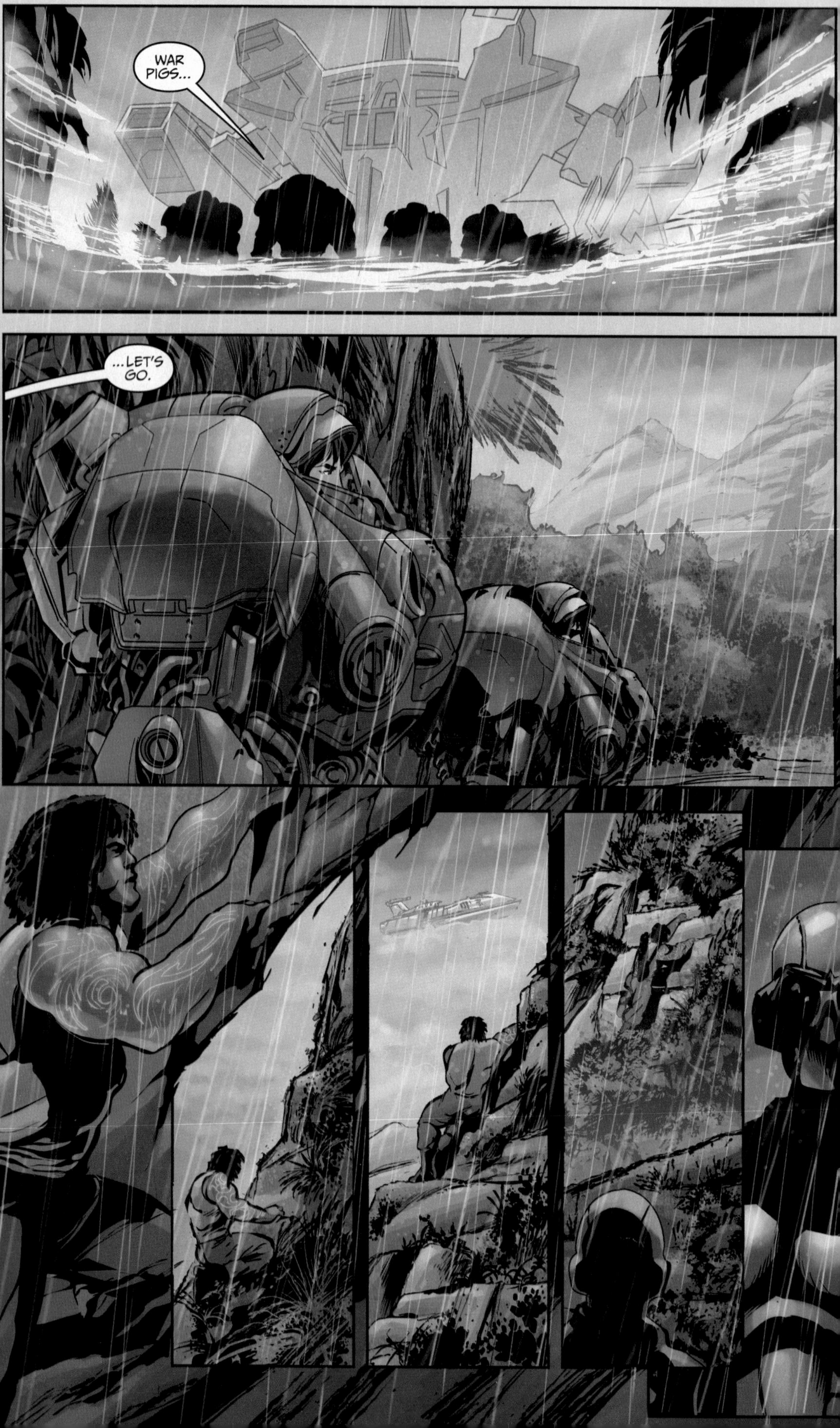
WAR PIGS...
...LET'S GO.

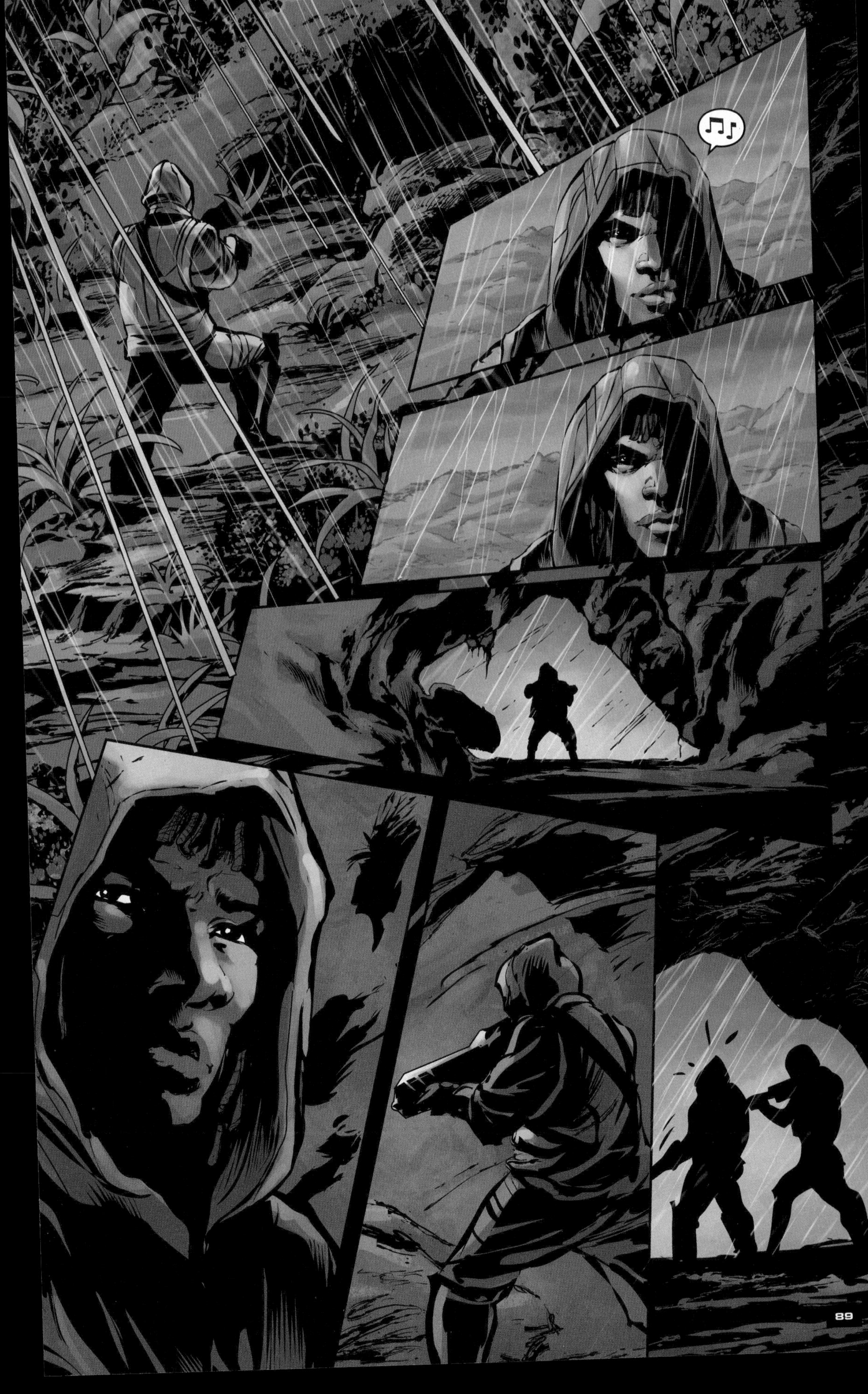

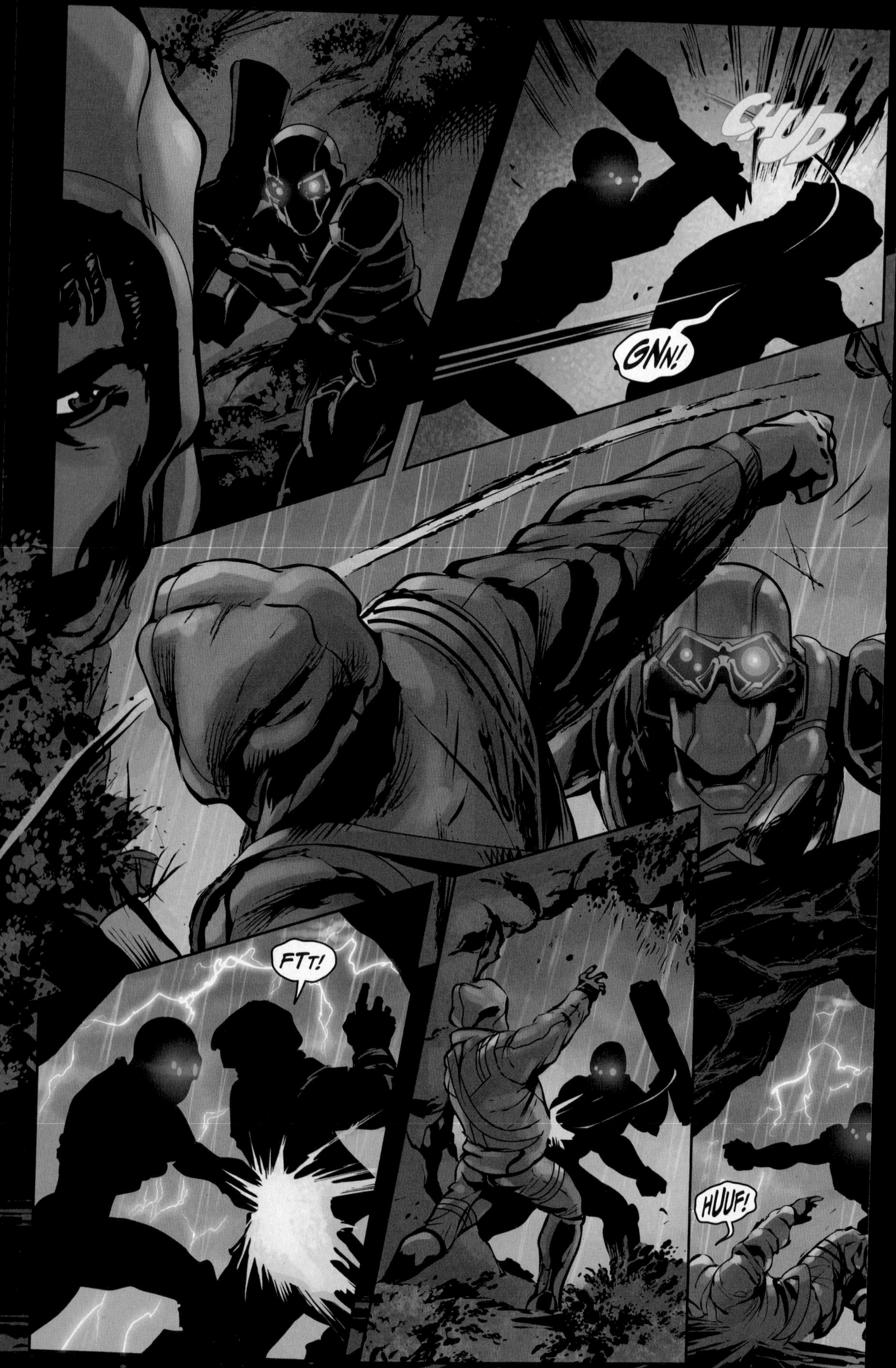
CHUD
GNN!
FTT!
HUUF!

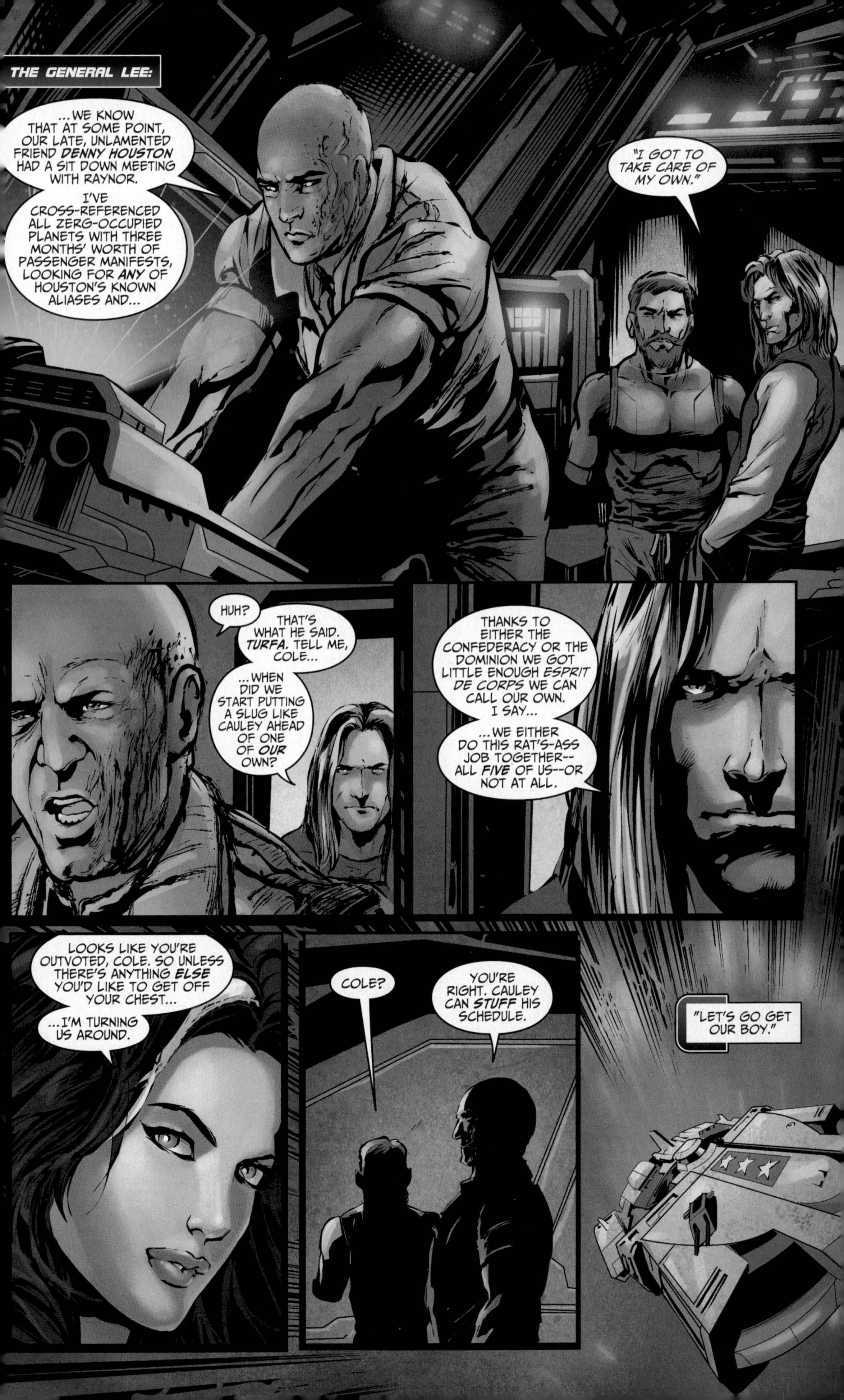
THE GENERAL LEE:
...WE KNOW THAT AT SOME POINT, OUR LATE, UNLAMENTED FRIEND DENNY HOUSTON HAD A SIT DOWN MEETING WITH RAYNOR.
I'VE CROSS-REFERENCED ALL ZERG-OCCUPIED PLANETS WITH THREE MONTHS' WORTH OF PASSENGER MANIFESTS, LOOKING FOR ANY OF HOUSTON'S KNOWN ALIASES AND...
"I GOT TO TAKE CARE OF MY OWN."
HUH?
THAT'S WHAT HE SAID. TURFA. TELL ME, COLE...
...WHEN DID WE START PUTTING A SLUG LIKE CAULEY AHEAD OF ONE OF OUR OWN?
THANKS TO EITHER THE CONFEDERACY OR THE DOMINION WE GOT LITTLE ENOUGH ESPRIT DE CORPS WE CAN CALL OUR OWN. I SAY...
...WE EITHER DO THIS RAT'S-ASS JOB TOGETHER--ALL FIVE OF US--OR NOT AT ALL.
LOOKS LIKE YOU'RE OUTVOTED, COLE. SO UNLESS THERE'S ANYTHING ELSE YOU'D LIKE TO GET OFF YOUR CHEST...
...I'M TURNING US AROUND.
COLE?
YOU'RE RIGHT. CAULEY CAN STUFF HIS SCHEDULE.
"LET'S GO GET OUR BOY."

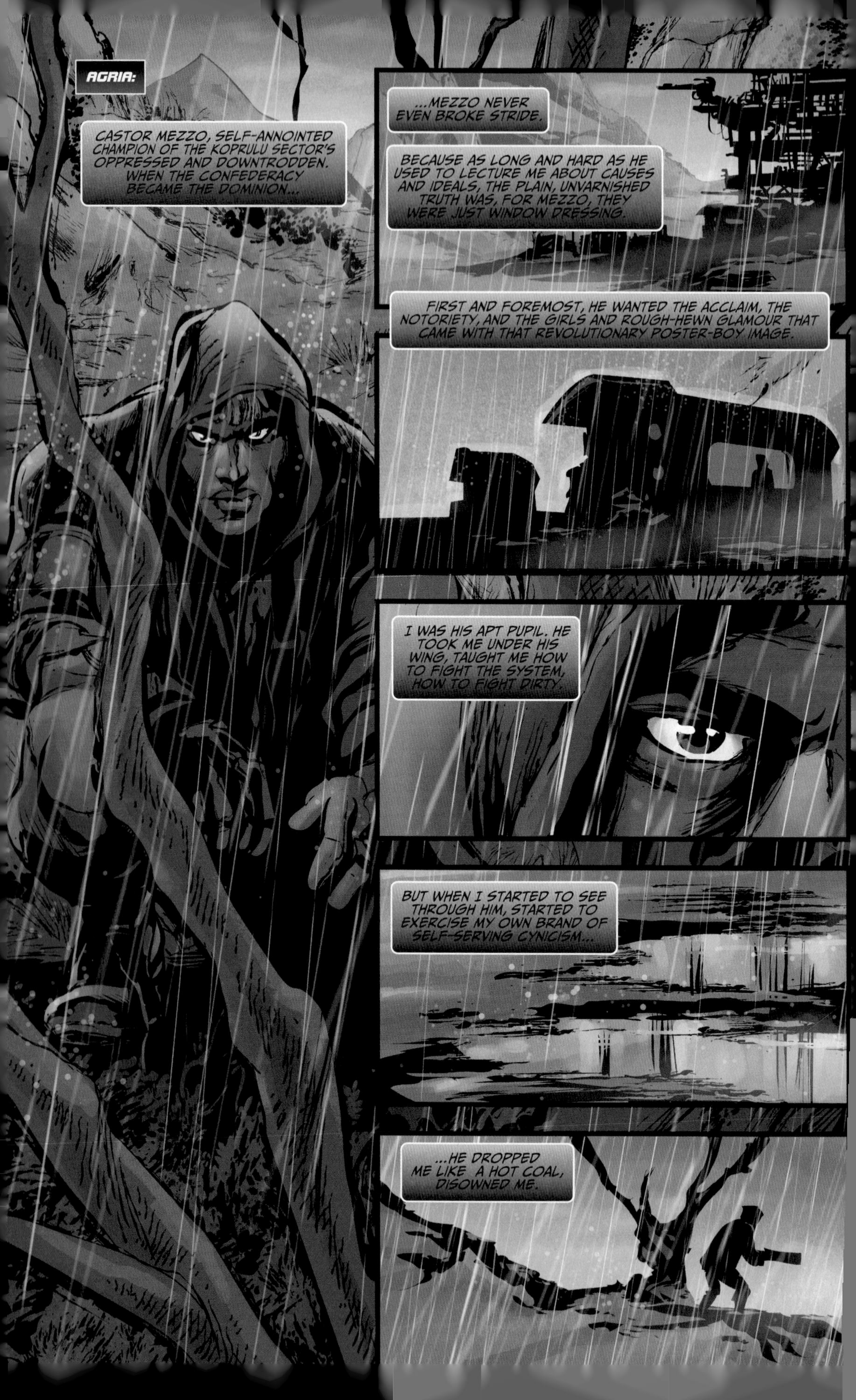
AGRIA:
CASTOR MEZZO, SELF-ANNOINTED CHAMPION OF THE KOPRULU SECTOR'S OPPRESSED AND DOWNTRODDEN. WHEN THE CONFEDERACY BECAME THE DOMINION...
...MEZZO NEVER EVEN BROKE STRIDE.
BECAUSE AS LONG AND HARD AS HE USED TO LECTURE ME ABOUT CAUSES AND IDEALS, THE PLAIN, UNVARNISHED TRUTH WAS, FOR MEZZO, THEY WERE JUST WINDOW DRESSING.
FIRST AND FOREMOST, HE WANTED THE ACCLAIM, THE NOTORIETY, AND THE GIRLS AND ROUGH-HEWN GLAMOUR THAT CAME WITH THAT REVOLUTIONARY POSTER-BOY IMAGE.
I WAS HIS APT PUPIL. HE TOOK ME UNDER HIS WING, TAUGHT ME HOW TO FIGHT THE SYSTEM, HOW TO FIGHT DIRTY.
BUT WHEN I STARTED TO SEE THROUGH HIM, STARTED TO EXERCISE MY OWN BRAND OF SELF-SERVING CYNICISM...
...HE DROPPED ME LIKE A HOT COAL, DISOWNED ME.

...JUST ALONG FOR THE RIDE.

MOVE IT. AND KEEP *BEHIND* ME. IT'S NOT MUCH OF AN EDGE, BUT I GOT A... *SENSE*...OF THESE PSI-BOYS!

YEAH?

YEAH. RESULT OF AN ABOVE AVERAGE PSI-INDEX OF MY OWN AN' HAVING A TELEPATH BURROWED IN MY HEAD A...WHILE...BACK...

BACK! GET BACK!

SHE'S HERE!

...ALL SHE HAD TO DO WAS SIT BACK...

THRRT

DUMB. DENSE. STUPID.

ONCE SHE KNEW I KNEW THE PLACES MEZZO MIGHT'VE HOLED UP IN...

...AND LET ME LEAD HER RIGHT TO HIM.

OH, SH--

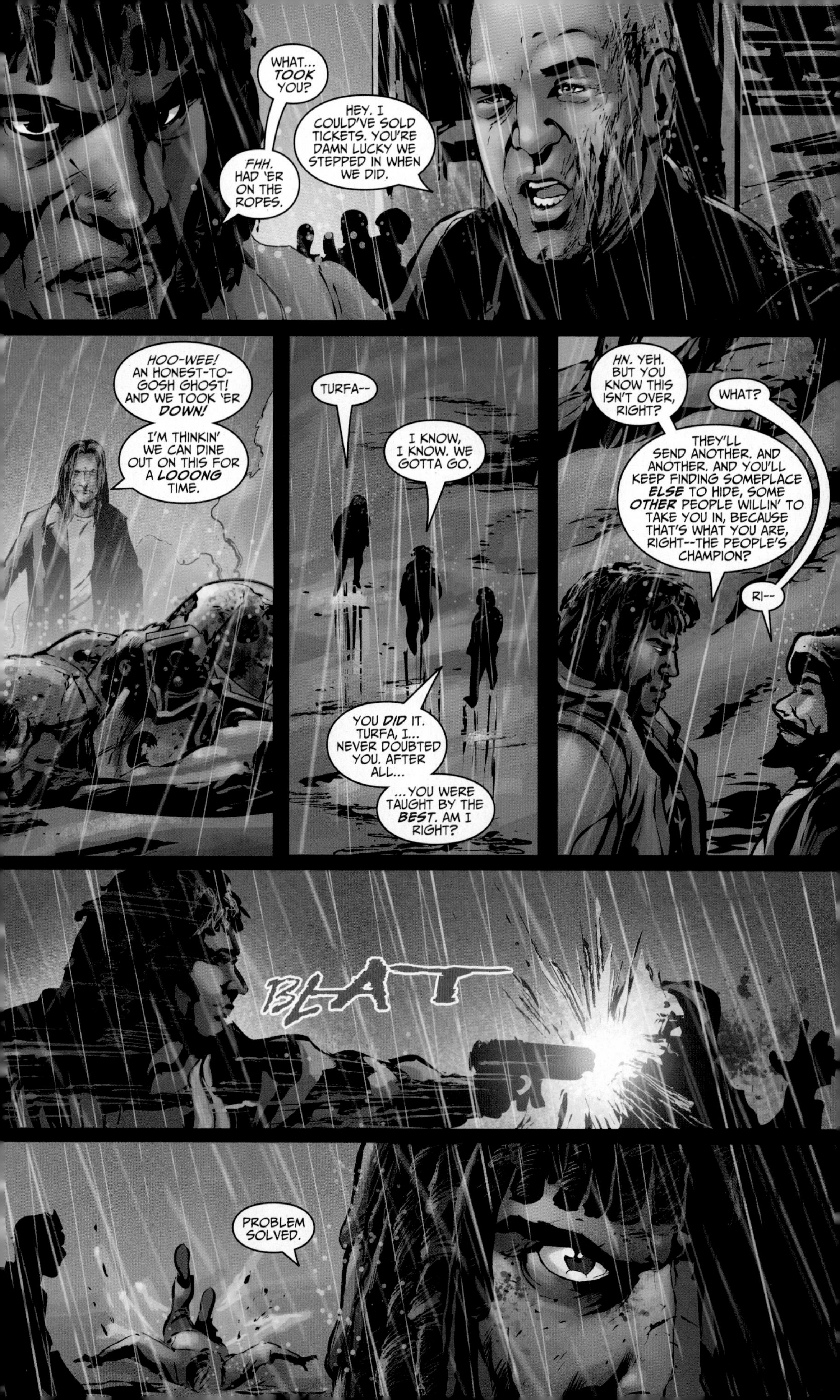
WHAT... *TOOK* YOU?
FHH. HAD 'ER ON THE ROPES.
HEY. I COULD'VE SOLD TICKETS. YOU'RE DAMN LUCKY WE STEPPED IN WHEN WE DID.
HOO-WEE! AN HONEST-TO-GOSH GHOST! AND WE TOOK 'ER ***DOWN!***
I'M THINKIN' WE CAN DINE OUT ON THIS FOR A ***LOOONG*** TIME.
TURFA--
I KNOW, I KNOW. WE GOTTA GO.
YOU ***DID*** IT. TURFA, I... NEVER DOUBTED YOU. AFTER ALL...
...YOU WERE TAUGHT BY THE ***BEST***. AM I RIGHT?
HN. YEH. BUT YOU KNOW THIS ISN'T OVER, RIGHT?
WHAT?
THEY'LL SEND ANOTHER. AND ANOTHER. AND YOU'LL KEEP FINDING SOMEPLACE ***ELSE*** TO HIDE, SOME ***OTHER*** PEOPLE WILLIN' TO TAKE YOU IN, BECAUSE THAT'S WHAT YOU ARE, RIGHT--THE PEOPLE'S CHAMPION?
RI--
BLAT
PROBLEM SOLVED.

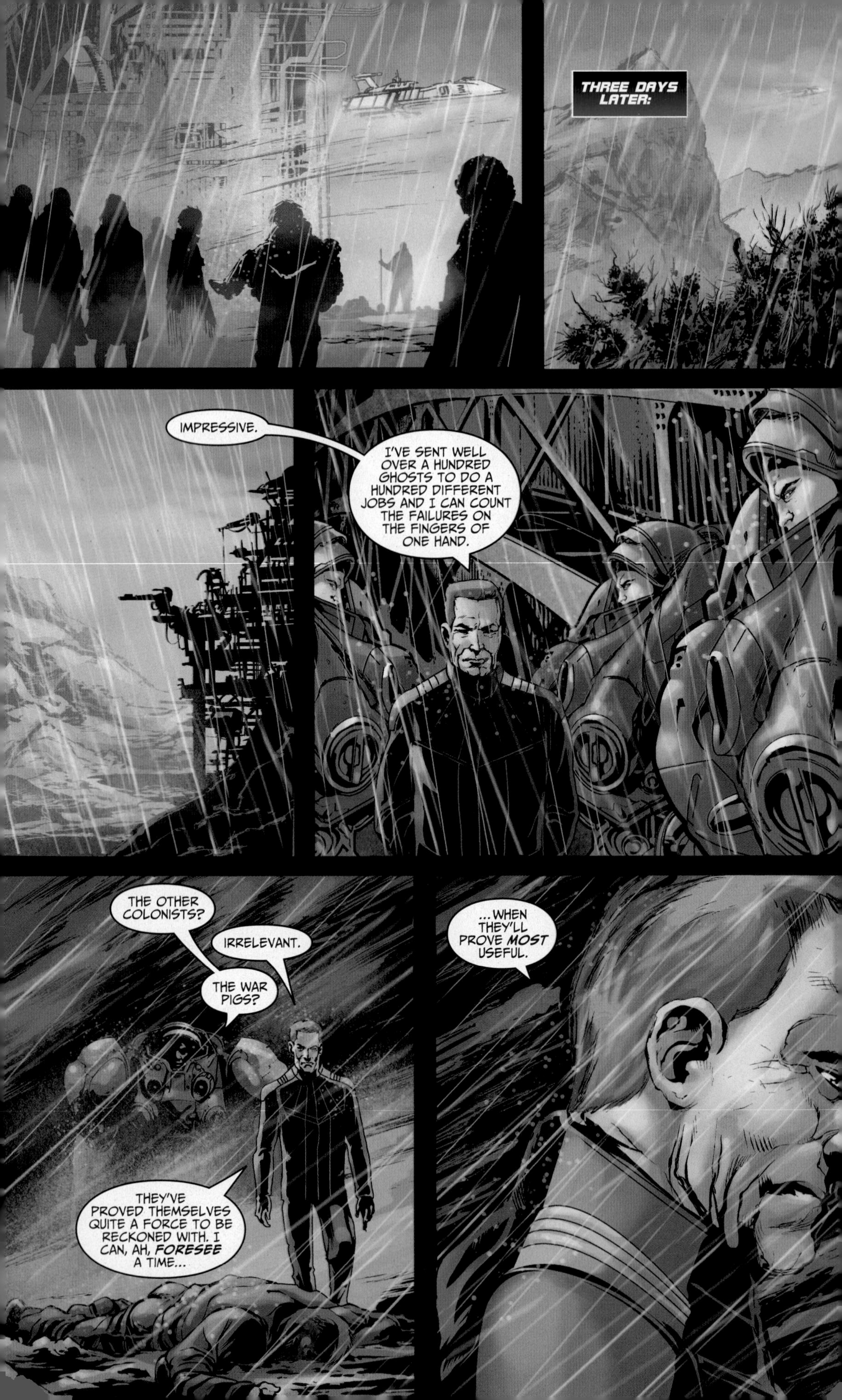
THREE DAYS LATER:
IMPRESSIVE.
I'VE SENT WELL OVER A HUNDRED GHOSTS TO DO A HUNDRED DIFFERENT JOBS AND I CAN COUNT THE FAILURES ON THE FINGERS OF ONE HAND.
THE OTHER COLONISTS?
IRRELEVANT.
THE WAR PIGS?
THEY'VE PROVED THEMSELVES QUITE A FORCE TO BE RECKONED WITH. I CAN, AH, *FORESEE* A TIME...
...WHEN THEY'LL PROVE *MOST* USEFUL.

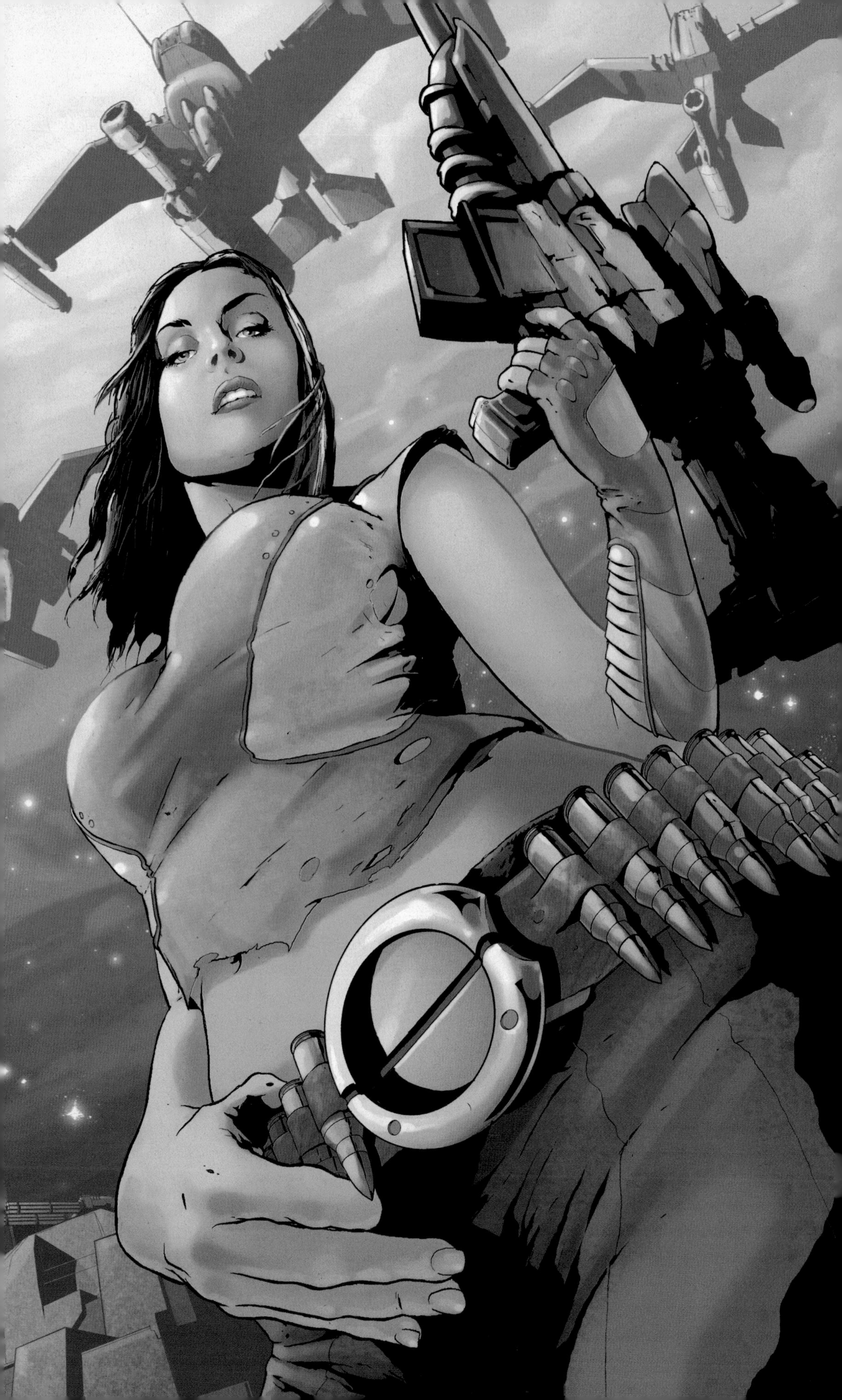

BRONTES. 2496:

AND BEYOND THAT, I SHALL DEMAND TRANSPARENCY IN *ALL* DEALINGS, BE THEY INTERNAL OR EXTERNAL...

THE ACCUSATIONS OF CORRUPTION IN THE SENATE MUST BE QUASHED ONCE AND FOR ALL...

...IF WE ARE TO BRING *ORDER* TO POLITICAL ANARCHY.

FIRST RULE: DON'T WATCH HIM.

WATCH THE CROWD.

LOOK FOR THAT ONE INDIVIDUAL WITH AN AXE TO GRIND AND THE MISGUIDED ZEAL TO FOLLOW THROUGH.

I FAIL WITHIN TWO MINUTES.

A NEW PERSONAL RECORD.

SECOND RULE: DON'T ALLOW YOURSELF TO BECOME ROMANTICALLY ENTANGLED WITH YOUR DESIGNATED "WARM BODY."

OOPS.

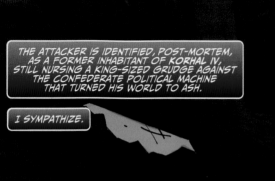

THE ATTACKER IS IDENTIFIED, POST-MORTEM, AS A FORMER INHABITANT OF *KORHAL IV*, STILL NURSING A KING-SIZED GRUDGE AGAINST THE CONFEDERATE POLITICAL MACHINE THAT TURNED HIS WORLD TO ASH.

I SYMPATHIZE.

TO A POINT.

NO, ABSOLUTELY *NOT.* I WILL NOT MAKE ANY STATEMENT TO THE EFFECT THIS WAS SOME *SONS OF KORHAL* ASSASSINATION PLOT. IT WASN'T.

JUST SOME LONE, MISGUIDED INDIVIDUAL WHO HAD LOST EVERYTHING. PRINT *THAT!*

IT HAS TO END.

I CAN'T BE OBJECTIVE. EVERY GUIDING PRINCIPLE I HAVE AND HOLD AS AN OPERATIVE IN THE *SPECIAL SERVICES* IS CURRENTLY BEING COMPROMISED.

NO, I'M SORRY, I CAN'T EXPLAIN. I JUST NEED TO BE REASSIGNED. I...

...CAN NO LONGER GUARANTEE SENATOR CANON'S SAFETY.

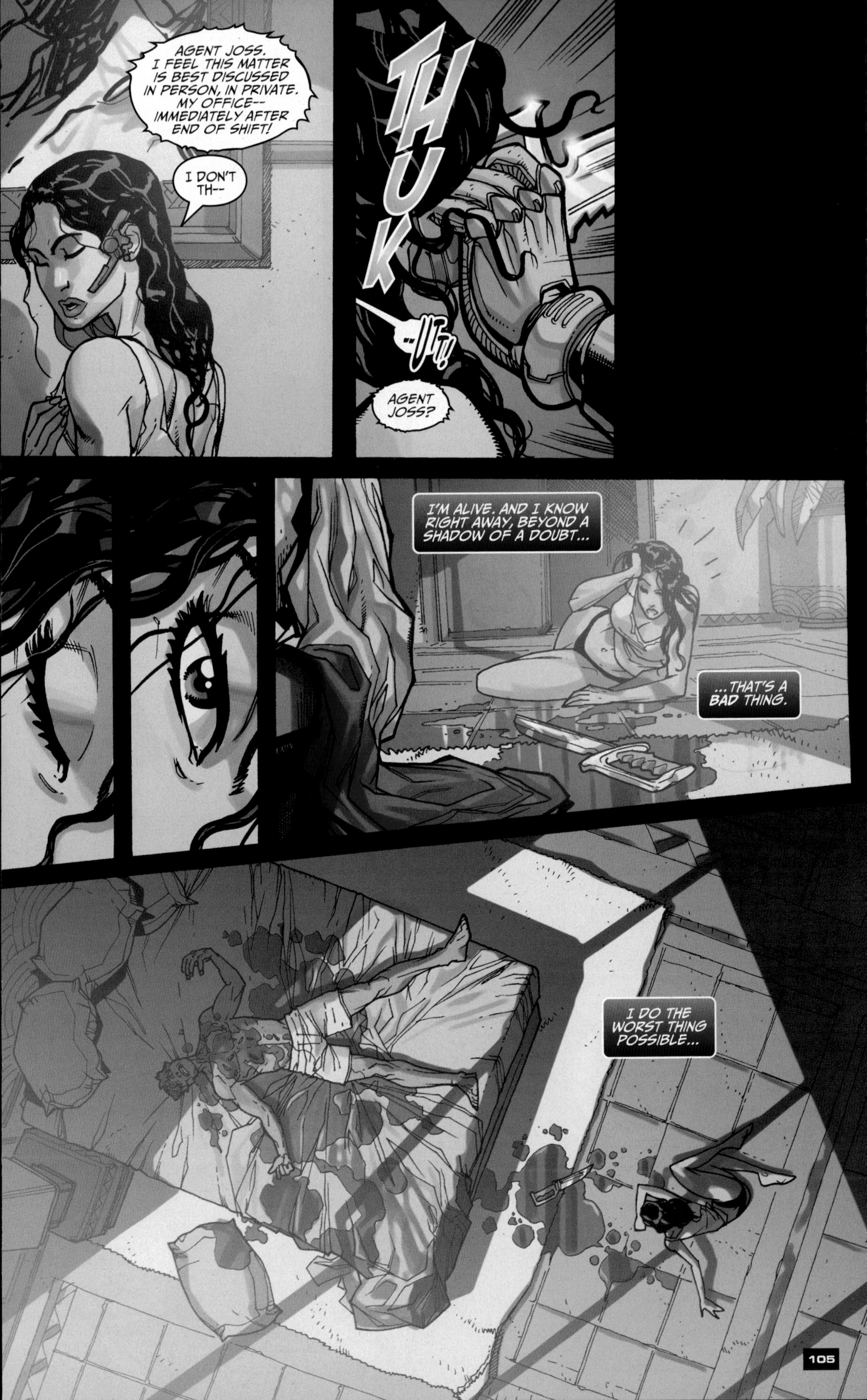
AGENT JOSS. I FEEL THIS MATTER IS BEST DISCUSSED IN PERSON, IN PRIVATE. MY OFFICE-- IMMEDIATELY AFTER END OF SHIFT!
I DON'T TH--
THUK
--UTT!
AGENT JOSS?
I'M ALIVE. AND I KNOW RIGHT AWAY, BEYOND A SHADOW OF A DOUBT...
...THAT'S A BAD THING.
I DO THE WORST THING POSSIBLE...

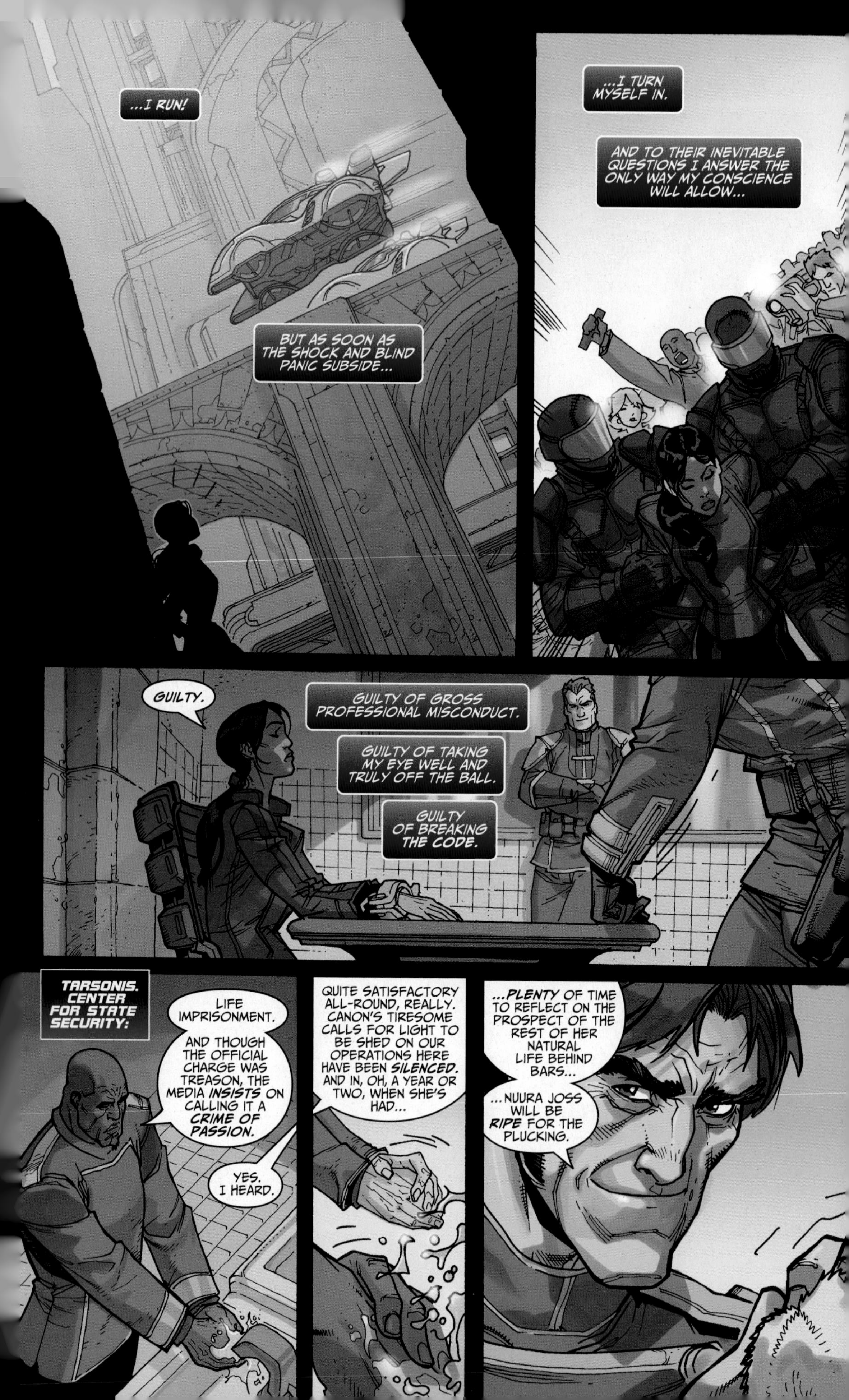
...I RUN!
BUT AS SOON AS THE SHOCK AND BLIND PANIC SUBSIDE...
...I TURN MYSELF IN.
AND TO THEIR INEVITABLE QUESTIONS I ANSWER THE ONLY WAY MY CONSCIENCE WILL ALLOW...
GUILTY.
GUILTY OF GROSS PROFESSIONAL MISCONDUCT.
GUILTY OF TAKING MY EYE WELL AND TRULY OFF THE BALL.
GUILTY OF BREAKING THE CODE.
TARSONIS. CENTER FOR STATE SECURITY:
LIFE IMPRISONMENT.
AND THOUGH THE OFFICIAL CHARGE WAS TREASON, THE MEDIA INSISTS ON CALLING IT A CRIME OF PASSION.
YES. I HEARD.
QUITE SATISFACTORY ALL-ROUND, REALLY. CANON'S TIRESOME CALLS FOR LIGHT TO BE SHED ON OUR OPERATIONS HERE HAVE BEEN SILENCED. AND IN, OH, A YEAR OR TWO, WHEN SHE'S HAD...
...PLENTY OF TIME TO REFLECT ON THE PROSPECT OF THE REST OF HER NATURAL LIFE BEHIND BARS...
...NUURA JOSS WILL BE RIPE FOR THE PLUCKING.

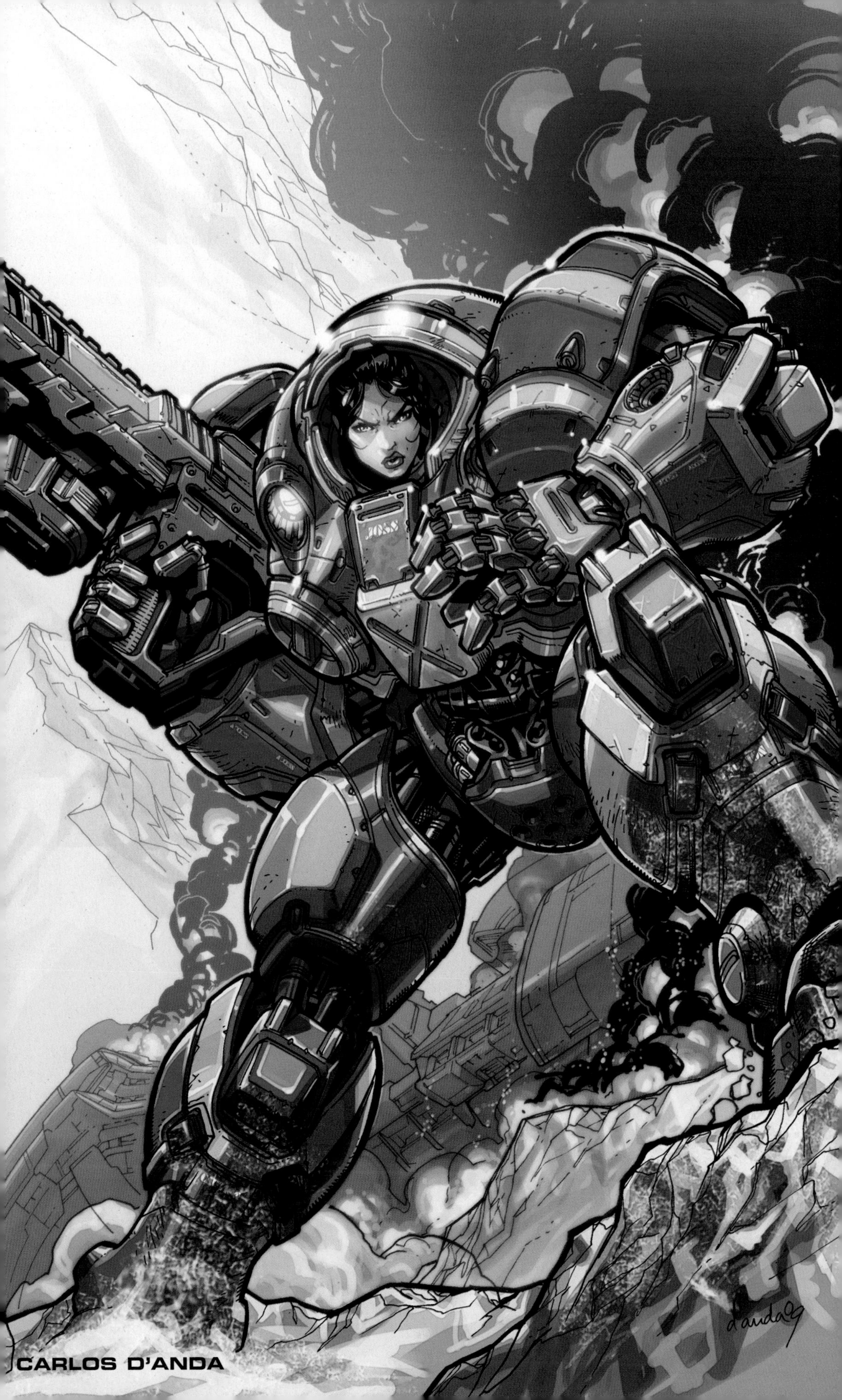

CARLOS D'ANDA

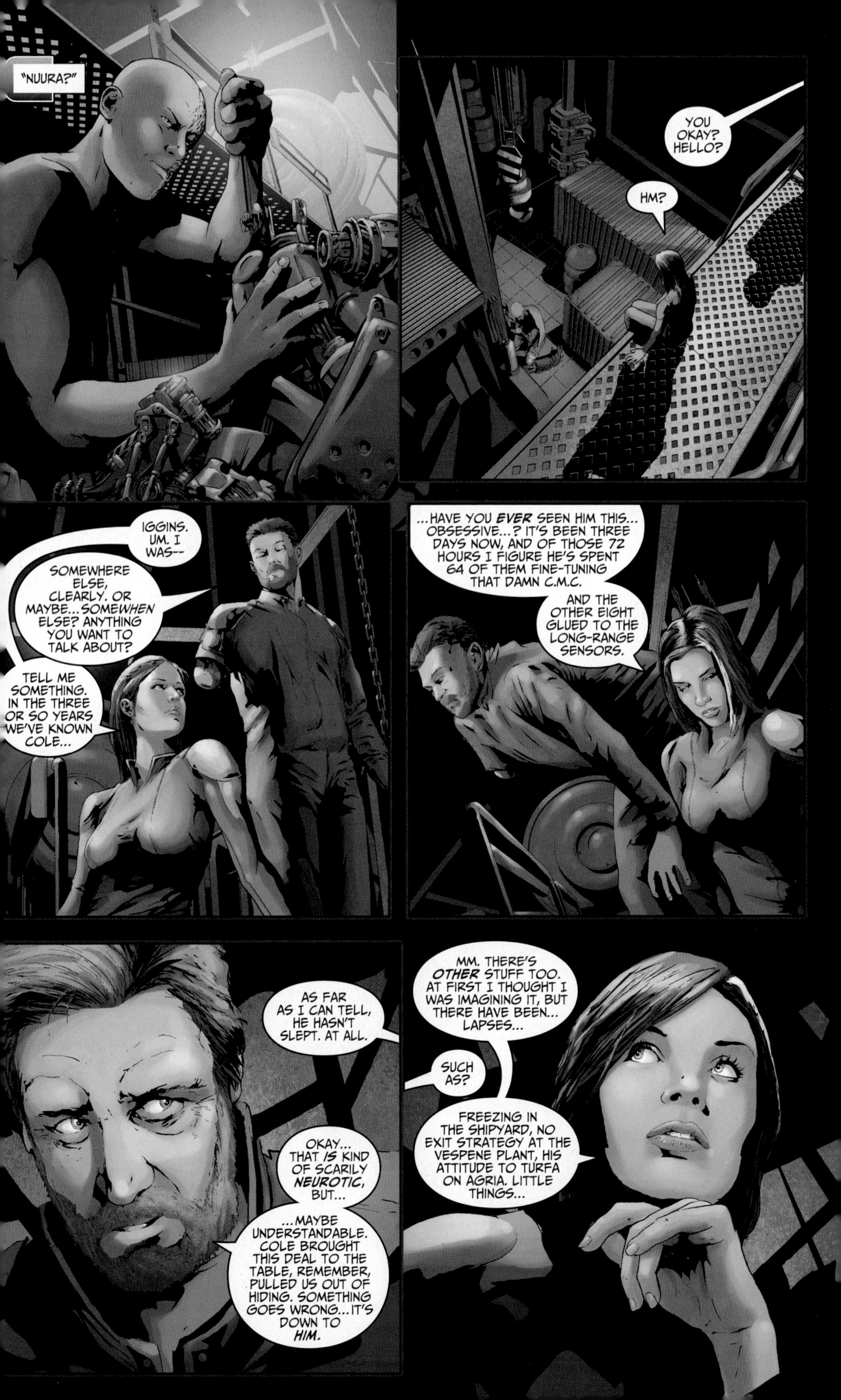
"NUURA?"
YOU OKAY? HELLO?
HM?
IGGINS. UM. I WAS--
SOMEWHERE ELSE, CLEARLY. OR MAYBE... SOMEWHEN ELSE? ANYTHING YOU WANT TO TALK ABOUT?
TELL ME SOMETHING. IN THE THREE OR SO YEARS WE'VE KNOWN COLE...
...HAVE YOU EVER SEEN HIM THIS... OBSESSIVE...? IT'S BEEN THREE DAYS NOW, AND OF THOSE 72 HOURS I FIGURE HE'S SPENT 64 OF THEM FINE-TUNING THAT DAMN C.M.C.
AND THE OTHER EIGHT GLUED TO THE LONG-RANGE SENSORS.
AS FAR AS I CAN TELL, HE HASN'T SLEPT. AT ALL.
OKAY... THAT IS KIND OF SCARILY NEUROTIC, BUT...
...MAYBE UNDERSTANDABLE. COLE BROUGHT THIS DEAL TO THE TABLE, REMEMBER, PULLED US OUT OF HIDING. SOMETHING GOES WRONG... IT'S DOWN TO HIM.
MM. THERE'S OTHER STUFF TOO. AT FIRST I THOUGHT I WAS IMAGINING IT, BUT THERE HAVE BEEN... LAPSES...
SUCH AS?
FREEZING IN THE SHIPYARD, NO EXIT STRATEGY AT THE VESPENE PLANT, HIS ATTITUDE TO TURFA ON AGRIA. LITTLE THINGS...

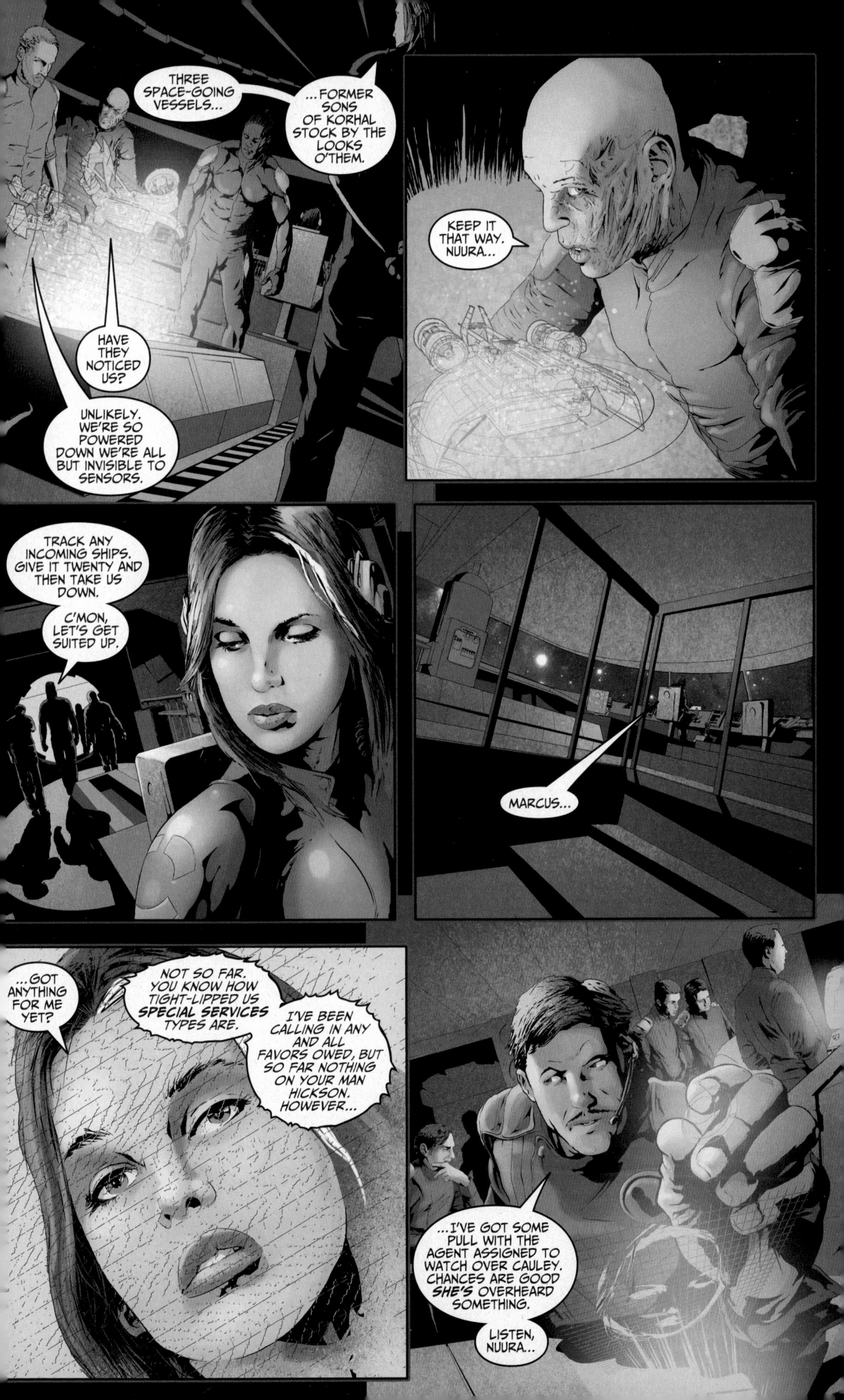
THREE SPACE-GOING VESSELS...
...FORMER SONS OF KORHAL STOCK BY THE LOOKS O'THEM.
HAVE THEY NOTICED US?
UNLIKELY. WE'RE SO POWERED DOWN WE'RE ALL BUT INVISIBLE TO SENSORS.
KEEP IT THAT WAY. NUURA...
TRACK ANY INCOMING SHIPS. GIVE IT TWENTY AND THEN TAKE US DOWN.
C'MON, LET'S GET SUITED UP.
MARCUS...
...GOT ANYTHING FOR ME YET?
NOT SO FAR. YOU KNOW HOW TIGHT-LIPPED US SPECIAL SERVICES TYPES ARE.
I'VE BEEN CALLING IN ANY AND ALL FAVORS OWED, BUT SO FAR NOTHING ON YOUR MAN HICKSON. HOWEVER...
...I'VE GOT SOME PULL WITH THE AGENT ASSIGNED TO WATCH OVER CAULEY. CHANCES ARE GOOD SHE'S OVERHEARD SOMETHING.
LISTEN, NUURA...

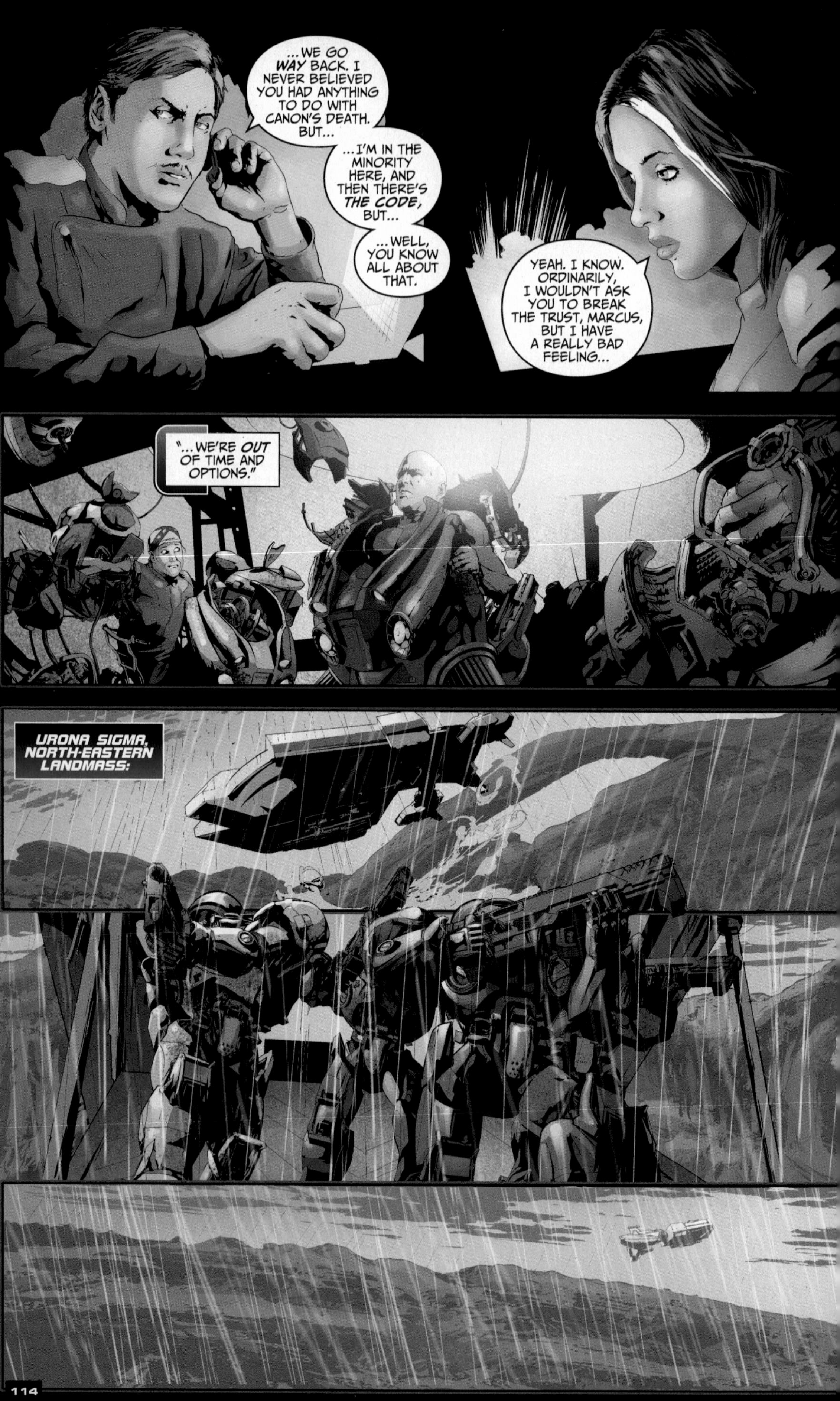
...WE GO WAY BACK. I NEVER BELIEVED YOU HAD ANYTHING TO DO WITH CANON'S DEATH. BUT...
...I'M IN THE MINORITY HERE, AND THEN THERE'S THE CODE, BUT...
...WELL, YOU KNOW ALL ABOUT THAT.
YEAH. I KNOW. ORDINARILY, I WOULDN'T ASK YOU TO BREAK THE TRUST, MARCUS, BUT I HAVE A REALLY BAD FEELING...
"...WE'RE OUT OF TIME AND OPTIONS."
URONA SIGMA, NORTH-EASTERN LANDMASS:

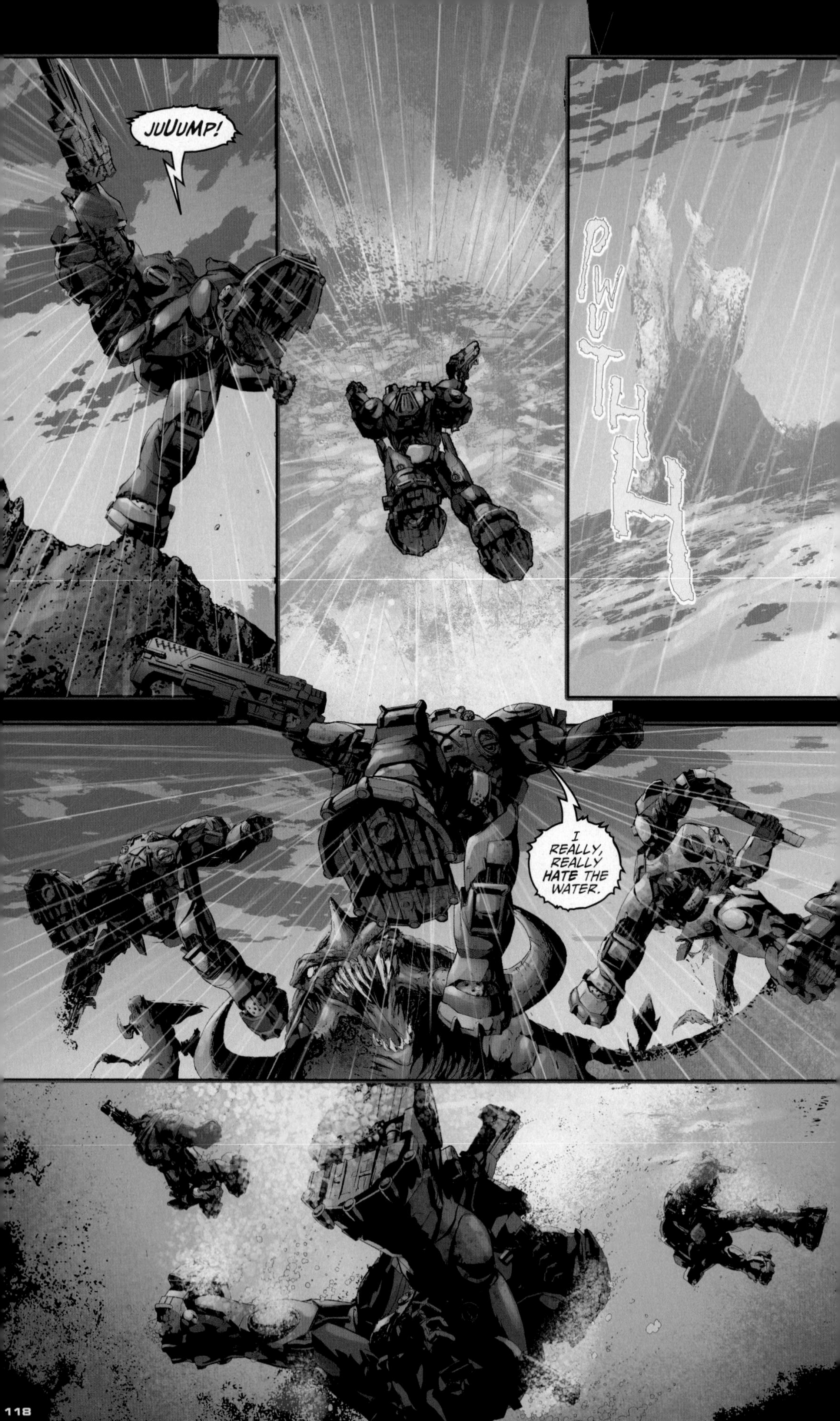
JUUUMP!
PWUTHH
I REALLY, REALLY HATE THE WATER.

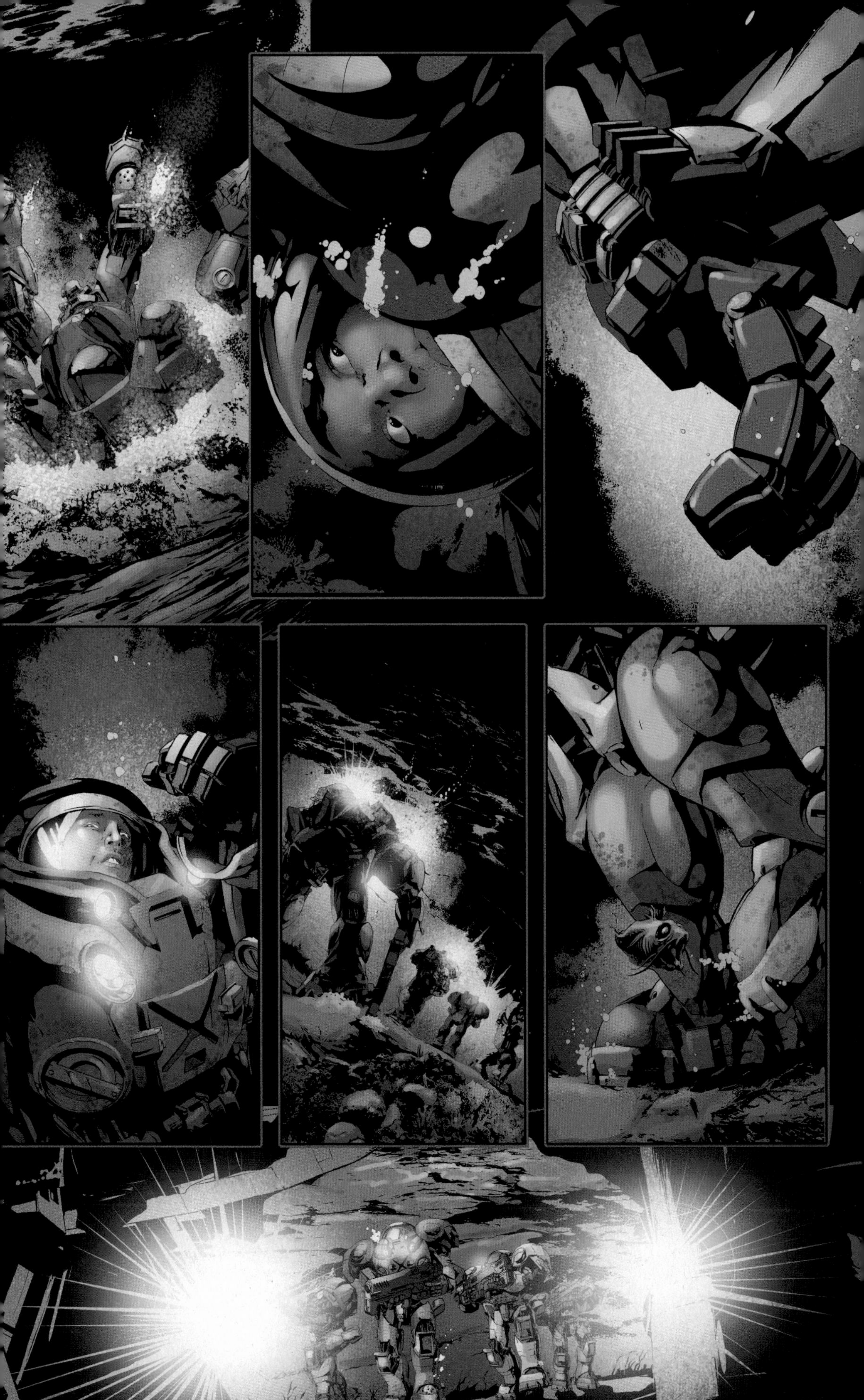

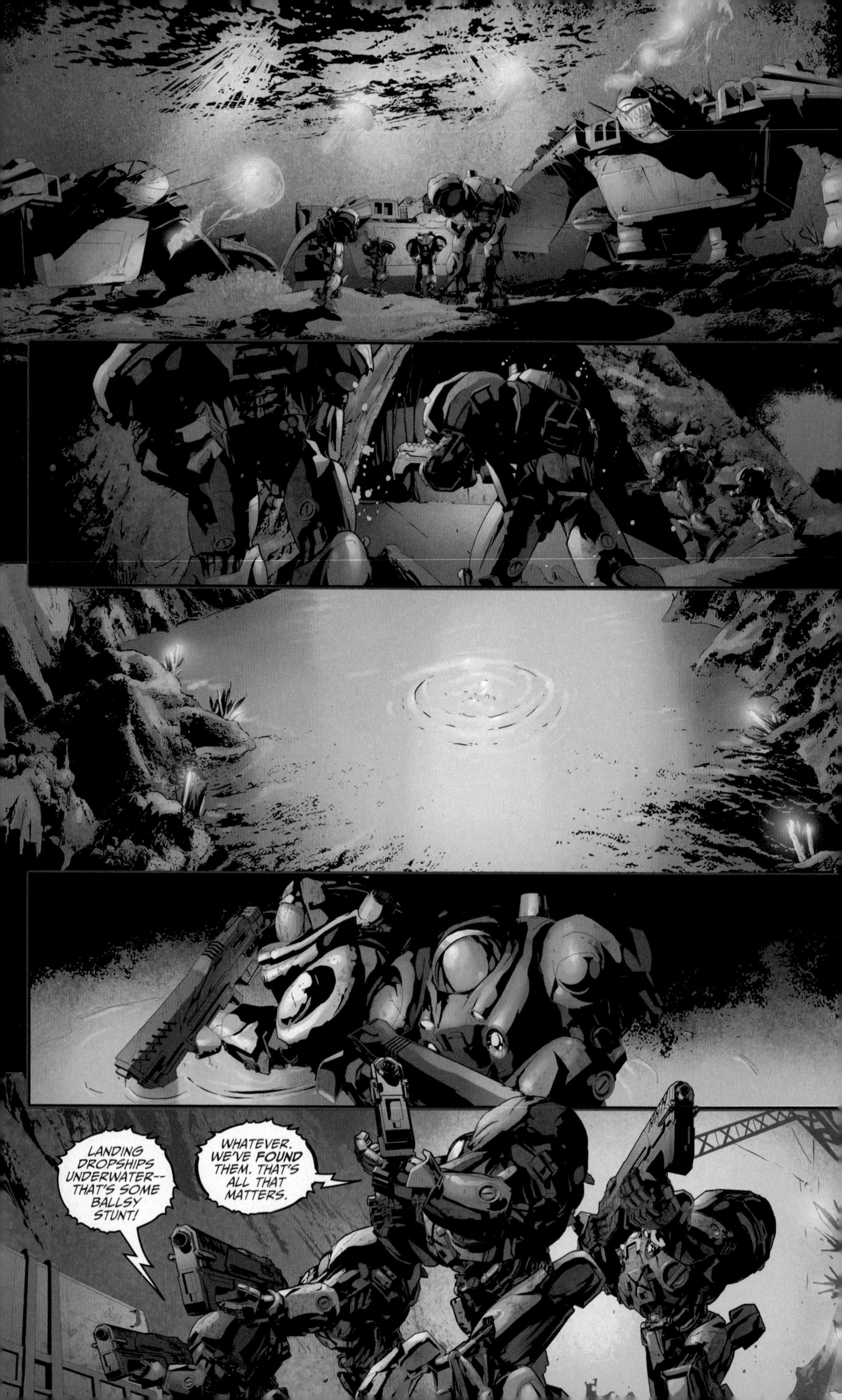
LANDING DROPSHIPS UNDERWATER-- THAT'S SOME BALLSY STUNT!
WHATEVER. WE'VE FOUND THEM. THAT'S ALL THAT MATTERS.

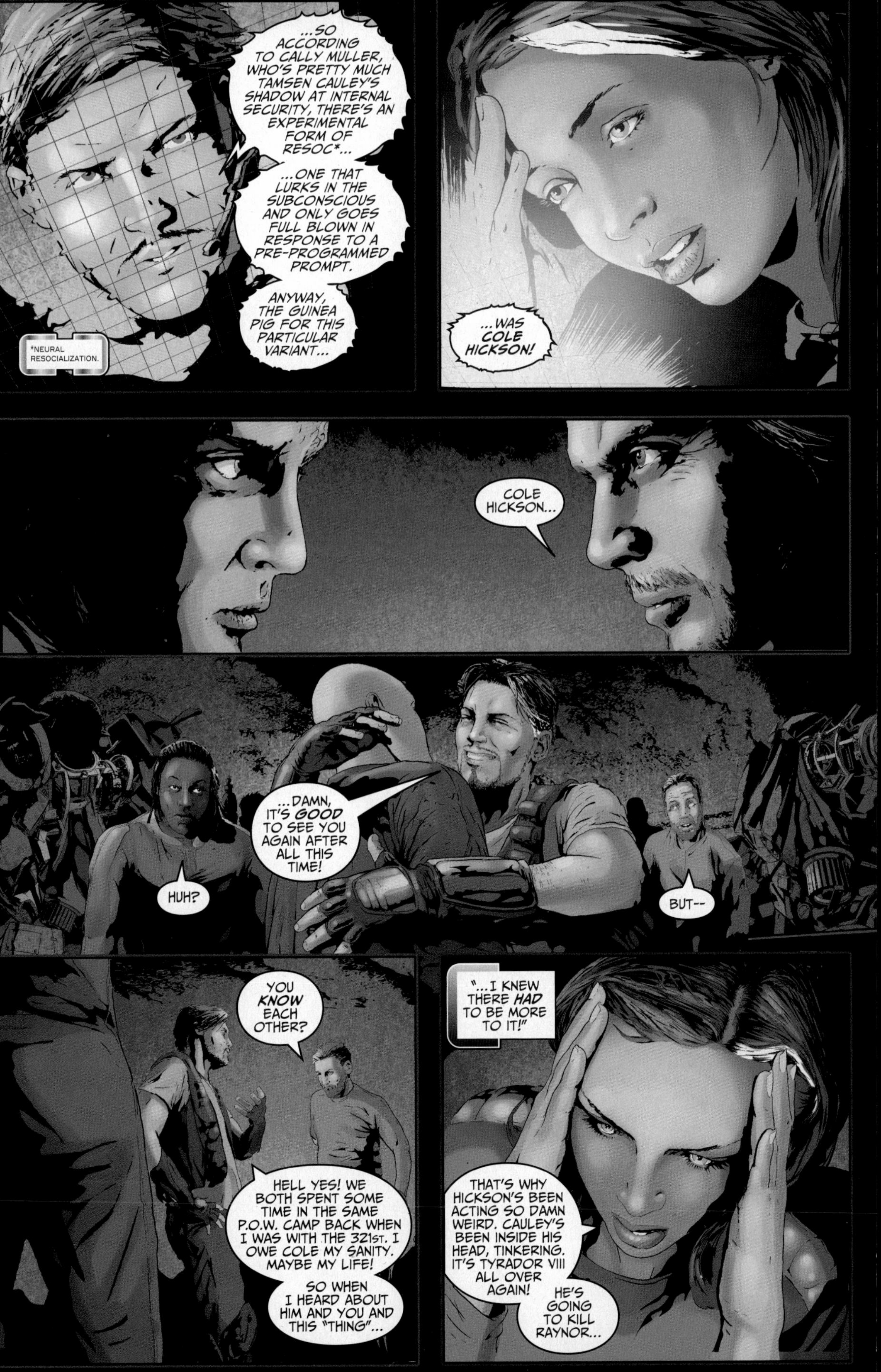

...SO ACCORDING TO CALLY MULLER, WHO'S PRETTY MUCH TAMSEN CAULEY'S SHADOW AT INTERNAL SECURITY, THERE'S AN EXPERIMENTAL FORM OF RESOC*...
...ONE THAT LURKS IN THE SUBCONSCIOUS AND ONLY GOES FULL BLOWN IN RESPONSE TO A PRE-PROGRAMMED PROMPT.
ANYWAY, THE GUINEA PIG FOR THIS PARTICULAR VARIANT...
*NEURAL RESOCIALIZATION.
...WAS COLE HICKSON!
COLE HICKSON...
...DAMN, IT'S GOOD TO SEE YOU AGAIN AFTER ALL THIS TIME!
HUH?
BUT--
YOU KNOW EACH OTHER?
HELL YES! WE BOTH SPENT SOME TIME IN THE SAME P.O.W. CAMP BACK WHEN I WAS WITH THE 321ST. I OWE COLE MY SANITY. MAYBE MY LIFE!
SO WHEN I HEARD ABOUT HIM AND YOU AND THIS "THING"...
"...I KNEW THERE HAD TO BE MORE TO IT!"
THAT'S WHY HICKSON'S BEEN ACTING SO DAMN WEIRD. CAULEY'S BEEN INSIDE HIS HEAD, TINKERING. IT'S TYRADOR VIII ALL OVER AGAIN!
HE'S GOING TO KILL RAYNOR...

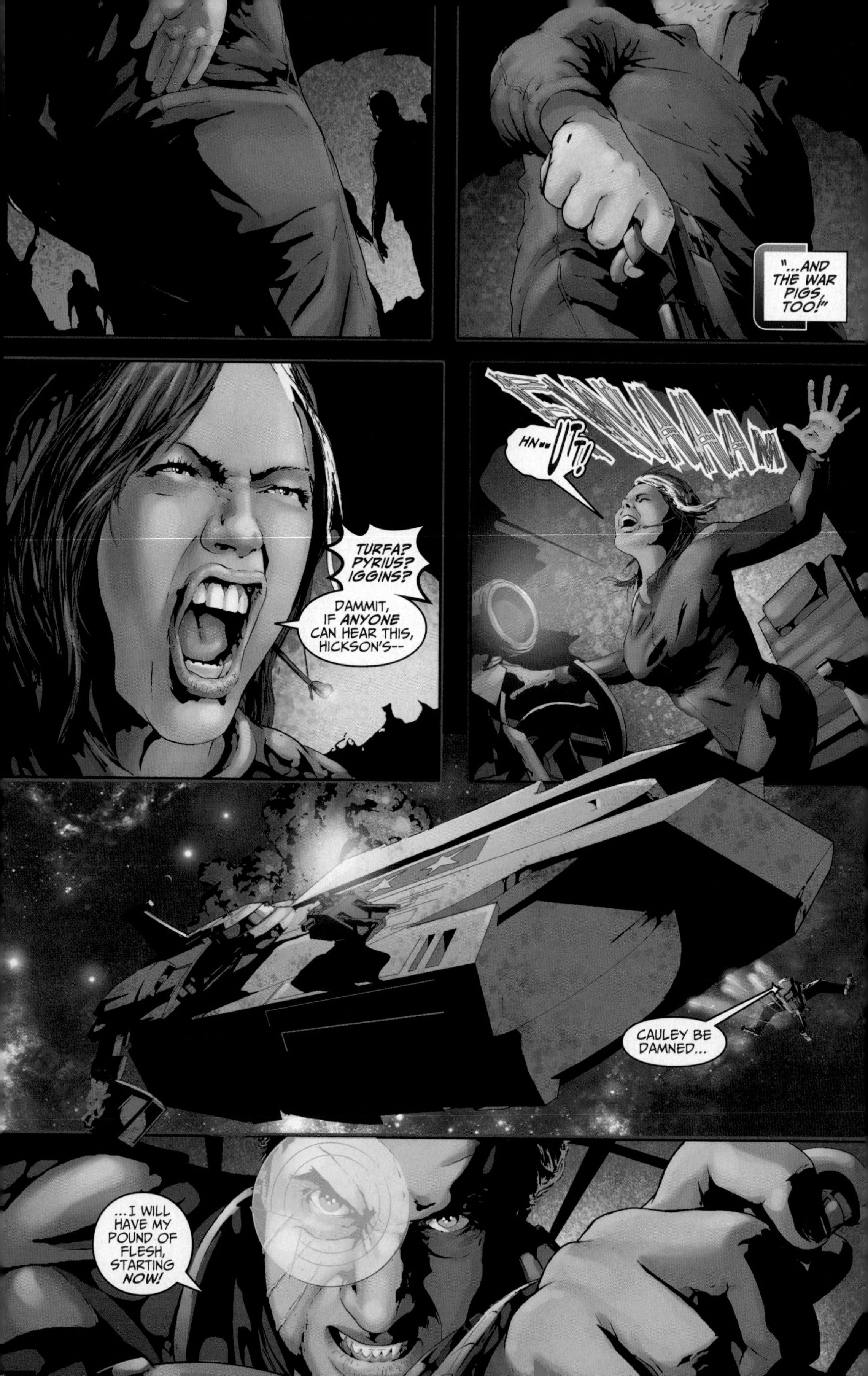
"...AND THE WAR PIGS, TOO!"
TURFA? PYRIUS? IGGINS?
DAMMIT, IF ANYONE CAN HEAR THIS, HICKSON'S--
HN-- UFF!
CAULEY BE DAMNED...
...I WILL HAVE MY POUND OF FLESH, STARTING NOW!

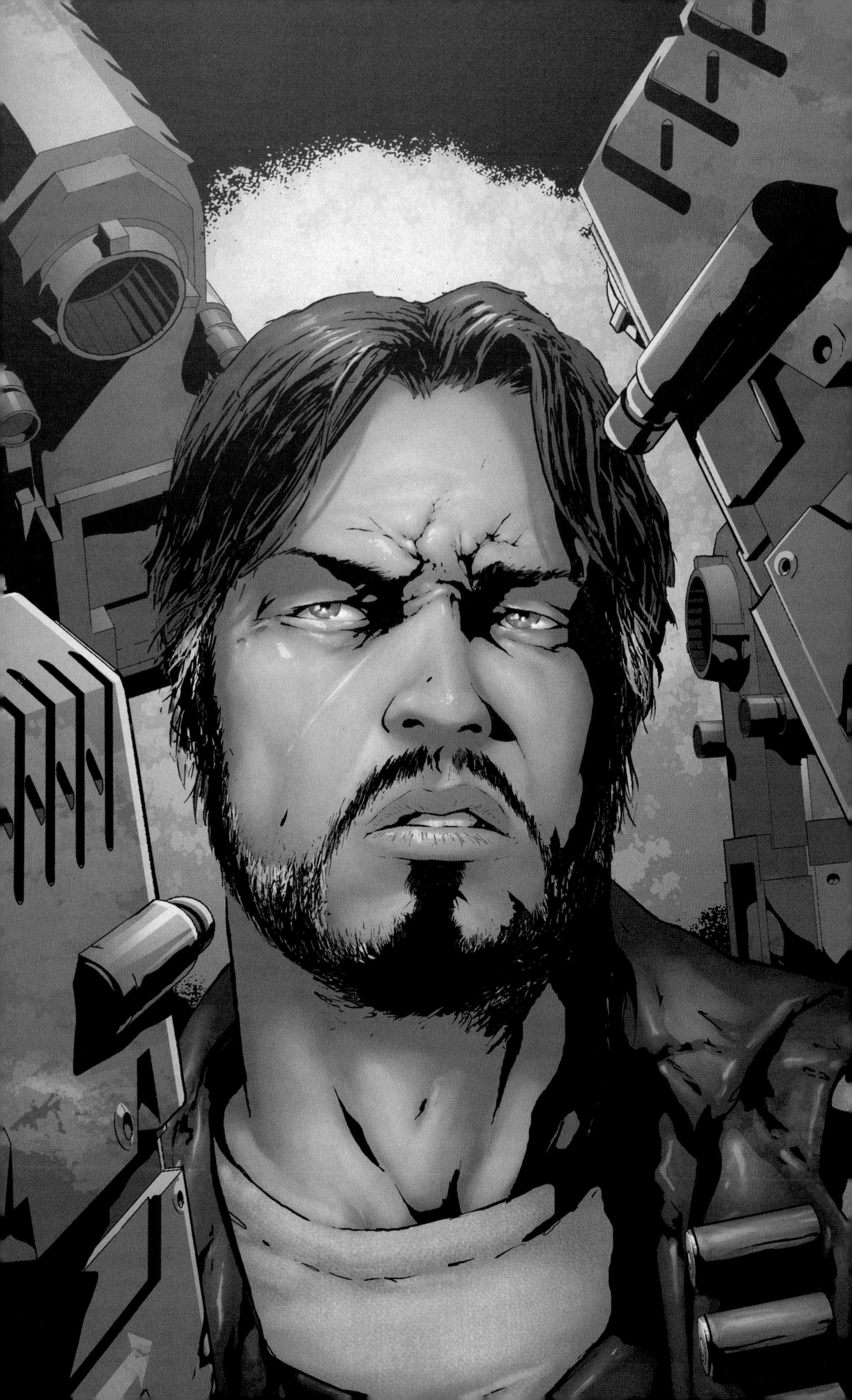

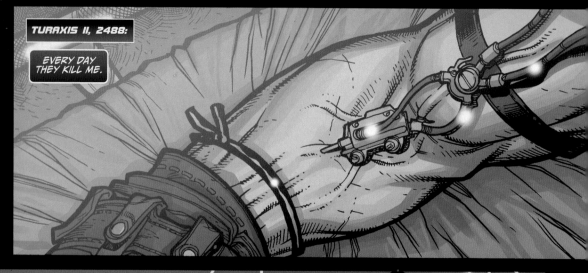

EVERY DAY THEY KILL ME.

THEN THEY BRING ME BACK.

CAN'T TELL IF IT'S TORTURE OR AN EXPERIMENT.

EITHER WAY...

...IT PUSHES BODY... AND MIND... WAY PAST ANYTHING LIKE NORMAL!

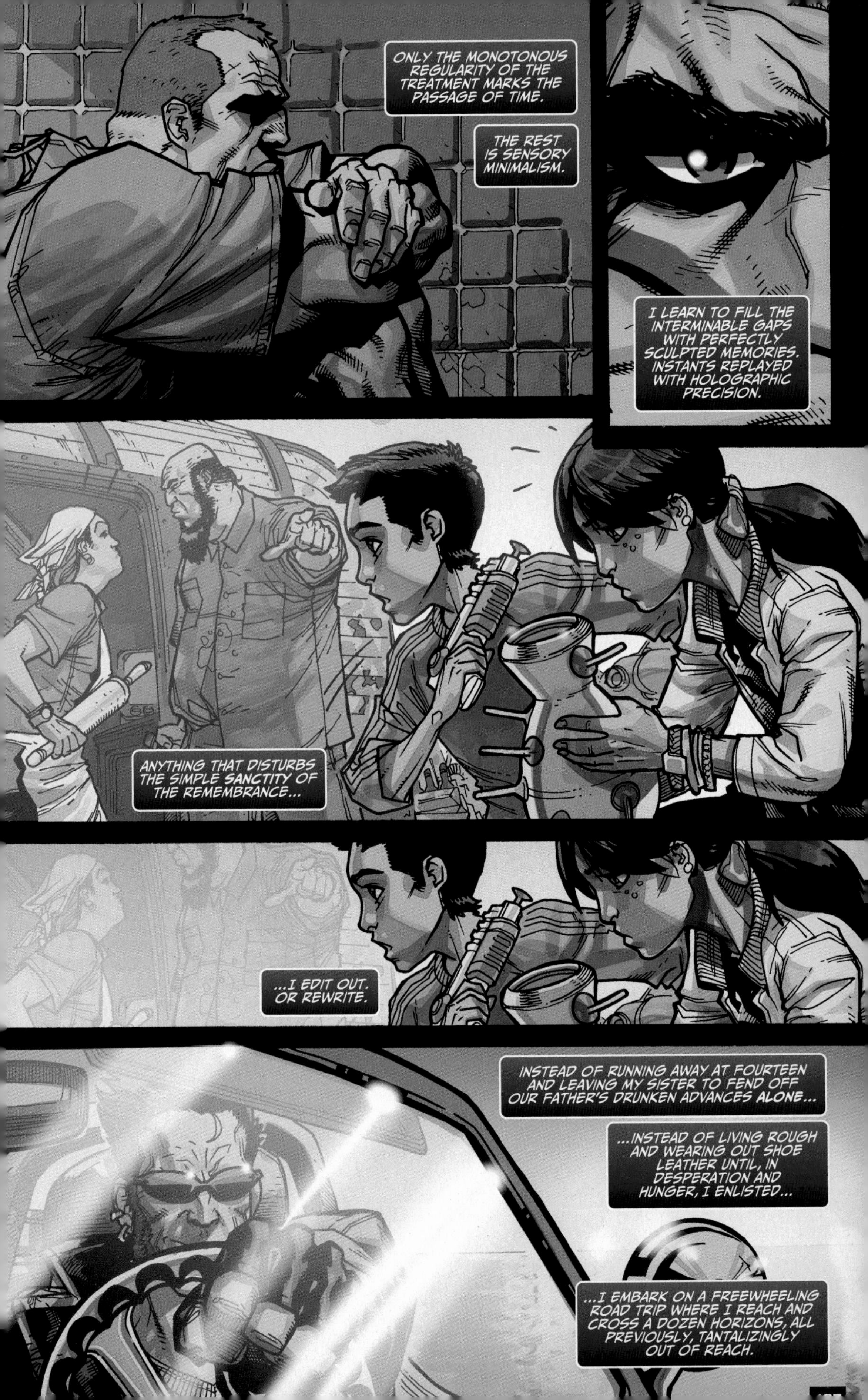
ONLY THE MONOTONOUS REGULARITY OF THE TREATMENT MARKS THE PASSAGE OF TIME.
THE REST IS SENSORY MINIMALISM.
I LEARN TO FILL THE INTERMINABLE GAPS WITH PERFECTLY SCULPTED MEMORIES. INSTANTS REPLAYED WITH HOLOGRAPHIC PRECISION.
ANYTHING THAT DISTURBS THE SIMPLE SANCTITY OF THE REMEMBRANCE...
...I EDIT OUT. OR REWRITE.
INSTEAD OF RUNNING AWAY AT FOURTEEN AND LEAVING MY SISTER TO FEND OFF OUR FATHER'S DRUNKEN ADVANCES ALONE...
...INSTEAD OF LIVING ROUGH AND WEARING OUT SHOE LEATHER UNTIL, IN DESPERATION AND HUNGER, I ENLISTED...
...I EMBARK ON A FREEWHEELING ROAD TRIP WHERE I REACH AND CROSS A DOZEN HORIZONS, ALL PREVIOUSLY, TANTALIZINGLY OUT OF REACH.

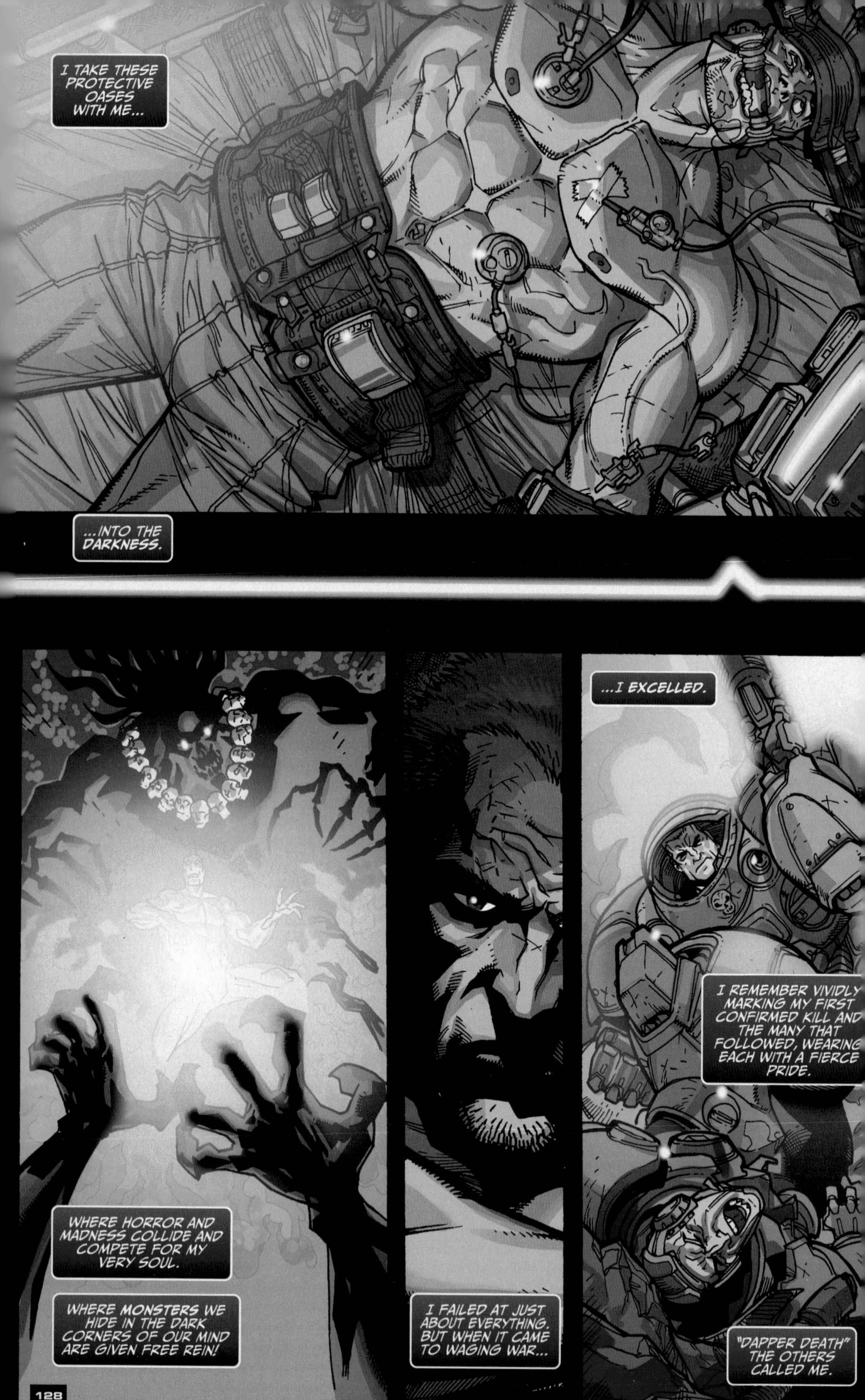

I TAKE THESE PROTECTIVE OASES WITH ME...
...INTO THE DARKNESS.
WHERE HORROR AND MADNESS COLLIDE AND COMPETE FOR MY VERY SOUL.
WHERE MONSTERS WE HIDE IN THE DARK CORNERS OF OUR MIND ARE GIVEN FREE REIN!
I FAILED AT JUST ABOUT EVERYTHING. BUT WHEN IT CAME TO WAGING WAR...
...I EXCELLED.
I REMEMBER VIVIDLY MARKING MY FIRST CONFIRMED KILL AND THE MANY THAT FOLLOWED, WEARING EACH WITH A FIERCE PRIDE.
"DAPPER DEATH" THE OTHERS CALLED ME.

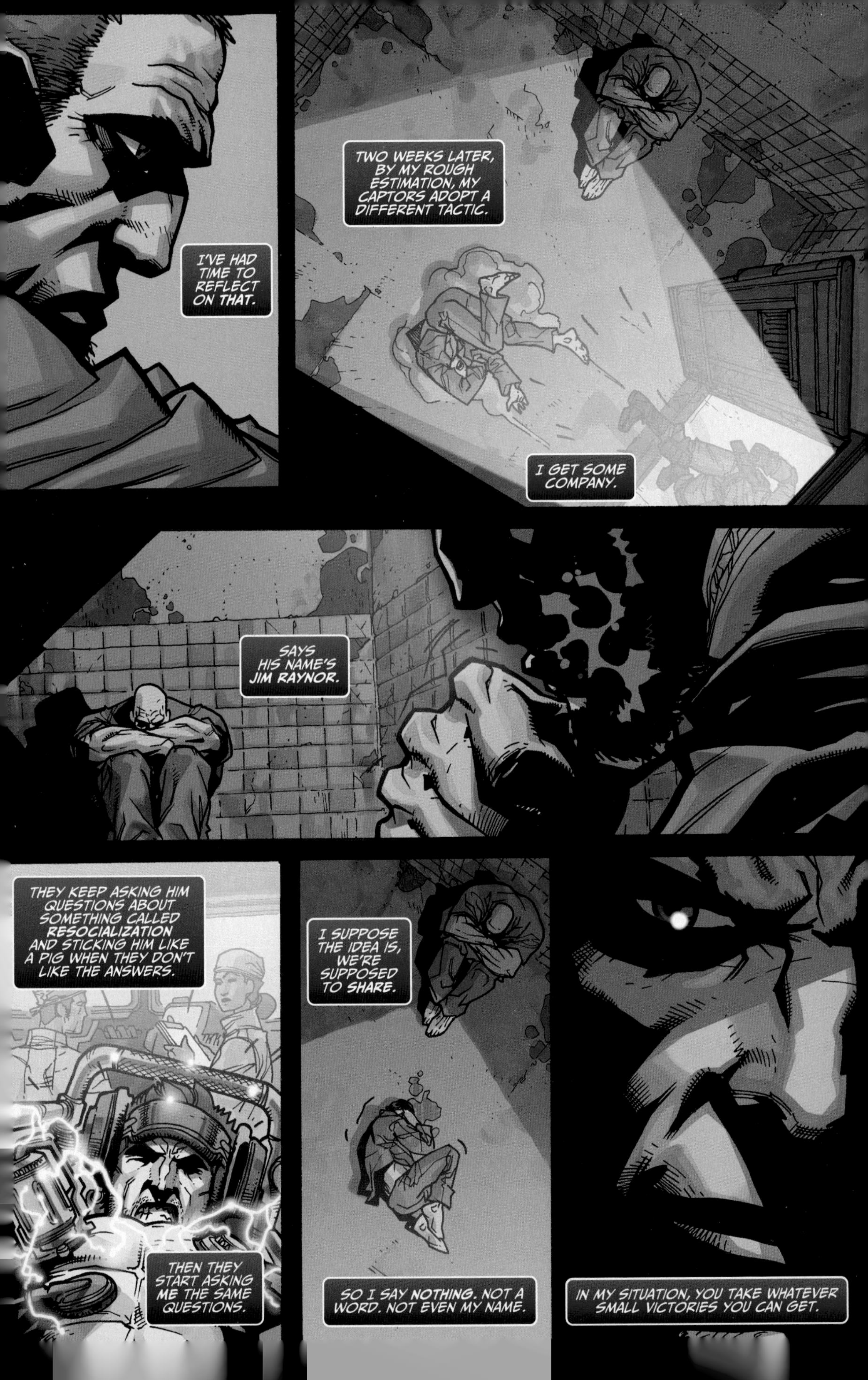
I'VE HAD TIME TO REFLECT ON THAT.
TWO WEEKS LATER, BY MY ROUGH ESTIMATION, MY CAPTORS ADOPT A DIFFERENT TACTIC.
I GET SOME COMPANY.
SAYS HIS NAME'S JIM RAYNOR.
THEY KEEP ASKING HIM QUESTIONS ABOUT SOMETHING CALLED RESOCIALIZATION AND STICKING HIM LIKE A PIG WHEN THEY DON'T LIKE THE ANSWERS.
THEN THEY START ASKING ME THE SAME QUESTIONS.
I SUPPOSE THE IDEA IS, WE'RE SUPPOSED TO SHARE.
SO I SAY NOTHING. NOT A WORD. NOT EVEN MY NAME.
IN MY SITUATION, YOU TAKE WHATEVER SMALL VICTORIES YOU CAN GET.

ANYWAY, RAYNOR TALKS ENOUGH FOR THE BOTH OF US.

...SEE, MY DAD, HE DIDN'T EXACTLY TEACH ME RIGHT AND WRONG, MORE WHERE TO DRAW THE LINE. IT WAS A KIND OF *IN-THE-TRENCHES* PHILOSOPHY, ADAPTABLE...

AT FIRST I PHASE HIM OUT, DISLOCATE, TAKING REFUGE IN ONE OF MY MANY MENTAL SPIDER HOLES.

BUT EVENTUALLY, MAYBE BY OSMOSIS, I START TO GET THE SENSE OF A GOOD MAN, A DECENT MAN, KNEE-DEEP IN EVENTS HE'S ONLY NOW BEGINNING TO GRASP.

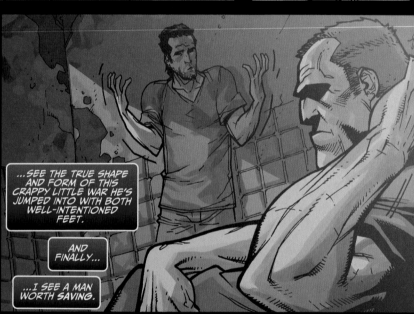

...SEE THE TRUE SHAPE AND FORM OF THIS CRAPPY LITTLE WAR HE'S JUMPED INTO WITH BOTH WELL-INTENTIONED FEET.

AND FINALLY...

I SEE HIM SLOWLY DISCERN THE LIES HE'S BEEN TOLD...

...I SEE A MAN WORTH SAVING.

PLAIN TRUTH IS, THE GUILD WARS ONLY SERVED TO CHISEL THE ROUGH EDGES OFF MY LATENT SOCIOPATHIC TENDENCIES.

BUT IN JAMES RAYNOR I SEE HOPE...AND SOME SMALL MEASURE OF PERSONAL SALVATION.

IF I CAN TEACH HIM, SHOW HIM HOW TO RESIST, HOW *NOT* TO LET THEM BREAK HIM...

...MAYBE, JUST MAYBE, I'M NOT A COMPLETELY LOST CAUSE!

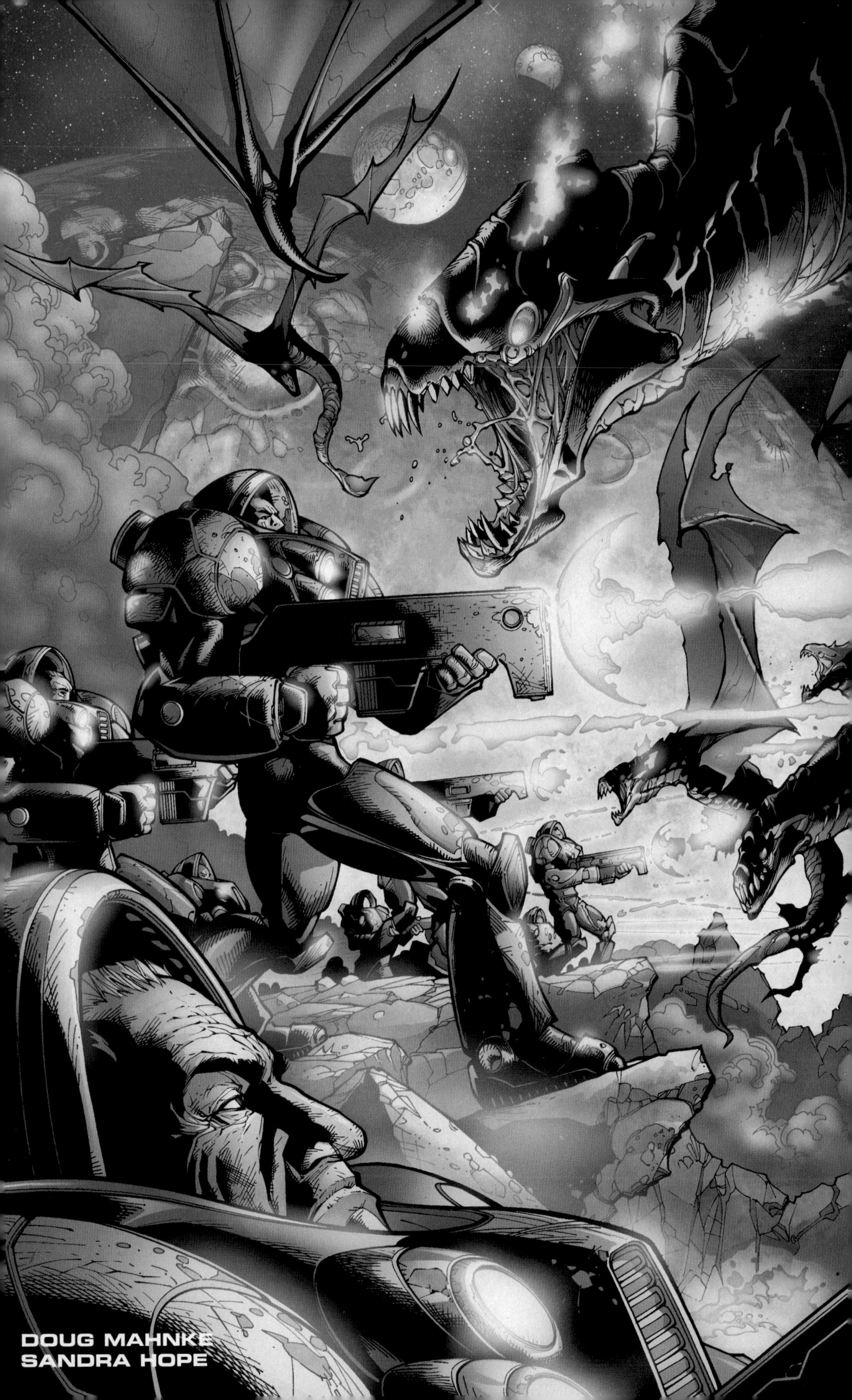
DOUG MAHNKE
SANDRA HOPE

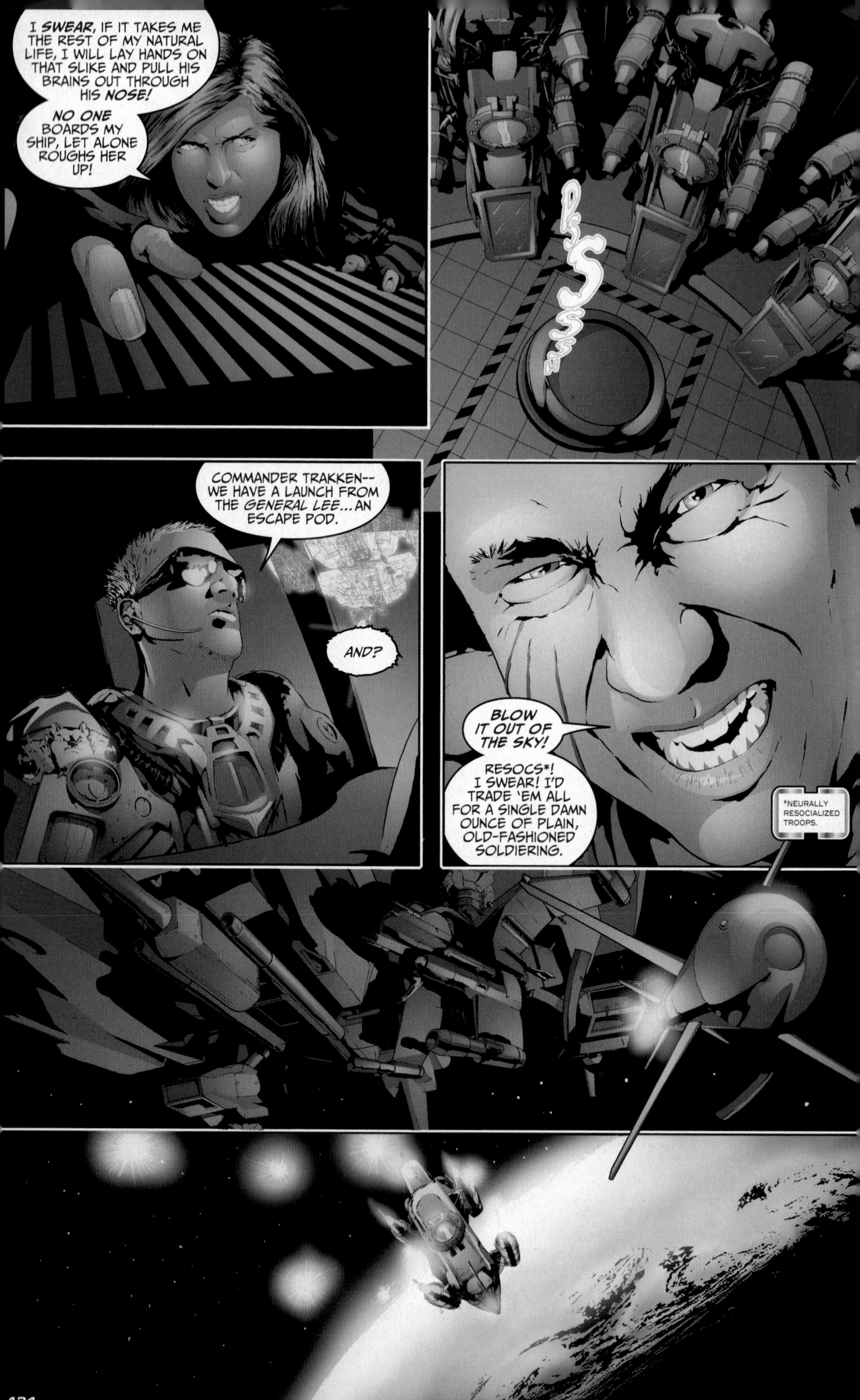
I SWEAR, IF IT TAKES ME THE REST OF MY NATURAL LIFE, I WILL LAY HANDS ON THAT SLIKE AND PULL HIS BRAINS OUT THROUGH HIS NOSE!
NO ONE BOARDS MY SHIP, LET ALONE ROUGHS HER UP!
COMMANDER TRAKKEN-- WE HAVE A LAUNCH FROM THE GENERAL LEE... AN ESCAPE POD.
AND?
BLOW IT OUT OF THE SKY!
RESOCS*! I SWEAR! I'D TRADE 'EM ALL FOR A SINGLE DAMN OUNCE OF PLAIN, OLD-FASHIONED SOLDIERING.
*NEURALLY RESOCIALIZED TROOPS.

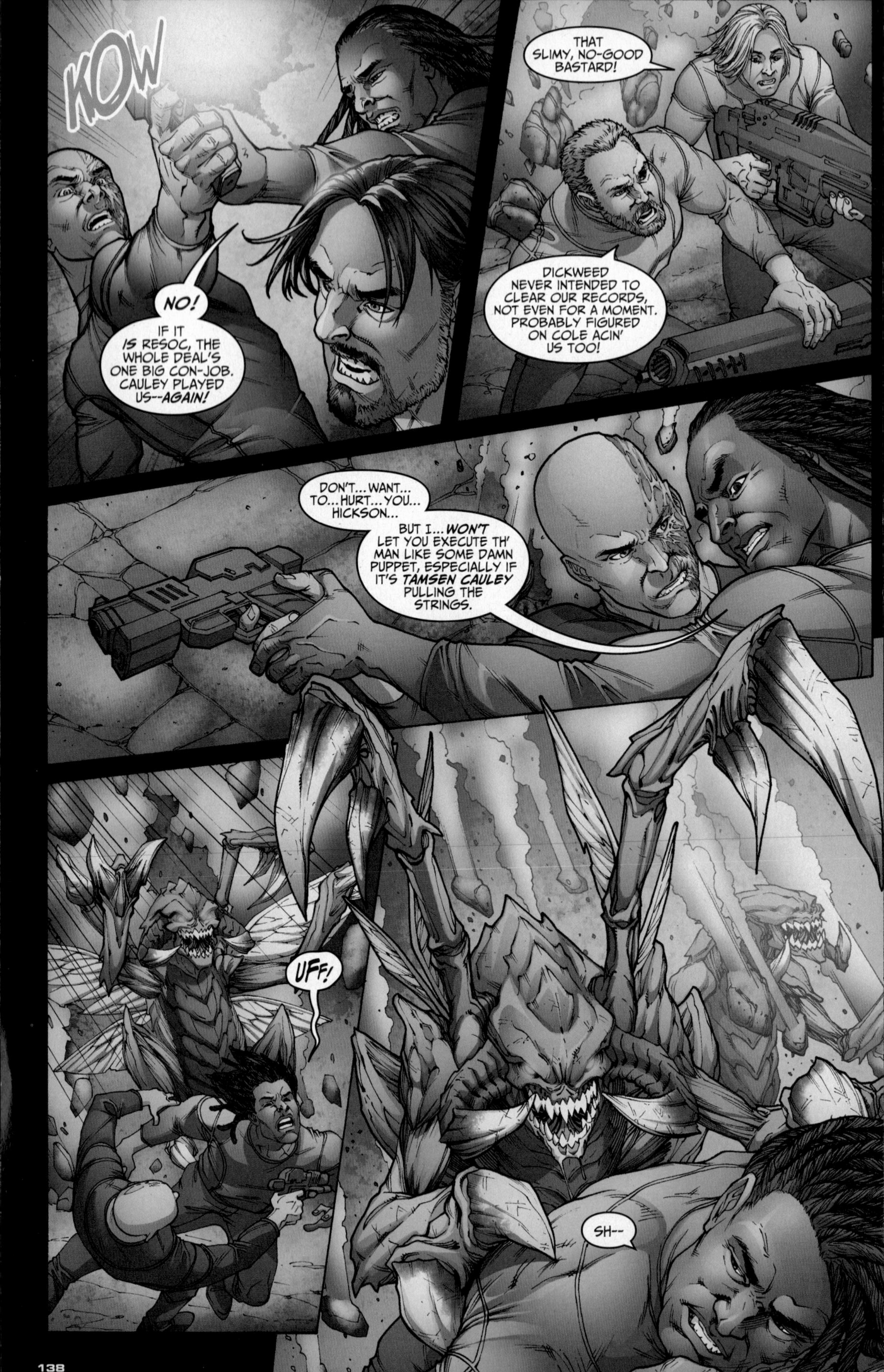
KOW
NO!
IF IT IS RESOC, THE WHOLE DEAL'S ONE BIG CON-JOB. CAULEY PLAYED US--AGAIN!
THAT SLIMY, NO-GOOD BASTARD!
DICKWEED NEVER INTENDED TO CLEAR OUR RECORDS, NOT EVEN FOR A MOMENT. PROBABLY FIGURED ON COLE ACIN' US TOO!
DON'T...WANT... TO...HURT...YOU... HICKSON...
BUT I...WON'T LET YOU EXECUTE TH' MAN LIKE SOME DAMN PUPPET, ESPECIALLY IF IT'S TAMSEN CAULEY PULLING THE STRINGS.
UFF!
SH--

BRAK
BRAK
BRAK

WHERE'S THE *CHIEF?* ANYONE SEE WHAT HAPPENED TO HIM?

DON'T KNOW. WITH THE MERCS... I THINK. WE GOT SEPARATED WHEN THE EFFING ROOF DROPPED IN ON US.

OH... *GREAT!* ZERG CAN SWIM! CAN THIS DAY *GET* ANY WORSE?

WE'VE *GOT* TO REACH THE WATER AND GET TO A DROPSHIP!

TROUBLE IS, THE ZERG ARE BETWEEN US... AND IT.

AN' ALL THAT DEBRIS MAKES A HEADLONG DASH SUICIDAL.

YOU GOT A BACK DOOR?

REMEMBER I TOLD YOU ABOUT THOSE PROTOSS, THE ONES WHO WARNED ME ABOUT YOUR LITTLE HUNTING EXPEDITION?

UH-HUH.

BHOOOF

YEAH. BUT IT'LL TAKE *TIME* TO REACH THE SURFACE, AND TIME'S AN ISSUE.

HOW SO?

WELL... THEY TOLD US THEY'D BE *BACK.* WE WERE PACKING UP, READY TO GO, WHEN YOU SHOWED UP.

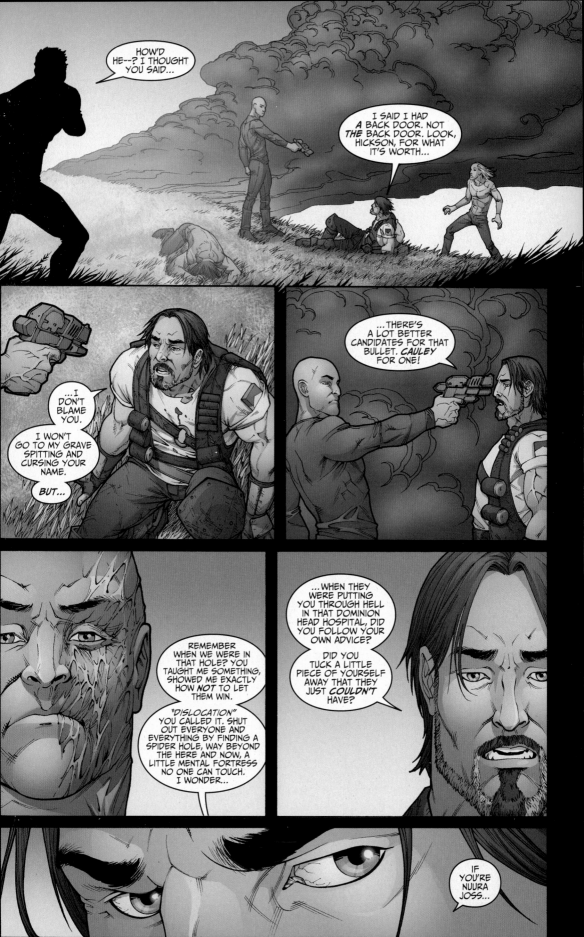

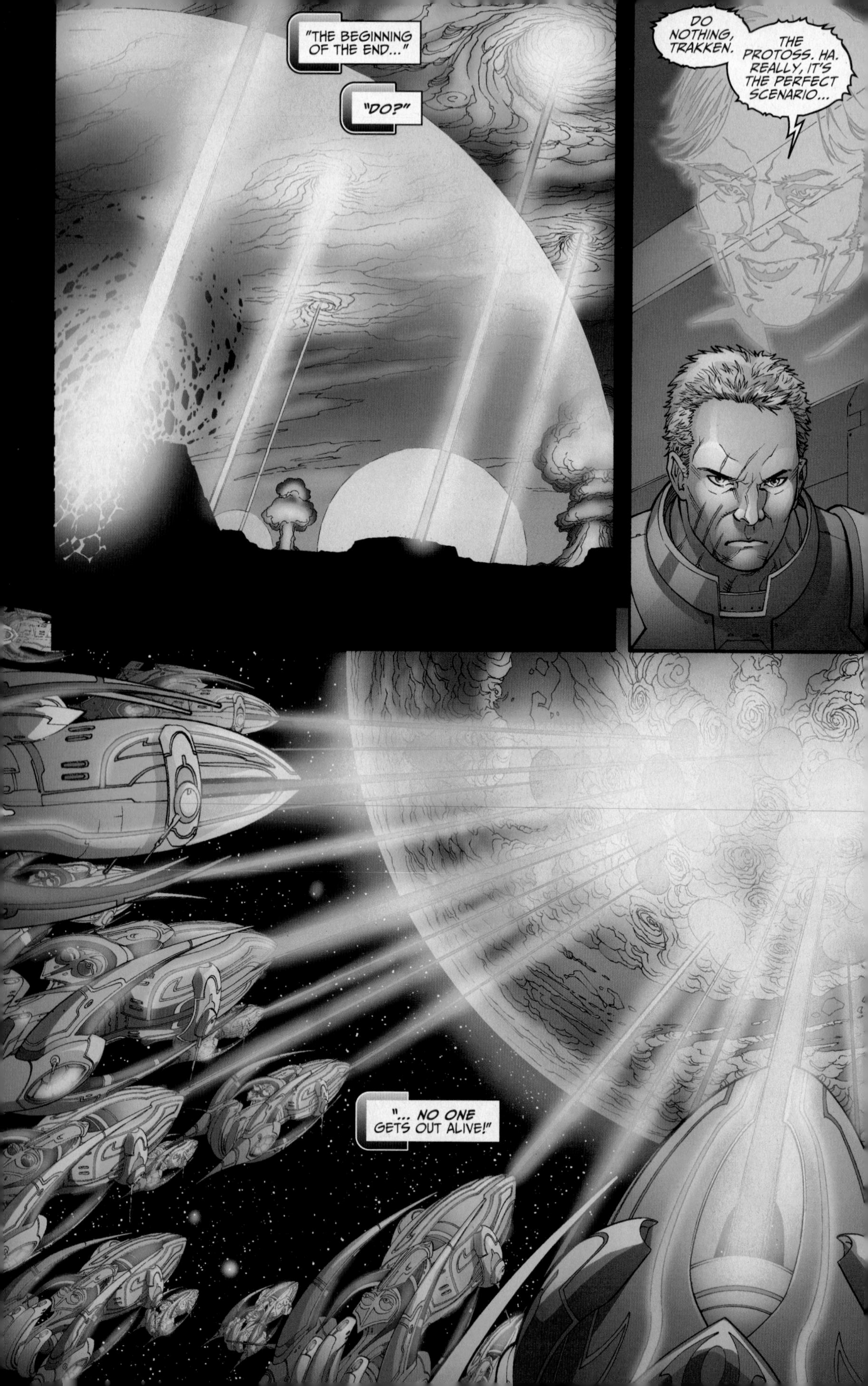
"THE BEGINNING OF THE END..."
"DO?"
DO NOTHING, TRAKKEN.
THE PROTOSS. HA. REALLY, IT'S THE PERFECT SCENARIO...
"... NO ONE GETS OUT ALIVE!"

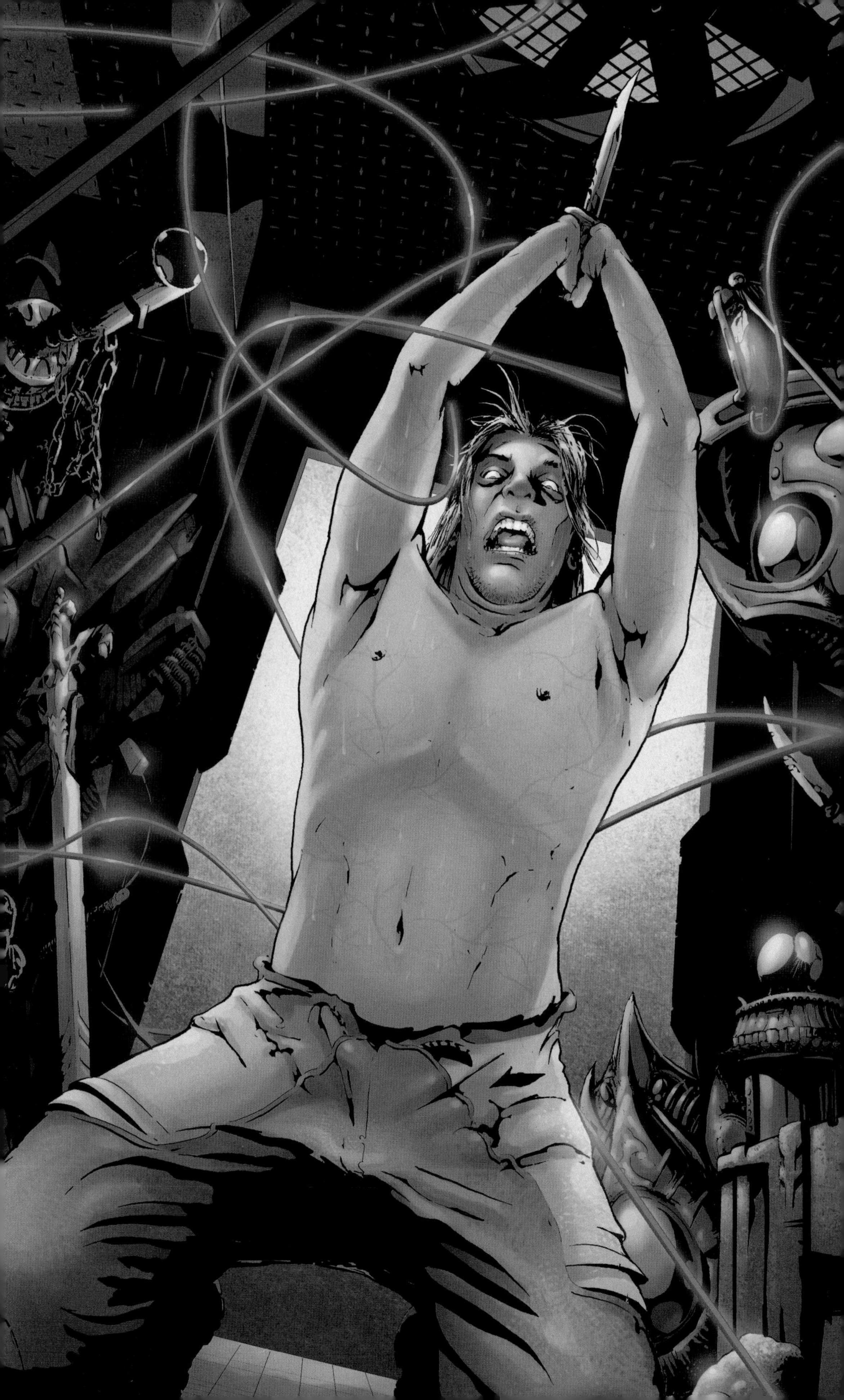

TARSONIS, NEW GETTYSBURG-- CENTRAL DISTRICT OF TARSONIS CITY, 2483:

BY DAY, I'M A RESPECTABLE MAN-ABOUT-TOWN. AN ENTREPRENEUR. TRUE...

...I DEAL IN HAB, TURK AND OTHER CONTROLLED SUBSTANCES, BUT IT'S GAINFUL ENTERPRISE NONETHELESS.

BY NIGHT...

...IT ALL SHADES A LITTLE DARKER.

THAT ALWAYS BOIL DOWN TO KILLING A LOT OF INCONVENIENT PEOPLE.

IN RETURN FOR THE UNHAMPERED FURTHERANCE OF MY PHARMACEUTICAL ENTERPRISES, I DO THE POWERS-THAT-BE A FEW SUB-RADAR FAVORS.

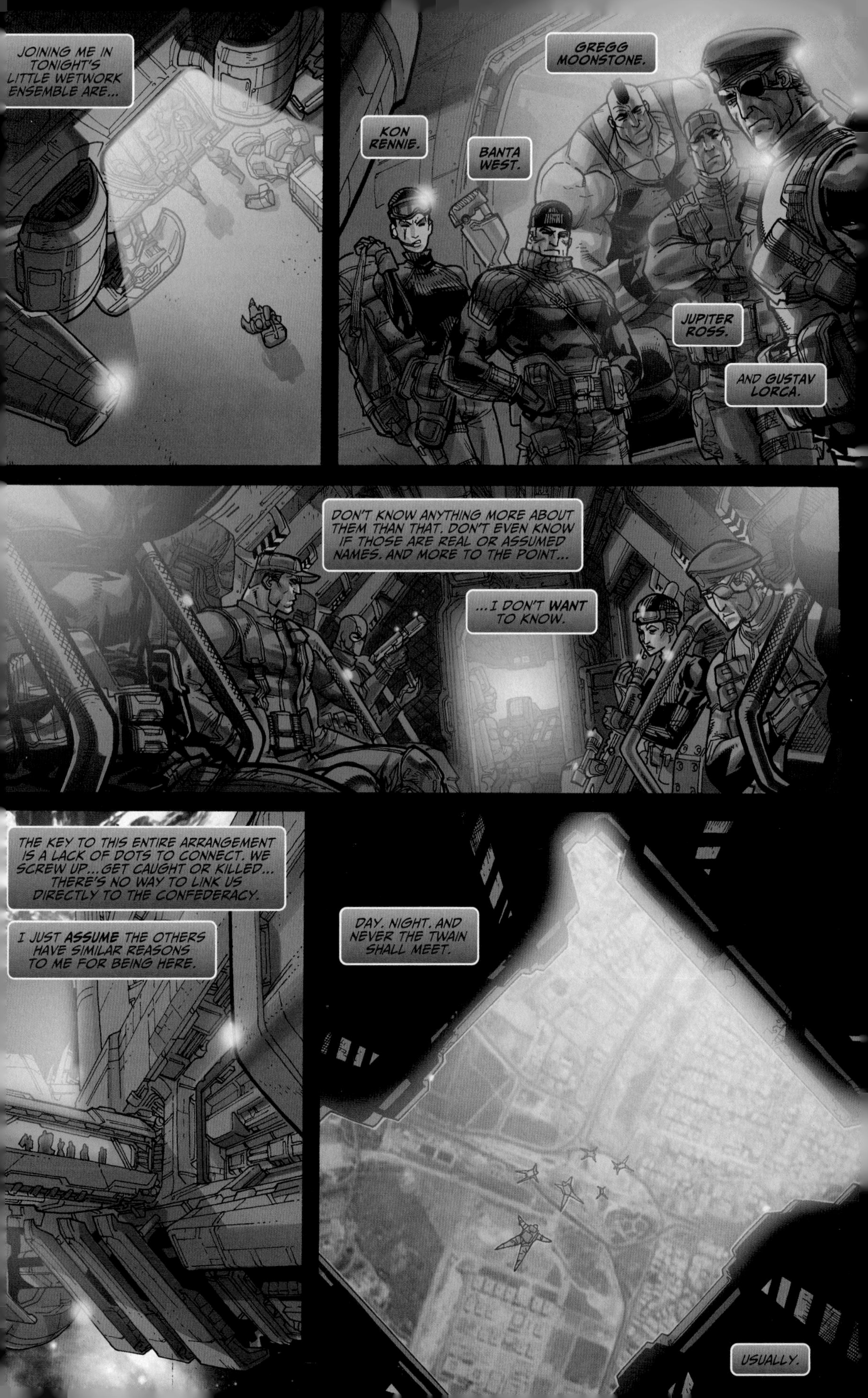
JOINING ME IN TONIGHT'S LITTLE WETWORK ENSEMBLE ARE...
GREGG MOONSTONE.
KON RENNIE.
BANTA WEST.
JUPITER ROSS.
AND GUSTAV LORCA.
DON'T KNOW ANYTHING MORE ABOUT THEM THAN THAT. DON'T EVEN KNOW IF THOSE ARE REAL OR ASSUMED NAMES. AND MORE TO THE POINT...
...I DON'T WANT TO KNOW.
THE KEY TO THIS ENTIRE ARRANGEMENT IS A LACK OF DOTS TO CONNECT. WE SCREW UP...GET CAUGHT OR KILLED... THERE'S NO WAY TO LINK US DIRECTLY TO THE CONFEDERACY.
I JUST ASSUME THE OTHERS HAVE SIMILAR REASONS TO ME FOR BEING HERE.
DAY. NIGHT. AND NEVER THE TWAIN SHALL MEET.
USUALLY.

I FIGURE TO DO THE OFFICIAL JOB--WHICH IS DELETING A BUNCH OF V.I.P.s, ALL COZIED UP TOGETHER IN THIS HOUSE HERE FOR SOME BIG POW-WOW...

THIS TIME I SET UP A LITTLE SIDE DEAL.

...AND PICK UP A CONSIGNMENT OF BOG.

WITH NEITHER PARTY ANY THE WISER.

RISKY, SURE. BUT THE PROFIT MARGINS ON BOG--SOMETHING OF A RARE COMMODITY ON TARSONIS--MAKE IT WORTH COMPROMISING MY OWN RULES.

IT NEVER EVEN CROSSES MY MIND I MAY HAVE ALSO COMPROMISED THE ENTIRE MISSION...

...UNTIL MUCH TOO LATE.

WARP

I'M INTERROGATED. STRANGELY...

...THEY'RE LESS CONCERNED WITH MY NOCTURNAL ACTIVITIES AND MORE ACTIVELY INTERESTED IN THE NINE-TO-FIVE.

THEY WANT TO KNOW ALL ABOUT MY DISTRIBUTION NETWORK, MY CLIENT BASE. IN PARTICULAR...

THEN I'M GIVEN THE TOUR...

...MY MORE ESTEEMED CUSTOMERS IN THE CONFEDERATE HIERARCHY.

YOU UNDERSTAND ABOUT CUTTING, YES?

THIS IS WHERE WE CUT, BUT NOT TO MAXIMIZE PROFIT. OH, NO.

WE CUT WITH BOURAS, VIVISTYRCHNINE, ZETOX...

I DON'T KNOW ALL THE NAMES, BUT ENOUGH TO GRASP THE INTENT. GENETIC ACCELERANTS, APPETITE SUPPRESSANTS, BIO-MOLECULAR TOXINS, ANTI-COHESIVES...

...A COCKTAIL OF SLOW, DEBILITATING DEATH IN A CANDY SHELL.

WE ARE ALWAYS EXPERIMENTING, LEARNING. NEW VARIATIONS. SO EXTRA RAW MATERIALS...

...ARE ALWAYS WELCOME.

I'M GIVEN A CHOICE: RETURN TO MY OLD LIFE, BE THE MULE FOR THEIR DESIGNER BULLETS, OR END IT HERE, LIKE MOONSTONE AND THE OTHERS.

153

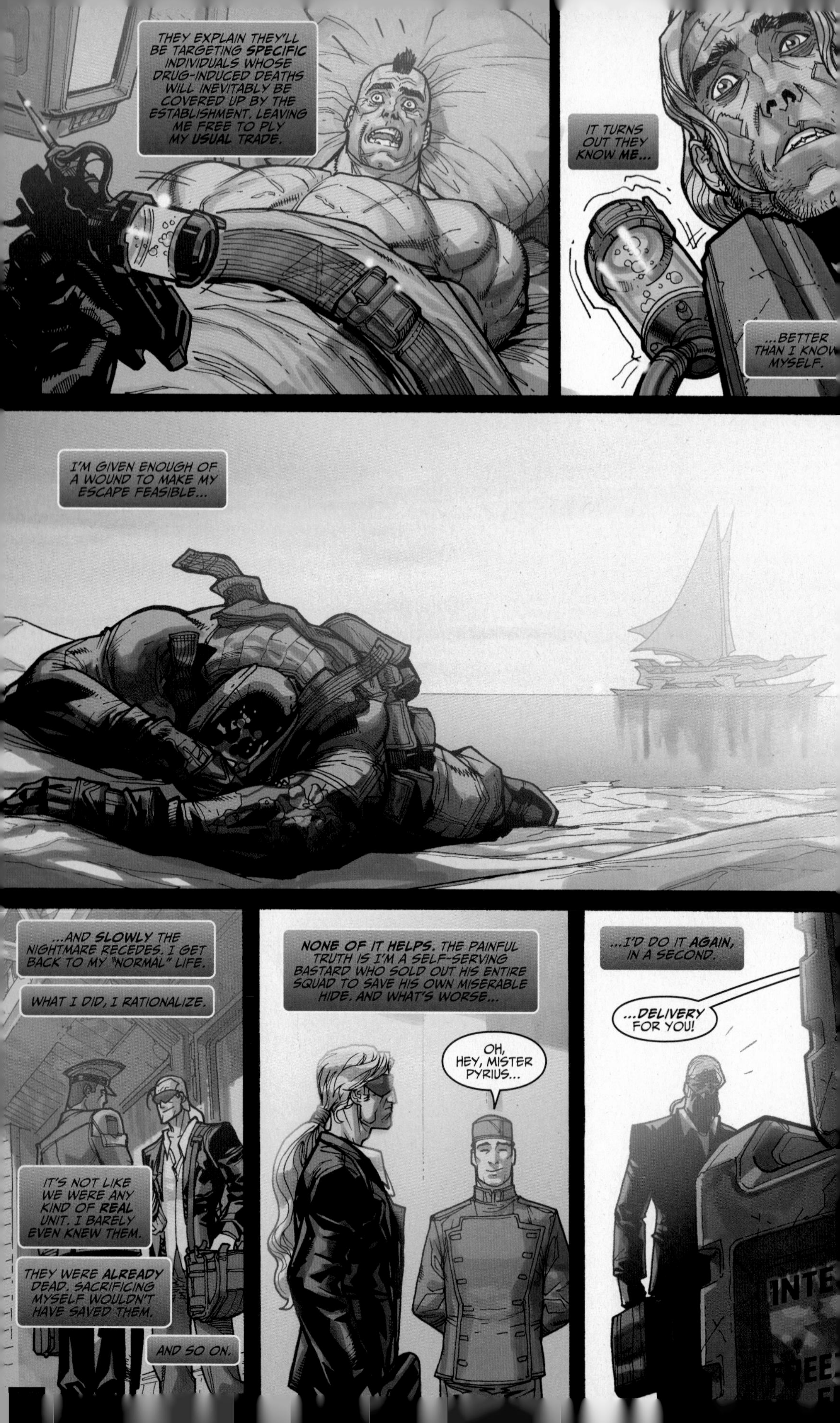
THEY EXPLAIN THEY'LL BE TARGETING SPECIFIC INDIVIDUALS WHOSE DRUG-INDUCED DEATHS WILL INEVITABLY BE COVERED UP BY THE ESTABLISHMENT. LEAVING ME FREE TO PLY MY USUAL TRADE.
IT TURNS OUT THEY KNOW ME...
...BETTER THAN I KNOW MYSELF.
I'M GIVEN ENOUGH OF A WOUND TO MAKE MY ESCAPE FEASIBLE...
...AND SLOWLY THE NIGHTMARE RECEDES. I GET BACK TO MY "NORMAL" LIFE.
WHAT I DID, I RATIONALIZE.
IT'S NOT LIKE WE WERE ANY KIND OF REAL UNIT. I BARELY EVEN KNEW THEM.
THEY WERE ALREADY DEAD. SACRIFICING MYSELF WOULDN'T HAVE SAVED THEM.
AND SO ON.
NONE OF IT HELPS. THE PAINFUL TRUTH IS I'M A SELF-SERVING BASTARD WHO SOLD OUT HIS ENTIRE SQUAD TO SAVE HIS OWN MISERABLE HIDE. AND WHAT'S WORSE...
OH, HEY, MISTER PYRIUS...
...I'D DO IT AGAIN, IN A SECOND.
...DELIVERY FOR YOU!

SHAWN MOLL
DOUG MAHNKE

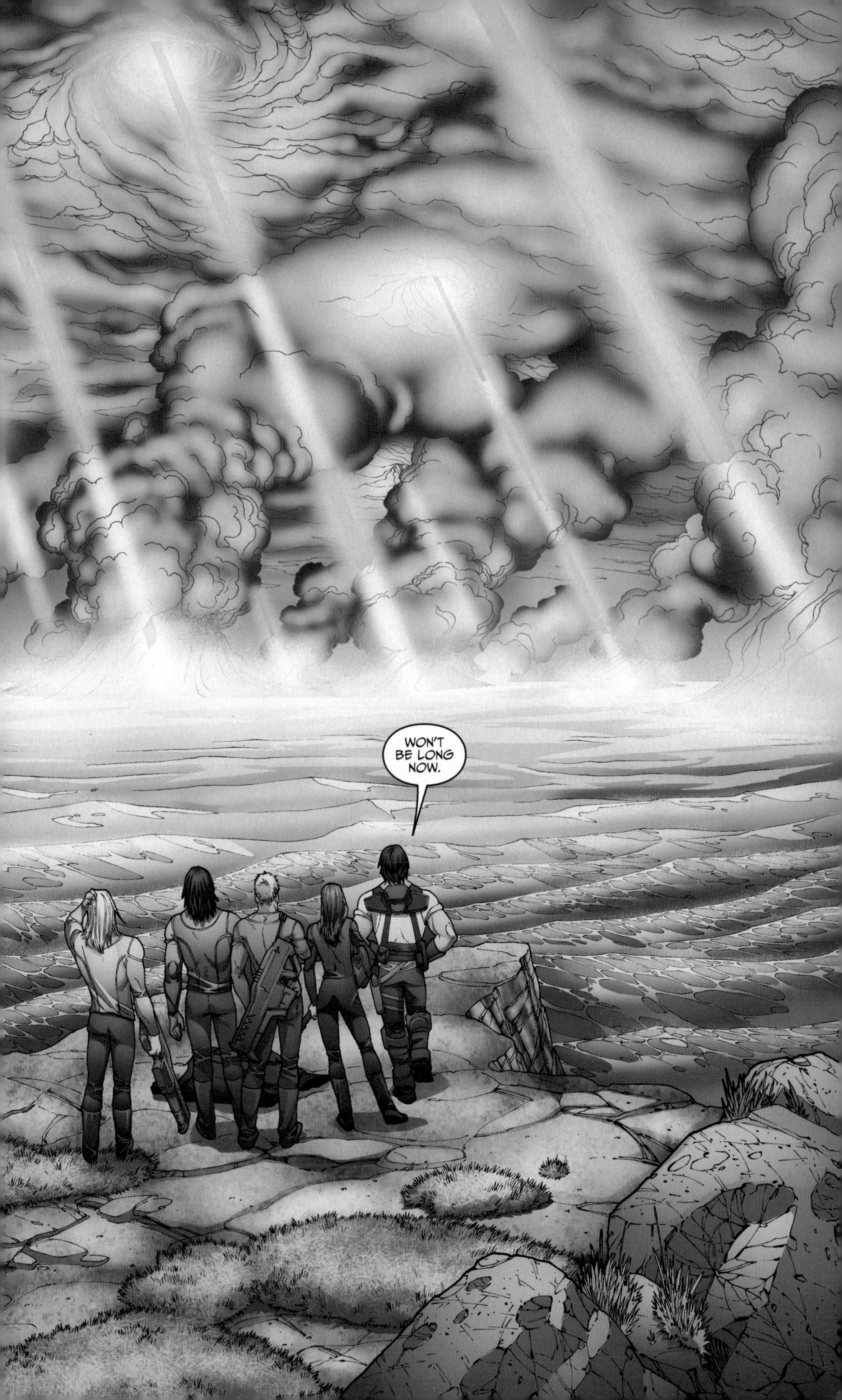
WON'T BE LONG NOW.

SCREW CAULEY!

HE MAY BE CONTENT TO SIT BACK AND WATCH THIS PLAY OUT FROM A SAFE DISTANCE, BUT I'M *NOT!*

GET ME A DROPSHIP PREPPED FOR LAUNCH.

I'VE WAITED YEARS FOR THIS OPPORTUNITY. AND NOW IT'S FINALLY COME, I NEED TO SEE HICKSON'S EYES POP AS MY HANDS CLOSE ON HIS NECK, HEAR VERTEBRAE CRACK AS I TWIST.

THE MILITARY SHRINKS WHO POKED AND PRODDED ME AFTER LOS ANDARES HAD A WORD FOR IT...

"...CLOSURE."

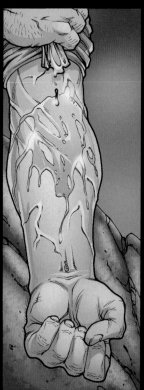

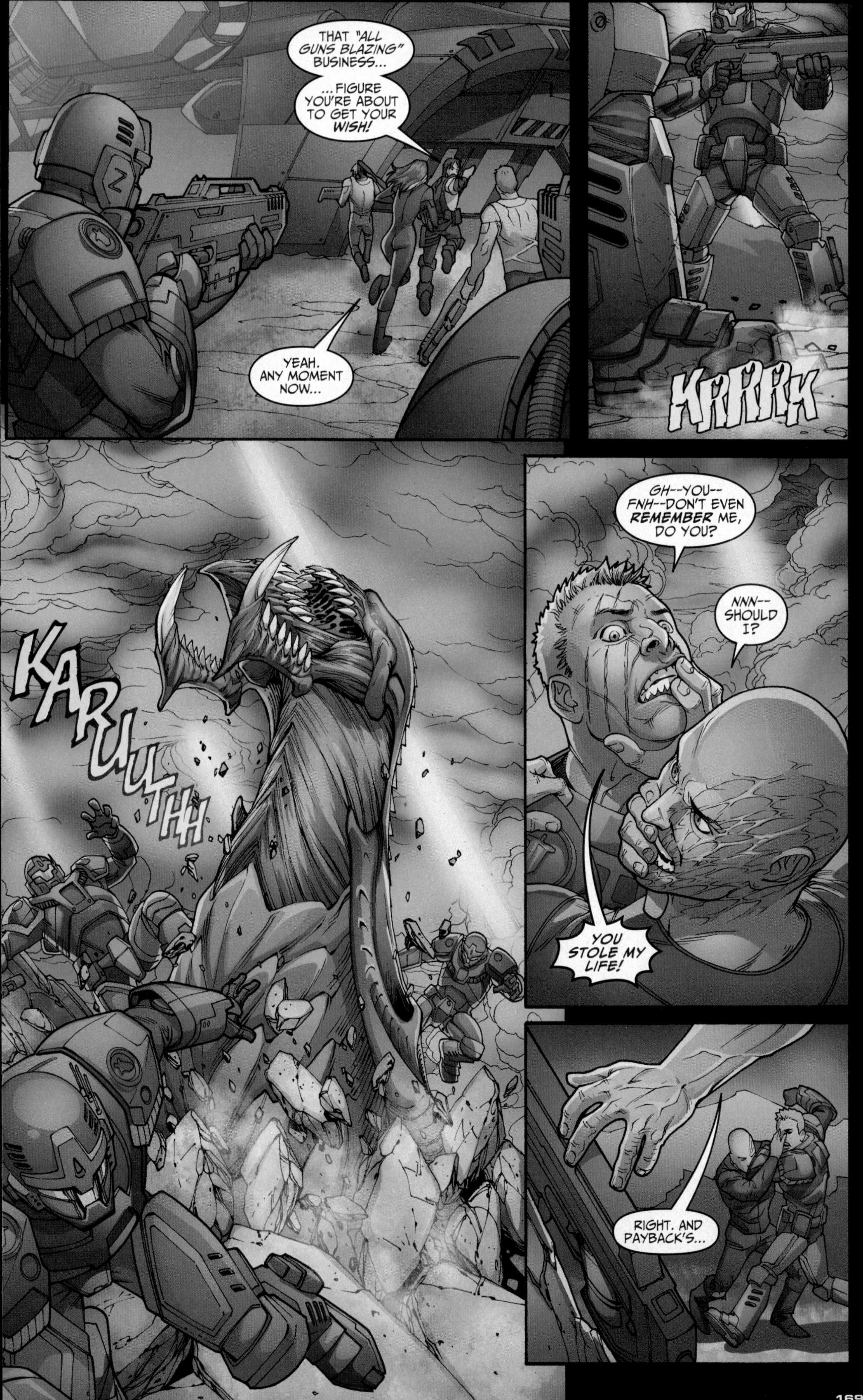
THAT "ALL GUNS BLAZING" BUSINESS...
...FIGURE YOU'RE ABOUT TO GET YOUR WISH!
YEAH. ANY MOMENT NOW...
KRRRK
KARUUUTHH
GH--YOU--FNH--DON'T EVEN REMEMBER ME, DO YOU?
NNN--SHOULD I?
YOU STOLE MY LIFE!
RIGHT. AND PAYBACK'S...

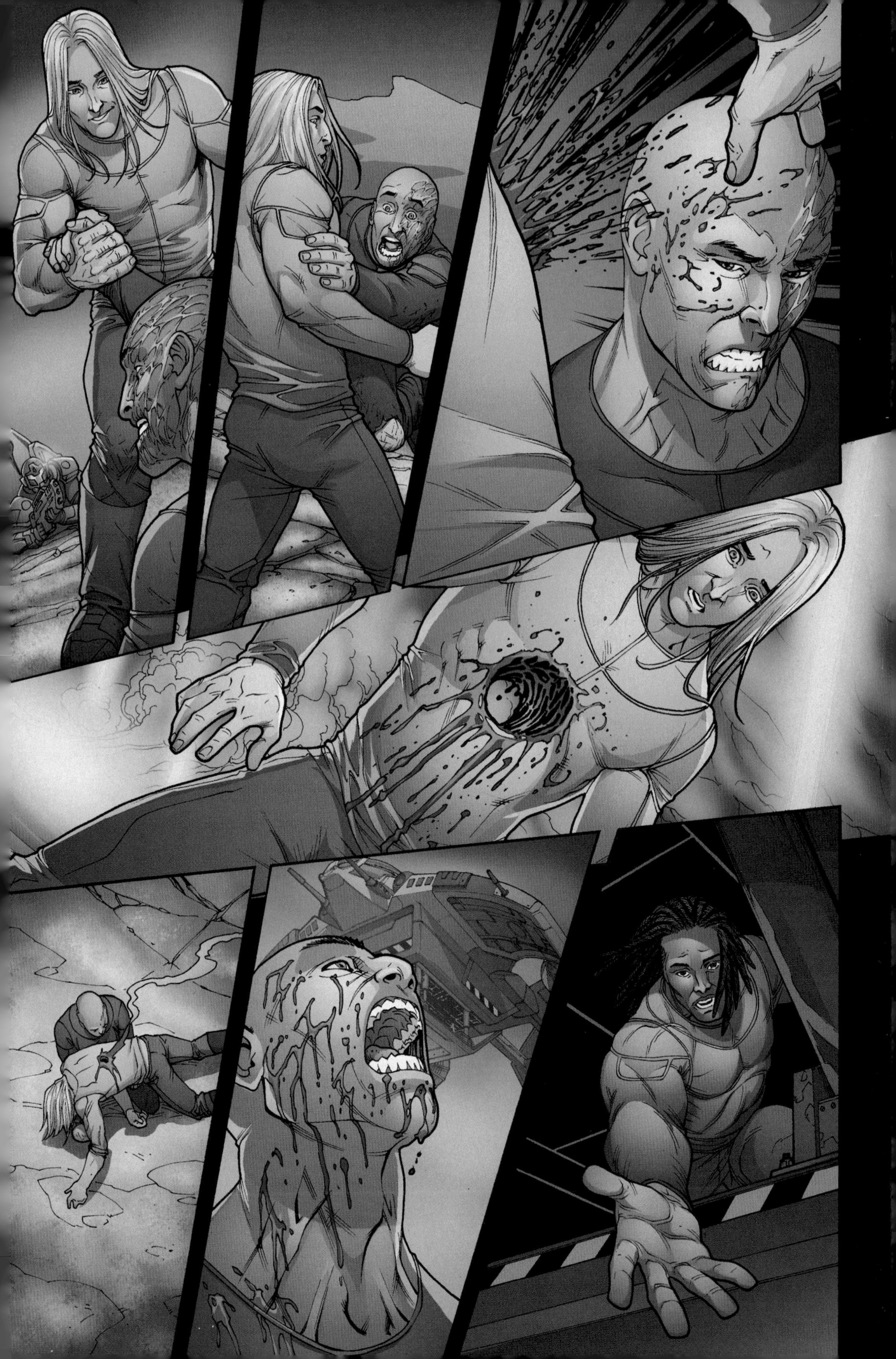

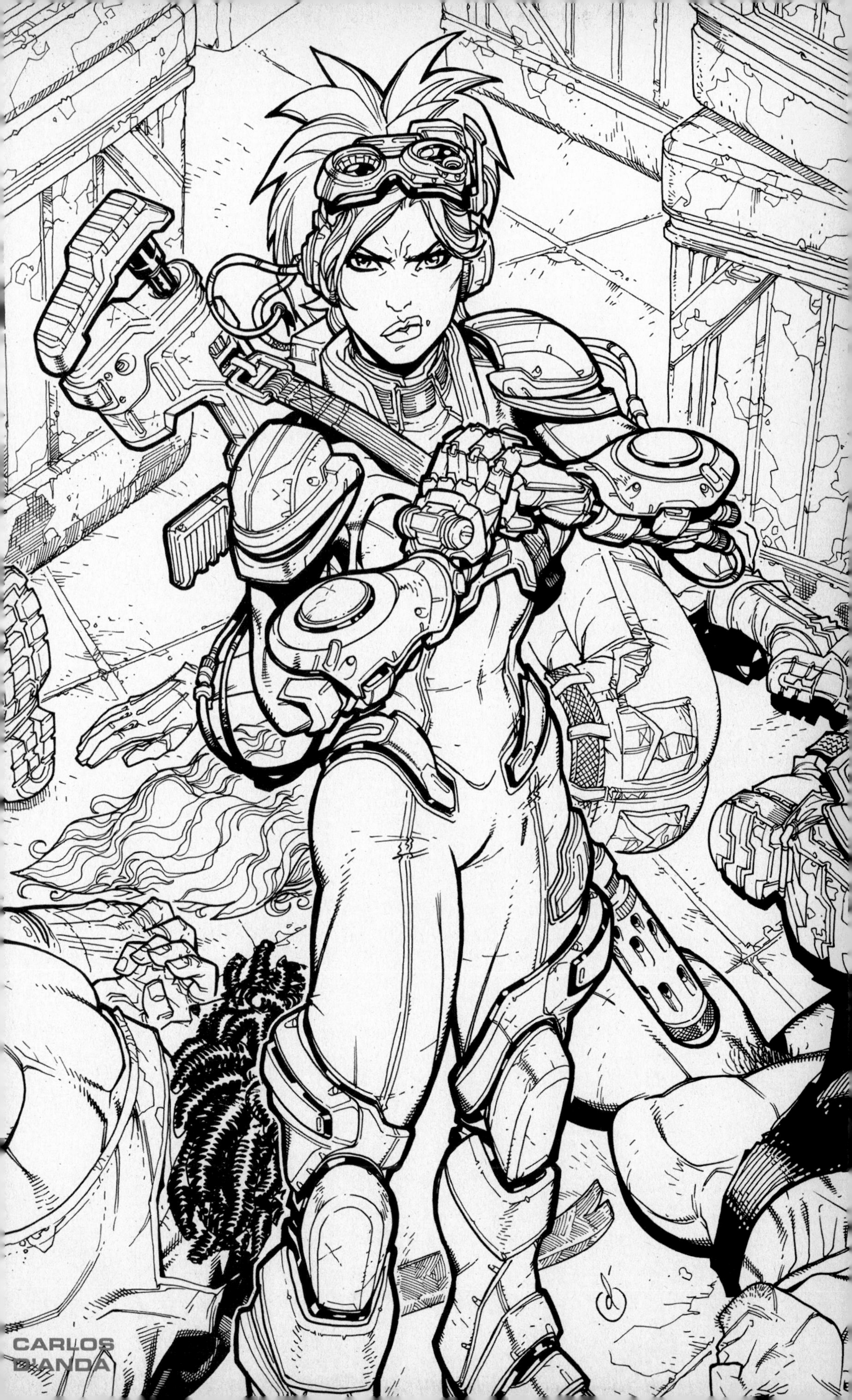
CARLOS
D'ANDA

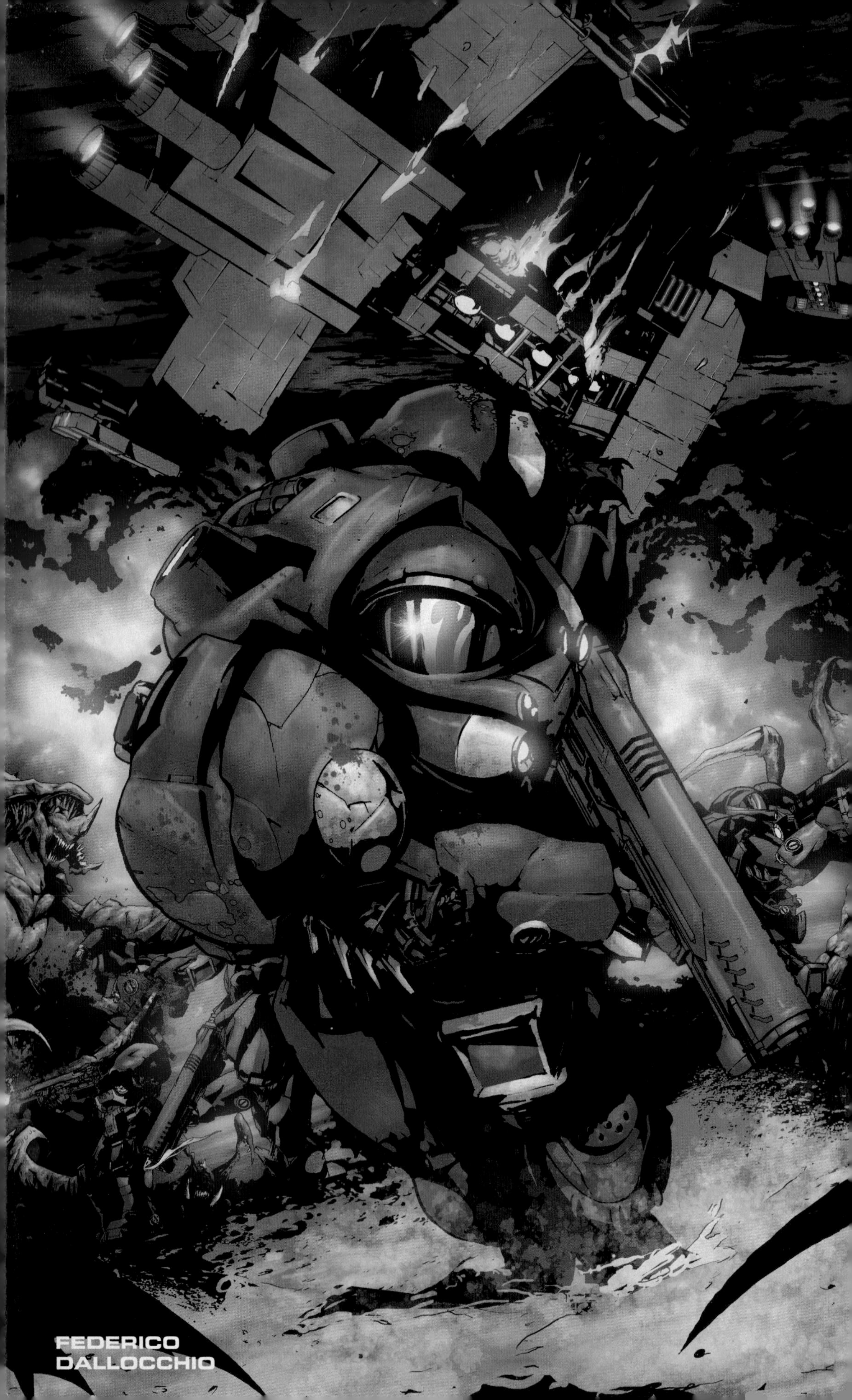
FEDERICO
DALLOCCHIO

WORLD OF WARCRAFT®

An amnesiac washes up on the shores of Kalimdor, starting the epic quest of the warrior Lo'Gosh, and his unlikely allies Broll Bearmantle and Valeera Sanguinar. Striking uneasy relationships with other races, as well as each other, they must fight both the Alliance and the Horde as they struggle to uncover the secrets of Lo'Gosh's past! Written by Walter Simonson (THE JUDAS COIN, *Thor*) and illustrated by **Ludo Lullabi** (*Lanfeust Quest*) and **Sandra Hope** (JUSTICE LEAGUE OF AMERICA), this is the latest saga set in the **World of Warcraft**!

WORLD OF WARCRAFT
Book Two

WORLD OF WARCRAFT
Book Three

WORLD OF WARCRAFT
Book Four (Coming Fall 2010)

WORLD OF WARCRAFT
ASHBRINGER

Simonson
Buran • Bowden

Simonson
Simonson • Bowden

Simonson
Simonson • Bowden

Neilson • Lullabi
Washington

SEARCH THE **GRAPHIC NOVELS SECTION** OF
WILDSTORM.COM
FOR ART AND INFORMATION ON ALL OF OUR BOOKS!